THE MASK AND

PAOLO GERBAUDO

The Mask
and the Flag

Populism, Citizenism and Global Protest

HURST & COMPANY, LONDON

First published in the United Kingdom in 2017 by C. Hurst &
Co. (Publishers) Ltd.,
41 Great Russell Street, London, WC1B 3PL
© Paolo Gerbaudo, 2017
All rights reserved.
Printed in the United Kingdom by Bell and Bain Ltd, Glasgow

The right of Paolo Gerbaudo to be identified as the author
of this publication is asserted by him in accordance with the
Copyright, Designs and Patents Act, 1988.

A Cataloguing-in-Publication data record for this book
is available from the British Library.

ISBN: 9781849045568

This book is printed using paper from registered sustainable
and managed sources.

www.hurstpublishers.com

CONTENTS

LISTS OF TABLES, FIGURES, AND IMAGES

Tables

Figures

Images

ACKNOWLEDGEMENTS

I would like to acknowledge some of the people whose contributions have been indispensable in the researching and writing of this book. First and foremost, I must thank the 140 interviewees that contributed to this research. Their willingness to engage in conversations about these movements' nature and meanings—and strengths and weaknesses—has allowed me to benefit from an insider perspective and to learn about the concerns, fears and hopes of organisers and participants.

My gratitude also goes to all those who helped me get through the travails of researching and writing this book. Anastasia Kavada, Alperen Atik, Eleftheria Lekakis, Magnus Ryner, Stathis Kouvelakis, Patrick McCurdy, Laura Burocco, Orsan Senalp, D.E. Wittkower, and Kenzie Burchell were of great assistance by reading and commenting on an early draft of the manuscript. Hannah el-Sisi, Mario Michelini, Gennaro Gervasio, Sofia de Roa, Javier Toret, Segundo Gonzalez, Jorge Moruno, Eirini Gaitanou, Katerina Anastasiou, Arnau Monterde, Antonio Calleja-López, Rodrigo Nunes, Amy Holmes, Jo Ris, Jerome Roos, Tzortzis Rallis, and Baki Youssoufou have been very helpful in providing me local contacts and knowledge of the regions covered in the book. Alex Foti has been an invaluable reader and critic, providing insightful comments throughout the process and prompting me to strengthen my argument and make it more accessible.

The conversations with other colleagues and friends including Geoffrey Pleyers, Tim Jordan, Nick Couldry, Veronica Barassi, Emiliano Treré, Alice Mattoni, Kevin McDonald, Rosemary Blecher, Patricia Ferreira-Lemos, Bue Rübner Hansen, Stefania Milan, Anne Alexander, Donatella Della Porta, George Souvlis, Alberto Toscano, Roberto Roccu, Emanuele

ACKNOWLEDGEMENTS

Toscano, Mario Pianta, Richard Barbrook, Stathis Kouvelakis, Jodi Dean, Matteo Mameli, Emanuele Ferragina, Alessandro Arrigoni, Samuele Mazzolini, Ben Little, and Mark Coté have contributed to shaping my understanding of the current political situation and the position of protest movements. My thanks also go to Jack McGinn who has meticulously edited my text, and to all the team at Hurst Publishers for their support and patience during the long gestation of the manuscript. Particular gratitude goes to my partner Lara, without whose empathy and acute observations of social reality writing this book would have taken twice as much time, and to my parents for their constant moral support.

This book is dedicated to the memory of Giulio Regeni, an Italian PhD student at Cambridge University who was kidnapped in Cairo on the fifth anniversary of the Egyptian revolution—25 January 2016—and whose body was found a week later with signs of torture. Likewise I dedicate it to the thousands of Egyptians who have been imprisoned, tortured, killed and "disappeared" for political reasons since the beginning of the 2011 revolution, and to all those participants in similar movements worldwide who have suffered police brutality and repression.

INTRODUCTION

People shouldn't be afraid of their government. Governments should be afraid of their people.

V for Vendetta[1]

In the wake of the 2008 financial crisis the world has been experiencing a veritable political earthquake. Economic distress produced by the Great Recession coupled with profound distrust in political and business elites has spawned new populist movements on the Left and the Right, upsetting the heretofore dominant order—firmly established since the 1980s under the aegis of neoliberalism—and raising both hopes of change and concurrent fears of instability. The once triumphant gospel of globalisation is in crisis, as is the faith in the self-regulating power of the markets, long accepted by the entire political mainstream. The system of representation offered by the political parties and trade unions of the post-war era seems incapable of addressing emerging popular demands. Protest movements against governments and banks have not been this strong since the Great Depression, and at every election voters punish incumbents and vote against the establishment. Revolutions, long presumed to be relics of the past, have made a comeback on the world scene, as have coup d'états, as has been seen in Egypt and Turkey. Donald Trump and Bernie Sanders in the US, Podemos and Ciudadanos in Spain and the Five Star Movement in Italy, Nigel Farage in "Brexit" Britain and Ada Colau in cosmopolitan Barcelona, are all conflicting yet interrelated signal shifts of this emergent political horizon, where traditional ideologies and social cleavages are given short shrift.

One phenomenon has epitomised more than any other this era of crisis, revolutions, and emancipatory possibilities: the movement of the

1

squares. The moniker "movement of the squares", along with similar terms such as "occupation movements" or "occupy movements," has been used to describe an array of protest movements that have emerged in different countries the world over, protesting against neoliberalism, extreme economic inequality, austerity policies, and lack of democracy. The initial spark for this global upheaval came from the revolutions of the "Arab Spring", where millions demonstrated for democracy against rusting dictatorships. Taking inspiration from Egypt's 25 January revolution in 2011, with its all-out occupation of Tahrir Square in central Cairo leading to the ouster of Hosni Mubarak, protesters the world over occupied central public squares and erected protest camps, lasting for weeks or even months, as a means to capture public attention and challenge power-holders.

In May 2011 Spanish protesters occupied Puerta del Sol in Central Madrid to voice widespread anger against greedy bankers and corrupt politicians. The Indignados found an immediate echo in Greece—a country on the brink of bankruptcy, forced to accept a humiliating bailout program sponsored by the IMF and the European Central Bank—with the occupation of Syntagma Square in front of the Hellenic Parliament. The Arab and European mobilisations were followed by Occupy Wall Street in the US where next to the New York Stock Exchange, the centre of global finance, protesters occupied Zuccotti Park. Though all these occupations were eventually dismantled or evicted, they provided a new protest blueprint for activists the world over. In 2013 Turkey and Brazil witnessed the rise of similar popular movements, taking public spaces to protest against the authoritarianism and corruption of their governments. The latest in this series of popular mobilisations was the 2016 "Nuit Debout" movement in France, which saw the occupation of Paris' Place de la République in protest against a new labour law, and the disconnection between political elites and ordinary citizens.

These movements—often misunderstood and sometimes maligned as inchoate "flash in the pan" spasms—deserve close attention if we are to understand the political horizon that has unfolded in the aftermath of the 2008 crash, and in order to devise progressive political strategies suiting this time of crisis in the neoliberal order. Due to its global scale and profound social and political impact, the movement of the squares may well be remembered alongside such other revolutionary years as the

INTRODUCTION

French Revolution of 1789, the 1848 Spring of Nations, the 1968 student movement, and the 1989 anti-communist protests. Mobilising millions of people, and winning the battle for public opinion, the protest wave of 2011–16 managed to fire up a powerful sense of possibility for radical political change as no other movement in decades had done. Some of these movements, such as the revolutions of the Arab Spring, overthrew regimes; others, such as those in Spain and Greece, led to the downfall of elected governments; all of them have thoroughly shaken and transformed their respective political systems. In fact, these upheavals became widely seen as the moment of foundation of a "new politics," which in the aftermath of the mobilisations led the rise of new left-wing formations like Podemos in Spain and radical political leaders like Bernie Sanders in the US. As argued by Christos Giovanopoulos, a 44-year-old Greek activist, the movement of the squares "changed the whole political imagination, the entire political landscape." But what actual change did the protest wave starting in 2011 bring about? Wherein lies its novelty vis-à-vis previous movements? And what can it reveal about contemporary society and its dilemmas at a time of systemic crisis and instability?

Some answers to these questions can be found in two symbols that often appeared next to one another among the protesting crowds gathered in the occupied squares. On the one hand there was the mask popularised by the international computer "hacktivist" group Anonymous: borrowed from the cult movie *V for Vendetta* and its main character V, and in turn inspired by the English anti-hero Guy Fawkes. On the other hand we saw national flags being waved in demonstrations and clashes in countries struck by this protest wave. These two striking images condense the two main political orientations—neo-anarchism and left-wing populism— that have met, mixed and clashed in the movements of 2011–16, giving way to the "new politics" of citizenism: an emerging ideology of the indignant citizen, that pits the self-organised citizenry against economic and political oligarchies, and pursues the reclamation and expansion of citizenship, seen as the necessary foundation of a true democracy.

The mask of Guy Fawkes is the most widely known symbol of the revolutions of 2011; ubiquitous in occupied squares and demonstrations, and reproduced in the millions while being incorporated into thousands of internet memes. At its core this smiling and moustached mask "signifies freedom of a distinctively left-libertarian sort," as Lewis Call has argued.[2] This symbol evokes that neo-anarchist influence that has been a constant in the arc of protest movements of post-industrial societies, starting with the student protests of 1968 and culminating in the anti-globalisation movement of the 1990s and 2000s. This political and cultural tendency—which has influenced radical feminism, environmentalism, the squatter movement, Marxist autonomism, anti-capitalist direct action, and hacker culture—exuded a palpable distrust for large-scale institutions such as multinational corporations, banks, and governments: neo-anarchist *bêtes noires* accused of controlling people's lives and deprived them of freedom.

In the positive, "the mask" expresses faith in the democratic power of "autonomous" individuals and self-organising collectives, as seen in a number of movement practices, from the self-management ethos of the '68 occupiers to the self-government of the Zapatistas in Mexico; the use of consensus-based decision-making by anti-globalisation activists in their direct-action movements; and the new practices of online collaboration in the open-source software movement and in hacker collectives, such as Anonymous and Lulzsec that have led a number of cyber-attacks against corporations and security agencies, and in support of various protest movements. Informed by notions of spontaneity and autonomy—staples of post-'68 alternative movements—this neo-anarchist orientation proposes an idea of grassroots democracy based on the principle of "horizontality," which opposes the presence of leaders and hierarchical structures.

The flag evokes something altogether different; strictly speaking flags denote control over an at least partly territorially defined political community. Official and revolutionary national flags have been ubiquitous in the Arab Spring that altered the map of Northern Africa and the Middle East beyond recognition, where they symbolised these movements' appeal to popular unity against the regimes. Furthermore, national flags have been flown in Greece in various demonstrations and protest camps as a way to express a demand for national independence against the perceived turn towards economic colonisation by Germany, but also in Brazil, Turkey, and the US, to express a sense of national unity and popular solidarity in the face of common enemies. Also in Spain where the official flag was taboo during the first Indignados protests due to its association with Franco's dictatorship, a flag did eventually appear in the "civic tide" demonstrations of 2012 and 2013, as the people waved the tricolour of the Spanish Republic defeated in the 1936–9 civil war, its connotations being both anti-fascist and anti-monarchical.

Image 0.1: Protester wearing a Guy Fawkes mask and various European national flags at anti-TTIP protest in Brussels, 16 October 2015 (Courtesy Michael Channan)

Alongside other cultural tropes widely seen in these movements, such as the use of local idioms and folk culture, and various unifying popular symbols, "the flag" manifests the surprising revival in contemporary protest of democratic populism: a populism of a very different sort to the right-wing and xenophobic proposals of the likes of new US President Donald Trump and "Brexit" champion Nigel Farage. This political orientation, which combines appeals to the people with a mostly benevolent patriotism, can be traced back to a number of progressive political movements, including the Narodniks,[3] the egalitarian Russian movement demanding the emancipation of peasants, and the progenitors of the term "populism"; the Chartists in Britain, who demanded a people's Charter guaranteeing basic democratic rights;[4] the People's Party in the

US who fought against robber barons, railroad tycoons, and the gold standard at the end of the nineteenth century;[5] and more recently the pink wave of Latin American socialist populism, represented by Hugo Chávez and Evo Morales among others. Furthermore, populist appeals to the people against the institutions have been implicit in many recent environmental, pro-democracy and anti-corruption mobilisations in Europe and the US. At its heart democratic populism contains a yearning for popular sovereignty,[6] understood as the collective control of a political community over its own destiny against the interference of various oligarchies: the Troika, global markets, financial speculators, lobbyists, and corrupt and authoritarian politicians, accused of rendering democracy and citizenship devoid of any substance.

The mask and the flag, the political traditions they allude to, and the social demands they express, seem at first sight irreconcilable. It is true that anarchism and democratic populism, two lesser-known leftist ideologies when compared to social-democracy and communism, share common origins in the political turmoil of the nineteenth century, at the time of the battle between autocratic regimes and emerging popular movements. This was seen most glaringly in the case of the Russian Narodniks: a populist movement at the dawn of the creation of the modern Left which deeply influenced Mikhail Bakunin, later to become the most influential figure of early anarchism.

Since those foundational times, however, anarchism and left-wing populism seem to have become increasingly at loggerheads. Anarchism espoused a politics of anti-statism, seeing the state as the root of all domination. Populism instead adopted a statist orientation, seeing in the state the necessary embodiment of popular sovereignty, and a weapon against particularist interests, and thus calling for a reintegration of the atomised people with the institutions of the state. Moreover, where anarchism has been resolute in its rejection of leadership and hierarchy, inherent in its very etymology, democratic populist movements have been well known for their customary reliance on strong charismatic leadership, as epitomised by figures like Feargus O'Connor, the leader of the Chartists; William Jennings Bryan, the presidential candidate of the US People's Party; Lázaro Cárdenas in Mexico; and Hugo Chávez in Venezuela. Finally, where neo-anarchism has espoused a cosmopolitan vision of the world where national borders are meaningless, something recently strengthened by its association with hacker culture and its experience of global interaction via the internet, populism has often been accompanied by an appeal to national identity as a source of meaning, and to the nation as a space to exercise the power of the People.

Why have such conflicting orientations come together in the movement of the squares of 2011–16? And what does their surprising marriage tell us about the meaning of these movements and about the new battle-lines of contemporary politics?

The birth of citizenism

Under the enormous pressure of the economic crisis of 2007–8 and amidst a deep distrust of political institutions, the convergence between neo-anarchism and democratic populism in the occupied squares has given way to a hybrid political culture, which in this book I describe as *citizenism*. Citizenism is a term that had in fact already been utilised by the protesters themselves in a number of countries struck by the 2011 protest wave, from the Spanish *"ciudadanismo,"*[7] to the French *"citoyennisme,"*[8] to refer to, and often to criticise, the ideology of the movement of the squares, particularly what some radical Leftists saw as its excessive moderatism and inclusivity. Furthermore, references to the subjects of the "citizens" and the "citizenry", and description of these movements as "citizens' movements" also cropped up in other countries, as seen for example in the description of the Tahrir movement as *"harka el-muwatineen"* [Movement of the Citizens], or in the Greek movement's name, Aganaktismenoi Polites [Indignant Citizens]. If Marx famously quipped that the French revolution adopted "Roman costumes and […] Roman phrases,"[9] in its revival of the ancient history of the Roman Republic, one could say that the movement of the squares in turn adopted the phrases of the French revolution, and its ultimate hero: the insurgent *citoyen*.

Citizenism is the ideology of the "indignant citizen," a citizen outraged at being deprived of citizenship, chiefly understood as the possibility of individuals to be active members of their political community with an equal say on all important decisions, which is increasingly in question in the neoliberal "post-democratic" condition.[10] It is a populist ideology but a very peculiar one: a libertarian,[11] participatory, or leaderless populism; an "anarcho-populism," which articulates the neo-anarchist method of *horizontality* and the populist demand for *sovereignty*, the mass ambition of populist movements, with the high premium placed on individual participation and creativity by neo-anarchism. Within this emerging ideology, "the citizen" or "the citizenry," as a sort of libertarian and individualist variation on the subject of populism's "the People", has become the new revolutionary subject, and "citizenship," as a more participatory and bottom-up approach to the populist demand for popular sovereignty, the new revolutionary object.

This discourse of the citizen and citizenship was however not just a change in the political lexicon or rhetoric. The transformation it signals runs much deeper. It affects different dimensions of protest movements: their collective identity; their definition of the central political conflict; and their vision of an alternative society.[12]

First, citizenship, a notion long associated with a conservative political ethos and an attitude of submission to the *status quo*, was counter-intuitively cast as a radical sentiment and a source of collective identity for protest movements. The movement of the squares used the notion of citizenship, and the subjects of the citizen and the citizenry, rather than notions of class or gender-based and cultural identities, as a common denominator to bring together the disparate social fragments that feel at a disadvantage in a world in which 1 per cent of the population controls more wealth than the remaining 99 per cent.[13] These have included the lost generation of precarious youth, the squeezed middle seeing its economic security threatened, and the new poor affected by unemployment and low pay. It has been precisely the perception of a "lack of citizenship"; the awareness of its erosion and privatisation[14] due to the onslaught of financial markets, the weakening of the nation-state in a globalised era, and the crisis of mass membership organisations, which has made citizenship a signifier capable of uniting a multitude of grievances, demands and constituencies in a counter-hegemonic popular alliance. Citizenship is reclaimed as a source of dignity, in a world in which many feel humiliated by the arrogance of global financiers and an aloof political class.

Second, the central conflict of society in citizenism is not that between labour and capital, which dominated the political "imaginary"[15] of twentieth century left-wing movements. For the movement of the squares, the central antagonism has been between the Citizenry and the Oligarchy: the power of ordinary citizens versus the privilege of economic and political elites, financial markets, the super-rich, the Troika, technocrats and career politicians, all accused of ruling in spite of the views of the majority of the population. The widening gap between the super-rich and the rest; the collapse of the middle class and the rise of a lost generation of "graduates with no future";[16] the authoritarian behaviour evident in dictatorships and democratic governments alike; the endemic political corruption and the lack of trust in traditional parties; the inability of established civil society organisations and trade unions to cast themselves as defenders of collective interests; a closed-off political system,[17] largely indifferent to new demands: these grievances have been viewed as part of a larger political problem; the manifestation of an anti-democratic and oligarchic trend in government, that deprives ordinary citizens of their fundamental democratic rights and consequently also of their economic welfare and personal dignity.

Third, citizenism offers a view of a better society which centres on the notion of "real democracy,"[18] beyond the "sham democracy" controlled by lobbies, career politicians, and financiers. This effort of "democratising democracy", in the words of Wendy Brown, at a time at which it appears to have been hollowed out, has also resorted to the imaginary and language of citizenship. Protesters saw the reclaiming and expansion of citizenship, understood as a condition of political equality and a culture of active participation in the polity, as the best antidote against an oligarchic power that feeds precisely on the passivity and apathy of an atomised and unpoliticised population. This vision of a bottom-up reclamation of democracy, laying claim to the people's voice and participation in public life, was dramatised in the occupation of public squares the world over, which turned into contemporary "agoras": public spaces in which ordinary citizens could re-engage in the most basic of political acts, such as participating in public meetings and discussing political issues, with the ultimate aim of progressively constituting a power from below from which to challenge the power of those above.

The notion of citizenism, and the connected idea of a politics of radical citizenship, provides a condensed framework for understanding the transformation of protest movements and politics more generally in the era of the Great Recession. Firstly, citizenism signals a veritable change of paradigm in protest culture, which moves away from the minoritarian, countercultural and unequivocally anti-statist "politics of autonomy" of the anti-globalisation movement, and towards a majoritarian and counter-hegemonic politics of radical citizenship aiming at achieving systemic social and institutional change. Instead of pitting society against the state, and pursuing a "counter-power" against official power, as many anti-authoritarian and anarchist movements did in the aftermath of the 1968 student protests, the movement of the squares tried to build an "under-power", a power from below, which starting from the squares could progressively reclaim all levels of society, including state institutions. Citizenism needs to be understood as a progressive version of the populist turn evident in contemporary politics, while neoliberal hegemony fails. It demonstrates that populist sensibilities do not necessarily need to be turned towards xenophobic and authoritarian ends, as exemplified by the politics of Donald Trump, but can be geared towards a democratic and emancipatory direction. This is why analysing citizenism constitutes an urgent task for those interested in developing a progressive political agenda matching the conditions that have emerged in the aftermath of the 2008 financial crisis.

A global analysis of the occupation movements

Adopting citizenism as a guiding concept, this book aims at developing a global sociological analysis of the movement of the squares and the way it reflected an exceptional historical conjuncture marked by converging economic and political crises. Completed on the fifth anniversary of the 2011 upheavals it constitutes to date one of the most extensive (in terms of coverage) and intensive (in terms of depth of empirical research) analyses of this protest wave.[19] Furthermore, it looks at these movements' political ramifications and their spawning of new social and political organisations that are reshaping radical politics the world over. The book covers a total of nine case studies: the Arab Spring, with particular reference to Egypt and Tunisia; the Spanish Indignados and Greek Aganaktismenoi anti-austerity movements; Occupy Wall Street in the US and the UK, which effectively globalised the uprising; the Gezi Park protests in Turkey and the Movimento de Junho in Brazil in 2013, which shook their respective governments and showed the enduring vitality of the global uprising; and finally France's Nuit Debout protests in the spring of 2016.

The movements discussed in this book displayed a considerable degree of diversity in their composition, their ostensible aims, their relationship with power holders, and their discourses and practices. Some were more concerned with the economy, others were concerned with politics; some were more progressive, others were more conservative;

some confronted dictatorships, others elected governments; some have been more durable, others more evanescent. Yet, as we shall see, they all shared significant common features including their tactic of occupying public space for protest, resistance, and deliberation;[20] the adoption of a spirit of radical inclusiveness, epitomised by Occupy's slogan "We Are the 99 Percent"; the suspicion towards leaders, organised political groups and celebrities; the rejection of the Left/Right divide and of traditional ideological descriptions; the eschewal of militantism and a resort instead to amateur protest skills, as exemplified by the ubiquity of handmade protest signs; the use of social media such as Facebook and Twitter as mobilising platforms; the encompassing of demographics not traditionally seen in political demonstrations, including older people and those with more conservative beliefs; the prevalence of non-violent tactics; and the emphasis on participatory practices allowing all individuals to have a say in the process.

To explore these elements of commonality, which stand to signal the rise of a new global protest culture, between 2011 and 2016 I conducted extensive fieldwork, which allowed me to gather a large volume of qualitative data in the form of interviews, ethnographic observations, and archival and social media material, providing the foundations on which this study's theorising rests. Writing this book has involved first and foremost living through the protests in person, by travelling to and residing in the various cities where rebellions exploded as if via chain reaction. I had the opportunity to visit many of the key sites of this protest wave, including Tunis, Cairo, Athens, Madrid, Barcelona, Istanbul, New York, London, Rio de Janeiro, Sao Paulo and Paris, while protests raged in those countries. During these visits I immersed myself in the space these movements created, spending a lot of time in protest camps and exploring their manifold activities and events, from people's libraries, people's kitchens, assemblies, working groups and committees, to the stand-offs with security forces.

Especially important was to meet and interview these movements' protagonists, their organisers and participants, to get a sense of how they experienced the upheavals and understood their meaning, ends, prospects and impact. For each of the core countries covered in this book I conducted 15–25 in-depth interviews, for a total of 140 people (details are included in the appendix at the end of the book). These in-depth conversations provided me with a vivid picture of how the movement felt from the inside, and the different hurdles faced by its participants. Finally, I could also avail myself of data gathered during prior research on the anti-globalisation movement, during which I conducted fifty interviews with activists in Germany, Italy, and the UK, as well as my acquaintance with activism and related youth subcultures and countercultures. Unless otherwise cited, all direct quotes in this book originate from these interviews.

Besides the "live data" of observations and interviews which offered what anthropologists call a "thick account" of what these movements were and how they were experienced by their participants, the book has also drawn upon comprehensive archival research, comprising numerous statistics and key movement documents, including public resolutions, declarations of popular assemblies, and the manifestoes of various protest groups. These documents serve to cast light on the worldviews, self-definitions, and demands these movements have put forward.

The anarchist, Marxist, and techno-political views

Since its emergence the movement of the squares has been the object of an intense debate which has often appeared very tentative and discordant, not least because of the enigmatic character of these movements, and the difficulty of pigeon-holing them into familiar social and political categories. The academic discussion can be roughly categorised into three schools, each with their interpretations of these movements and particular political biases: the anarchist, the Marxist, and the techno-political view. The first two read these movements as prolongations of two familiar twentieth-century ideologies known for their mutual rivalry, while the third reads them as the necessary result of present technological and economic conditions. All these streams provide important insights into the nature of these movements: the influence of neo-anarchist culture; their status as history-changing "events"; their reclamation of a universalist and emancipatory narrative; and their reflection of digital technology and its potential for grassroots organisation. However, they fall short of identifying the novelties and elements of rupture vis-à-vis previous social movements, and in particular the anti-globalisation movement of the 1990s and early 2000s.

The analysis of the movement of the squares that has predominated within activist debates, especially in the US and northern Europe, is their interpretation as twenty-first-century anarchism, standing in direct continuity with the neo-anarchist section of the anti-globalisation movement. To this stream pertains the work of such self-declared anarchists and autonomists as David Graeber, Mark Bray, Raúl Zibechi, Marina Sitrin and Dario Azzellini.[21] These authors emphasise the anti-representational character of these movements and see their pursuit of direct democratic practices as proof of their adherence to neo-anarchist beliefs. Thus, David Graeber, influential activist and intellectual in both the anti-globalisation movement and Occupy movement was based on anarchist principles due to its use of "direct action, direct democracy, a rejection of existing political institutions and attempt to create alternative ones."[22] Mark Bray has described the Occupy movement as "an anti-capitalist, anti-authoritarian movement run by organisers with predominantly anarchist and anarchistic politics."[23] US political historian Michael Kazin has likewise portrayed Occupy activists as the "cyber-clever progeny of Henry David Thoreau and Emma Goldman" dreaming of a future of "self-governing communities" and animated by a "non-doctrinaire anarchism."[24] In their book *They Can't Represent Us!* Marina Sitrin and Dario Azzellini describe these movements as rejecting all forms of representation in the name of a neo-anarchist politics of "horizontality."[25]

While these interpretations have been most frequently made in reference to Occupy Wall Street, as a reflection of the popularity of anarchism in the US compared with other countries, they have also been seen in other contexts. Turkish writer Süreyya Evren argued that the protesters in Gezi Park used "anarchistic organisational principles" that were reminiscent of the themes of 1968.[26] Raúl Zibechi has described the movement in Brazil as animated by the neo-anarchist principles of "autonomy and horizontalism."[27] These authors are correct in identifying the presence of a neo-anarchist influence in these movements, seen in their participatory ethos and their adherence to the idea of horizontality. What they fail to notice, however, is that this neo-anarchist element is only one part of a mosaic comprised of various ideological orientations, among which democratic populism features most prominently, and neo-anarchism appears more in the guise of a residual ideological element, inherited from movements past.

The Marxist interpretation takes a more critical view of this protest wave. While not daring to say, as their anarchist colleagues do, that the movements belong to their own political camp—something which would be open to challenge due to the scarcity of self-declared communists in these movements—authors such as Alain Badiou,[28] Slavoj Žižek[29] and Jodi Dean read in them a political potentiality that furnishes fresh proof of the supposedly ever-green "communist hypothesis."[30] The protests of 2011 are seen, to use a typical Badiouan term, as an "event", a moment of rupture in the historical continuum that opens the possibility of a new emancipatory universalism beyond the folly of the present capitalist order. For the *doyen* of French radical thought, the wave of occupations revealed that "we find ourselves in a time of riots wherein a rebirth of History, as opposed to the pure and simple repetition of the worst, is signalled and takes shape."[31]

While complimenting these movements for demonstrating that history is not yet over, as infamously argued by one of liberal democracy's foremost apologists, Francis Fukuyama,[32] these Marxist scholars unsurprisingly harbour a scepticism towards them and their neo-anarchist elements. Thus Badiou criticises these movements both for being insurrectionary rather than revolutionary, and for substituting the "correct" demand for communism with the demand for democracy, which he, like others in the group, considers a fundamentally bourgeois con.[33] Jodi Dean has taken aim at the organisational practices of these movements arguing that they should abandon their belief in spontaneity[34] and organise as a party,[35] while Žižek has often lambasted the narcissism of their direct democracy practices. This literature is perceptive enough to see the self-indulgence of the politics of horizontality and spontaneity. Yet, by scrabbling to associate these movements with the communist cause, these scholars demonstrate scant connection with the feelings of participants on the ground, who, as we shall see in the course of the book, in fact hold short shrift for the lost cause of the Soviet Union and are more concerned with the issue of democracy than with the overthrow of capitalism.

The "techno-political" view does not derive the characteristics of these movements from a specific ideology, but rather from the material and technological conditions in which contemporary activists operate. It focuses on the "affordances" of digital communication technologies in the era of social media like Facebook and Twitter, and the way they have facilitated new forms of inter-personal interaction and social organisation. An abundant literature has explored this issue, including the work of W. Lance Bennett,[37] Manuel Castells, Jeffrey Juris, Javier Toret, Antonio Calleja-Lopez, John Postill, Arnau Monterde[38] and this author's previous book, *Tweets and the Streets*.[39] Famed sociologist of the network society Manuel Castells has argued that these "networked movements" are "largely made of individuals living at ease with digital technologies in the hybrid world of real virtuality," and are deeply influenced by the "culture of autonomy" of the internet.[40] Jeffrey Juris sees these movements' adoption of social media platforms leading to a transition of the "networking" logic of the anti-globalisation movement, to a logic of "mass aggregation", resulting in the huge crowds that gathered in the occupied squares.[41] These authors are right to highlight the role of digital connectivity in contemporary protest and its potential for grassroots organising. Indeed, as we will see, the values and worldview of these movements bear a strong connection to digital culture and hacker culture, and their techno-utopianism and techno-libertarianism. However, citizenism cannot be reduced to the affordances of digital communication alone; any evaluation needs to encompass the totality of contemporary social experience, and its emerging desires and fears at a time of systemic crisis.

The movement of the squares as a populist insurrection

There is a fourth possible interpretation of this protest movement, which informs the argument of this book and my understanding of citizenism. This view sees the 2011 and post-2011 mobilisations as manifesting a *populist turn* in protest culture, centring on the demand for popular sovereignty, economic equality and a restoration of the true spirit of democracy.[42] Since the beginning of the Great Recession there has been much discussion about a "populist zeitgeist"[43] seen in the rise of an array of populist phenomena on both the left and right wings of the political spectrum, including the rise of new parties such as Podemos and the Five Star Movement in Spain and Italy, the electoral growth of xenophobic formations like the Front National in France, and the emergence of anti-establishment candidates such as Bernie Sanders and Donald Trump in the US. As we will see in Chapter 2, populism is an eccentric ideology with both right and left-wing manifestations. The strand most relevant to understanding the movement of the squares is left-wing democratic populism, steeped in democratic passion and emancipatory fervour and with its roots in a number of people's movements, from the nineteenth-century reformers like the Russian Narodniks, the British Chartists, and the US People's Party, to the Latin American "pink wave" of Chávez and Morales.

Like other democratic populist movements, citizenism's central concern has been with the reclaiming of democracy, understood not simply as a set of procedures for the selection of ruling elites,[44] as proposed by Joseph Schumpeter, but rather as a substantive condition of equality and freedom "that constantly wrests the monopoly of public life from oligarchic governments, and the omnipotence over lives from the power of wealth," as argues French philosopher Jacques Rancière.[45] Counter to the republican emphasis on mixed government and representation, populism approaches democracy in its original and radical sense as people-power and popular self-government. For populists, democracy is thus deeply intertwined with the notion of popular sovereignty as enabling the majority of the population to exercise "a day to day influence on the conduct of society," in the words of Alexis de Tocqueville in *Democracy in America*.[46]

As we shall see, in the case of the 2011–16 public square occupations this customary populist demand for democracy and sovereignty was framed in protest discourse as depending on a bottom-up reclamation of citizenship rights, precisely because of the perception that their erosion in times of globalisation and financialisation is the factor that has allowed the establishment of the Oligarchy and the hollowing out of democracy.

My view of the movement of the squares and of citizenism as "neo-populist" has two important analytical and political implications.

First, this view locates the 2011 protest wave at an exceptional conjuncture of "regime crisis" or "organic crisis," in which, as Gramsci claims, "the old is dying and the new cannot be born," a moment at which progressive populist movements are more likely to arise.[47] The worst economic crisis of capitalism since the Great Depression of 1929—still hobbling the world as we continue through the second decade of the twenty-first century—and the deepening disaffection of citizens with the establishment, have contributed to hastening a crisis for the neoliberal order, with its faith in the self-regulating power of the market, which has dominated the world since the 1980s. The crisis of neoliberalism and the inability of established Left parties and civil society organisations—trade unions, co-operatives, associations—to give voice and weight to popular demands have created the space for new counter-hegemonic actors to arise on the back of broad social alliances that were previously inconceivable.

16

Secondly, the interpretation of the movement of the squares as populist highlights how, counter to what has been claimed by anarchist theorists, these mobilisations have not adopted a narrow anti-statist and anti-representational view. They have not aimed simply at creating forms of counter-power in civil society against political institutions. As will be seen when analysing the content of resolutions and declarations of popular assemblies, participants in the movement of the squares instead mostly saw in the opening-up of the state a necessary step towards reasserting popular sovereignty and confronting oligarchic power. This orientation marked a significant departure from the political logic of the anti-globalisation movement, which like many post-'68 anti-authoritarian movements before it saw the state as the enemy and not as a structure to be reclaimed. The return of a more pragmatic attitude towards political institutions goes a long way towards explaining why this protest wave has acted as the incubator for new political organisations and parties such as Podemos, and for the rise of left-wing political figures such as Bernie Sanders and Jeremy Corbyn.

Citizenism is, however, markedly different from traditional forms of populism in a number of respects. It is a populism with a libertarian twist, an "anarcho-populism" that reflects the influence of neo-anarchist culture in previous movements: it is populist in content, but libertarian or neo-anarchist in form. Also neo-anarchistic are its organisational structures, communicative practices, and protest tactics; but neo-populist the meanings, demands, and claims it conveys through such practices. Reflecting the libertarian primacy of the individual over the collective, and a concern for individual freedom, creativity, participation and self-realisation, long present in alternative movements and subcultures with their suspicion towards bureaucracy and large-scale organisations, citizenism appeals not to the People in its collectivity, but to the Citizen as the individual component of the People. It turns upside-down the modernist political imaginary of revolutions and popular movements, in which the citizen was seen simply as the "member" of the collective and totalising subject of the People, reflecting how references to "the People" smack too much of the distant upheavals of the nineteenth century and sound out of sync with the present era of individualism.[48] Citizenism is thus a populism for an individualised and digital era, informed by a suspicion towards organisations and by the libertarian ethos of digital culture, hacking, and open-source, yet also animated by a resurgent desire for community and collective solidarity in face of extreme inequality.

Such a libertarian twist has important consequences for organisational forms. Citizenism moves away from the traditional populist assumption about the need for a charismatic leader as the necessary unifying element of an otherwise divided population. This assumption is thematised by Ernesto Laclau when he argues that, "the equivalential logic leads to singularity, and singularity to an identification of the unity of the group with the name of the leader,"[49] a view which is informed by Gustave Le Bon's famous description of the emotional relationship between the crowd and the leader.[50] Counter to this leader-centric view, citizenism sees popular unity as emerging organically out of people's "crowding" online and offline, rather than depending on top-down intervention. Reflecting its incorporation of the neo-anarchist principle of horizontality, citizenism is thus a populism of the "leaderless people", in which the function of the charismatic leader is substituted by the self-organising power of the connected citizenry and by a number of unifying symbols and practices, from the occupied squares to social media and popular assemblies. The movements have however not been completely deprived of leadership. Rather leadership has taken more collective, diffused and interactive forms than those seen in the Old Left of trade unions and parties.

The articulation between libertarian and populist orientations has led to new discourses and practices that have captured the public imagination, at times torn between individualism and a new desire for solidarity, between the narcissism displayed in social networking sites and selfies, and a returning longing for community. But this hybrid ideology has also experienced notable frictions, reflecting the profound differences between its constituent inspirations. Populist and neo-anarchist orientations sometimes appeared to be at cross-purposes and more or less easily identifiable populist and anarchist factions within these movements took rather different views of the meaning and purpose of the occupations. For example, where for anarchists protest camps were seen as self-governed communes prefiguring a world without state and government, for populists they were instead meant to constitute a temporary rallying point for the reclamation of the entirety of society and its political institutions.

INTRODUCTION

2001–11: From counter-summits to public square encampments

This book is not an analysis of ideology as an abstract system of ideas, but rather of ideology as a lived texture of meaning, values and beliefs that pervades all the domains of activity of protest movements, and whose presence can be identified in their most concrete manifestations and the way they respond to overarching cultural motives. To conduct the present investigation we shall focus on two main levels: discourses and practices. The first encompasses the ways in which protest movements conceive of themselves, their adversaries, society, and their goals. The second includes the practices of communication, organisation and protest which these movements deploy in accordance with such discourses.

At the discourse level I will focus on two elements: *ideology*, understood as the general system of values and beliefs that structures these movements' worldview; and *identity*, understood as the subjective self-definition of protest movements. At the level of the analysis of practices, my study will focus instead on three issues: *communication practices* deployed by these movements, and the way in which they mobilise participants; the forms of protest often described as *protest tactics*; and finally the *forms of decision-making* and internal organisation. Other aspects that will be discussed include the geographic scale of protest action and its level of national and international coordination, and the connection between social movements and political institutions. Analysing these different levels of collective action will allow us to explore the concrete difference citizenism has made both to the way in which social movements operate internally, and how they interact with society at large.

To ascertain the specificity and novelty of the movement of the squares I will compare and contrast it with previous protest movements and in particular the anti-globalisation movement. This comparative approach stems from the recognition that no movement creates itself out of thin air; all reflect the deeds of their predecessors, inherit part of their language, aesthetics, and tactics, and absorb their victories and defeats. Yet protest movements are always also a reflection of the specific historical conjuncture they traverse, of the specific dilemmas and demands the present throws up. To them applies the Arab proverb, "men resemble their times more than they resemble their fathers", and this is particularly true at times of systemic crisis, the likes of which the world has been experiencing since the explosion of the financial crisis of 2008, which open the possibility for new actors to storm the political arena.

Table 0.1: Levels of analysis of protest culture

	Anti-globalisation movement	*Movement of the squares*
Discourses		
Ideology	Anarcho-autonomism (autonomy and diversity)	Citizenism (sovereignty and horizontality)
Identity	Countercultural/ minoritarian	Popular/majoritarian
Practices		
Communication	Indymedia, alternative mailing lists, hacker meetings	Facebook, Twitter, Tumblr, messaging apps, hackpads
Organisation	Collectives, spokes-councils, social forums, logic of networking	Popular assemblies, logic of "organisation of the disorganised"
Protest tactics	Counter-summits, blockades, block-ins, direct action	Protest encampments in central public spaces; impromptu marches
Scale and political outcomes		
Scale	Global space	National space with strong transnational connections
Relationship with institutional space	Civil society versus political society; uneasy collaboration with political parties; anti-statist attitude	Strategy of "assault on the institutions"; genesis and re-generation of leftist political parties; constitutional processes and civic campaigns

The obvious case for comparison with the movement of the squares is the anti-globalisation movement, the most important predecessor and inspiration for the 2011 wave (see Table 0.1). The anti-globalisation movement, also known as the global justice movement or alter-globalisation movement, is the wave of protest against capitalist globalisation that emerged around the turn of the millennium, and whose flash-points were large counter-summit demonstrations such as those against the WTO in Seattle in 1999, the World Bank and IMF in Prague in 2000, and the G8 in Genoa in 2001.[51] The anti-globalisation protest wave united different factions of the radical Left—Trotskyist groups, environmentalists, trade unions, and NGOs—in an unstable alliance of the radical Left after the defeat of the labour movement in the 1980s, the fall of the Berlin wall, and the newly rampant hegemony of neoliberalism. Within this motley crew the so-called "anarcho-autonomist" section, comprising both anarchist and Marxist autonomist groups—as manifested in a wide range of phenomena, from the anarchist Black Bloc to direct action environmentalist protests, and non-violent civil disobedience as practiced by groups such as the Tute Bianche [White Overalls][52] at counter-summit protests—exercised cultural hegemony over the whole movement, with its ideas of autonomy and the rejection of hierarchy influencing the entire movement. The anti-globalisation movement managed to mount an impressive challenge to the new regime of global governance, but was soon suffocated by police repression, in-fighting, and the "war on terror" that followed the 9/11 attacks, shifting attention away from its cause.

As we shall see, the relationship of the movement of the squares with the anti-globalisation movement is a complicated one. On the one hand, there are clear continuities between these two protest waves. Firstly, many of the older activists of the movement of the squares, those in their 30s and 40s, cut their teeth in the global counter-summits of the 1990s and 2000s. Secondly, the movement of the squares can be seen as a vindication of much of the analysis of the anti-globalisation movement and in particular its criticism of neoliberalism. Last but not least, the movement of the squares derived much of the organisational ethos and practice of the anti-globalisation movement, as seen for example in their consensus-based decision-making, their rejection of leadership and their use of direct action tactics. Despite this legacy, there is some evidence of rupture at the level of ideology, identity, and organisational practices that reflects the populist turn introduced by the 2011 upheavals, and the rise of citizenism. The 2011 generation of protesters spurned key beliefs and values of the anti-globalisation movement in order to respond to changing structural conditions and exploit the new political opportunities opening up for social movements.[53]

This change in spirit and attitude between the anti-globalisation movement and the movement of the squares is visible both at the level of "protest discourses" and "protest practices", the ideas guiding social movements and their concrete forms of action.

In terms of protest discourses the movement of the squares was characterised by its adoption of the highly inclusive subject of the citizen and the citizenry in opposition to oligarchic power, and by its focus on the political demands of democracy, sovereignty, and citizenship. Where the anti-globalisation movement criticised capitalism and multinational corporations, the movement of the squares took aim at the Oligarchy, understood as the unholy alliance between economic and political elites. Where the former espoused the value of autonomy, as the right to absolute self-determination of small social units, individuals, collectives or local communities, the latter reintroduced the more universalist principle of popular sovereignty, which affirms the supremacy of the people's general will, above and beyond the corporate or parochial interests of specific sections of society, or the sectarian orientations of various political groupings. Where global justice activists were mostly imbued with an antagonistic and minoritarian identity, connected with a moral valuing of minorities over majorities, the movement of the squares took the side of the majority, most glaringly expressed in Occupy's "We Are The 99 Percent" slogan. The anti-globalisation movement conceived of itself through the postmodern notion of "multitude," proposed by Antonio Negri and Michael Hardt,[54] and the connected ideas of the "network" and the "swarm." The occupation movements instead constantly referred to the unifying notion of the citizenry, and reclaimed the imaginary of the mass and the crowd. Finally, where the anti-globalisation movement was often characterised by a countercultural rejection of mainstream culture, the movement of the squares was marked by a counter-hegemonic appeal to reasonability and common sense; by a focus "on concrete things, things that affect ordinary people," as put by Spanish activist Javier Toret, a 37-year-old organiser and social media campaigner with ¡Democracia Real Ya! in Barcelona.

The populist turn could also be seen in protest practices: the movement of the squares' main novelty consisted of its development of a populist logic of mass mobilisation through a scaling-up of participatory practices, previously confined to anarchist and activist subcultures. Where the anti-globalisation movement constructed autonomous communication infrastructures, acting as Islands in the Net, the movement of the squares occupied the mainstream internet, unashamedly making use of corporate platforms such as Facebook, YouTube, and Twitter as means of mass outreach. Where global justice activists mostly pursued a "small group" politics, of collectives and affinity groups organised in flexible networks, the occupation movements constructed inclusive mass assemblies encompassing a diverse cross-section of the population. Finally, where the former erected its protest camps and occupations in peripheral areas, the latter occupied areas at the very centre of political and geographic space as a way to acquire high visibility and to be easily accessible to ordinary people. These strategic changes bespeak a different organisational logic. The anti-globalisation movement attempted to "organise the organised," to cluster together already active and organised sections of society. The movement of the squares instead tried to "organise the disorganised," to mobilise the unrepresented, with the aim of recomposing together the many "fragments" and "atoms" of an individualised and apolitical neoliberal society into a new collectivity.

Changes in protest discourse and practice ran in parallel with modifications in the scale of protest action and the relationship between protest movements and institutions. Where the anti-globalisation movement was characterised by its attempt to construct a global space of action, the movement of the squares instead focused on the national level, while at the same time constructing important transnational connections. Moreover, whereas the anti-globalisation movement was marked by an uneasy collaboration with political parties, the movement of the squares has led to the genesis of new political parties such as Podemos, the renewal of existing left-wing parties as with Syriza, and the propulsion of maverick politicians like Bernie Sanders and Jeremy Corbyn into the limelight. The anti-globalisation movement pursued a politics of the "society against the State"[55] that attempted to create spaces of autonomy and counter-power away from the control of state institutions. The movement of the squares instead inspired a strategy of an "assault on the institutions," that included an attempt at a radical transformation of state institutions and their opening up to the will of their citizens.

The movement of the squares was thus a sort of estranged child of the anti-globalisation movement. It kept with some of its predecessor's cultural motives—in particular with its libertarian emphasis on self-organisation, expressed in the principle of "horizontality," as a rejection of all forms of "vertical" hierarchy and formalised organisation—but also introduced radically different attitudes and ideas to match the rapid transformation of social conditions in the aftermath of the 2008 crisis and the political and geo-political quake it unleashed. Protest culture has

transitioned from the minoritarian antagonism of the politics of autonomy to a counter-hegemonic politics of radical citizenship that reinserts
an emphasis on collectivist notions of unity, solidarity and sovereignty,
and an expansive imaginary of mass mobilisation, one which had long
been eschewed by anti-authoritarian protest movements.

Besides developing an analysis of the movement of the squares, the
book also aims at a critical evaluation of its successes and failures. As we
shall see citizenism has proven well suited to the social experience of a
crisis-ridden post-industrial society, marked by a number of serious
obstacles for grassroots political organising, including extreme individualisation and social fragmentation; low levels of organisational affiliation;
political apathy, and distrust of traditional Left ideologies. This emerging
ideology has been able to appeal to different demographics, catering
both for the libertarian impulses of precarious middle class students and
for the populist drive of the many other demographics that joined this
protest wave, including the squeezed middle and the new poor. However,
these mobilisations were also soon crippled by a number of contradictions that reflect their difficulty in accommodating libertarian and populist orientations. This was most glaringly seen in the fizzling out of these
movements after a phase of momentous growth. Protest camps were
dismantled, assemblies shrunk and shrunk, and social media enthusiasm
turned into disappointment. The great hopes these upheavals had managed to conjure, and the sense of a global revolution, seemed to vanish
at almost the same speed at which they had made their spectacular
entrance onto the public stage.

While some commentators have taken these elements of weakness as
signifying the ultimate defeat of the movement of the squares, as we shall
see, this protest wave was a fundamental historical turning and a foundational development for a new wave of progressive politics that is currently challenging the neoliberal order. The public square occupations
turned into powerful rituals of popular communion, allowing an individualised and fragmented citizenry to regain collective solidarity, and
have acted as the "incubators" for new social campaigns, initiatives and
political organisations that have tried to bring the voice of protesters and
their demands to the institutions. This has been seen in the foundation
of new parties like Podemos in Spain, a general revival of Left politics as
seen in the re-foundation and victory of Syriza in Greece, the growth of
the Turkish Peoples' Democratic Party, the election of Jeremy Corbyn as

Labour leader in the UK, and the impressive performance of Bernie Sanders in the 2015–16 US Democratic Party primaries. These phenomena can be seen as the first inklings of a new Left for the twenty-first century, capable of responding to the challenges of a society marked by extreme inequality.

Thus the outcome of the movement of the squares has been mixed yet impressive in its long-term consequences. It is true that this protest wave did not deliver on its hyperbolic ambition of fomenting global revolution. But it ignited a powerful sense of possibility, condensed in the Indignados' appropriation of Obama's slogan "Yes we can," and instigated a general re-politicisation of society that will inform radical politics for years to come. It was both a destituent moment (a negative moment of "undoing" the political order, in Agamben's sense),[56] contesting the existing status quo, and a constituent moment, facilitating the construction of a new political space for the development of a progressive and democratic politics.

To explore this momentous protest wave the book begins by reconstructing its history and root causes. It goes on to discuss the discourses these movements developed, in particular with regards to their collective identity and ideology, their space of action and the practices they constructed in accordance with these discourses, with specific reference to their forms of mobilisation, protest tactics and practices of organisation. It concludes by evaluating their impact on civil society and political institutions.

Chapter 1 provides the historical, economic and political context for the ensuing analysis. I argue that these movements should be understood as a "protest mosaic", encompassing various regional clusters: the Arab Spring, the Mediterranean Indignados, Occupy Wall Street, and the protests in emerging economies like Turkey and Brazil. Furthermore, I locate the movement of the squares in the historical context of a phase of *interregnum* provoked by the economic crisis of 2007–08 and rising disaffection with political institutions that unlocked new pools of mobilisation for social movements, leading to the construction of a popular alliance that comprised the precarious youth of the lost generation, the squeezed middle, and the *nouveaux pauvres* created by the economic crisis.

In Chapter 2 citizenism is described as a hybrid compound that arises at the point of confluence between neo-anarchism and democratic populism. The movement of the squares combined the neo-anarchist principle of horizontality, prescribing a rejection of leaders and formal structures, with the populist idea of popular sovereignty, affirming the need for strong collective control over the economy and politics. This ideological mix informed the citizenist vision of "real democracy" encompassing both alternative democratic structures and a reclamation of existing democratic institutions, seen as a means to fight against the onslaught of the oligarchy.

Chapter 3 discusses the change in subjectivity and identity that accompanied the 2011 upheavals. These movements adopted a highly inclusive and syncretic popular identity which involved a shift from minoritarianism to majoritarianism, as exemplified in the famous "We Are The 99 Percent" slogan of Occupy Wall Street. However, this shift was not simply a return to the modernist imaginary of the People. The movement of the squares instead opted for the notion of the citizenry as a libertarian adaptation of the People, to emphasise the emergent and bottom-up nature of the contemporary revolutionary subject.

Chapter 4 examines the transformation of the scale and space of radical politics by the movement of the squares. While the anti-globalisation movement saw globalisation as a new political space that could supersede the (supposedly inherently conservative) nation-state, the movement of the squares re-centred the nation as the most important stage of political struggle. This trend was hailed as abandoning the naïve cosmopolitanism of previous protest movements and reclaiming a rootedness in national space. However, it also raised questions as to the ethical and political risks arising from the nationalist temptations inherent in populism.

Chapter 5 discusses the use of social media by protesters, and their contribution to the process of mobilisation. Activists made use of the outreach and participatory capabilities of corporate social networks such as Facebook and Twitter and utilised the many tropes of digital popular culture as a means to launch inclusive calls for participation. Countering the activist narrative that sees social media as engendering a radical redistribution of power and the elimination of leadership, I demonstrate how these practices see the emergence of new forms of leadership, epitomised by the role of social media activist teams: collectives responsible for managing the social media accounts of these movements.

Chapter 6 examines protest camps as the most iconic manifestation of the new "protest repertoire" introduced by the movement of the squares. While bearing some similarity to the protest camps of the anti-globalisation movement, the 2011 protest encampments had more public visibility and a more inclusive attitude towards movement outsiders. They were cast as open agoras—arenas of popular communion—in which a fragmented and individualised citizenry may rediscover collective solidarity and unity in the concrete experience of living and organising together in the camp. While useful as a means of dramatisation of the movement's spirit, this tactic often became a fixation, blocking the development of the movement.

Chapter 7 looks at processes of internal organisation and decision-making, and in particular popular assemblies, committees and working groups that emerged in the occupied squares. These movements saw a scaling up of the "direct democracy" practices of the anti-globalisation movement to unprecedented levels of participation, with assemblies becoming a sort of people's parliament opposed to the official parliament accused of betraying the people's will. However these events also laid bare the limits of consensus decision-making and horizontality in the construction of a mass movement, as seen in the sluggishness of many assemblies and the way they ended up alienating many newcomers.

Chapter 8 looks at the political outcome of these movements, and their reshaping of the political landscape in their respective countries. I argue that these movements' narrative of an assault on the institutions has overcome the sterile anti-statist view of many previous protest movements, including the latter's obstinacy in limiting themselves to merely a politics of resistance and counter-power. New single issue campaigns, alternative media and the revival of progressive politics, as seen in the electoral surge of democratic populist formations like Podemos in Spain and Syriza in Greece and the rise of radical candidates like Jeremy Corbyn and Bernie Sanders, have raised the hope of a political translation of this movement's momentum into a tangible change in government and policy.

The conclusion explores the implications of the movement of the squares and citizenism for contemporary society and for the construction of a progressive politics in the twenty-first century. I argue that the lasting contribution of these movements consists in their affirmation of a politics of radical citizenship, aimed at re-constructing democracy from the bottom-up, and in their organisational innovation pointing to the possibility of a compromise between the logic of participation and the logic of representation, which long appeared irreconcilable.

MOVEMENTS IN THE CRISIS
OF NEOLIBERALISM

We will not leave the squares until those who compelled us to come here leave the country: the governments, the Troika (EU, ECB, and IMF), the banks, the IMF Memoranda, and everyone who wants to exploit us. We send them the message that the debt is not ours.

Resolution of the People's Assembly of Syntagma Square, Athens,
27 May 2011[1]

From Egypt to Spain, from Greece to the US, from Turkey to Brazil and then France, the movement of the squares moved from East to West and then back in a dizzying succession of events, often described as a protest "contagion" which at its height, in the spring and summer of 2011, seemed truly unstoppable. Iconic public spaces—Tahrir Square in Cairo, Puerta del Sol in Madrid, Syntagma Square in Athens, Zuccotti Park in New York, Taksim Square in Istanbul, the Avenida Paulista in São Paulo, and Place de la République in Paris—were occupied by great protesting crowds and major protest camps, with hundreds of smaller occupations in local areas, reaching even into conservative backwaters such as Castilla y Leon in Spain and Mississippi in the United States. These mobilisations harnessed such strength that they often pushed governments to the brink of collapse. Their appearance took many by surprise, including seasoned activists from previous movements, as well as social and political scientists, who struggled to understand their nature and purpose. Why did this phenomenal protest wave emerge so unexpectedly? What were its root causes? And from where did it draw its support base?

The movement of the squares needs to be understood in the light of an exceptional historical conjuncture marked by the convergence between the economic crisis, spawned by the financial crash of 2007–8, and a crisis of legitimacy for political institutions, which has generated a historical situation bordering on the notion of Antonio Gramsci's "organic crisis". This is a situation in which, Gramsci argues, as the old regime dies, delinked from its social base and thus unable to address its demands, its death throes allow for the seeds of an alternative to emerge. These new actors take the form of "monsters," that is, phenomena that are complex and hybrid, and thus difficult to pigeon-hole in existing political categories.[2] As we shall see, this metaphor is very pertinent to the hybrid and enigmatic character of the movement of the squares, and their sometimes contradictory responses to the period of crisis and instability.

The upheavals of 2011 and since reflect the crisis of neoliberalism as both an economic and political doctrine. The collapse of the housing bubble in 2007–08 resulted in rising unemployment, foreclosures, indebtedness, and the depletion of public coffers to save ailing banks. Furthermore, it has exacerbated economic inequality that had been growing since neoliberalism established its dominance, and generated widespread anger and frustration among sectors of the population previously loyal to the neoliberal status quo. The economic crisis was compounded by and intertwined with a profound political crisis of legitimacy for liberal democracy, which had been brewing since the late 1990s. A long-term disaffection with a political system giving voters little choice and lobbyists more influence was exacerbated by a sense of betrayal: political elites seemed far more prepared to come to the rescue of reckless banks than to struggling citizens. This twin crisis has presented a challenge for the neoliberal consensus, firmly in place since the 1980s, which responded to the threat by enforcing privatisations and cutbacks on public spending. At the time of the protests neoliberalism remained the ideology of the commanding elites, even as they presided over a "zombie" state in the context of its declining hegemony and the rising discontent.[3]

Reading the present conjuncture as a moment of organic crisis goes a long way towards explaining the exceptional size and impact achieved by these protest movements, and the way in which they have managed to attract the sympathy of the majority of the population in their home countries. Furthermore, it provides a historical rationale to understand the way in which the movement of the squares has constructed a vast popular coalition comprising quite disparate social demographics, and in particular three social forces: the graduates without a future, of the so-called "lost generation"; the squeezed middle class; and the *nouveaux pauvres* mired with unemployment or miserly wages, which will be discussed at the end of this chapter.

A global protest mosaic

The 2011–16 occupation movements constitute a complex historical phenomenon due to the great number of countries, political cultures, issues, and events involved. Movements such as the Arab Spring, the Indignados, the Aganaktismenoi, Occupy Wall Street, the protests in Turkey and Brazil, and Nuit Debout on the one hand displayed specifically local characteristics and on the other raised similar grievances, used common symbols, and almost invariably adopted the same organisational practices, from assemblies to protest camps. These features enable us to look at these movements as not just sharing a temporal coincidence, but being genuinely part of a historic global upheaval, with a shared vision and shared aims. The protest wave beginning in 2011 can thus be best described as a "protest mosaic", a complex structure made up of different temporal and regional clusters of events, each with their own specificity, yet only understandable as part of a larger political picture.[4]

- The first cluster is the Arab Spring that saw revolutions in Tunisia, Egypt, Libya, Bahrain, Yemen and Syria, and protest movements in Morocco and Algeria, beginning in the first three months of 2011.
- The second cluster is the Mediterranean wave of the Indignados, which first struck in mid-May 2011 in Spain and made ripples in Greece at the end of May/beginning of June.
- The third cluster is the Occupy Wall Street protests, which had particular resonance in the Anglophone world, from Canada to Australia, starting in September 2011 in the United States and arriving in the UK in October.
- The fourth cluster comprises the 2013 protests in Turkey and Brazil, which given their simultaneity strongly inspired each other, and which share similarities due to the nations' statuses as emergent economies.
- The fifth cluster coincides with the 2016 Nuit Debout protests in France, which at the time of writing appears as a rather isolated epilogue of the movement of the squares.

The phenomena discussed in this book feature among the most significant examples of a larger array of popular and anti-establishment protest movements that have emerged in recent years and have shared similar discourses and tactics to the movement of the squares. Such movements include the 2009–11 Icelandic "saucepan revolution" against the government's handling of the financial crisis; the *Geração à Rasca* 2011 Portuguese anti-austerity mobilisation; the 2011 Israeli social justice protests against rising costs of living; the Italian Five Star Movement, an anti-establishment party launched by comedian Beppe Grillo which campaigned against political corruption; the Mexican #YoSoy132 student protests in 2012; the September 2012 Argentinian *cacerolazo* [literally "casserole", involving the banging of pots and pans] protests against corruption in Cristina Kirchner's government; the 2013–14 Ukrainian Euromaidan protests demanding autonomy from Russia and closer ties with Europe; the *forconi* [pitchfork] protest movement in Italy that emerged in December 2013; the 2013–14 Thai anti-government protests; and the Occupy Central protests in Hong Kong in the autumn of 2014. Some of these movements, such as the Israeli Indignados and Occupy Central in Hong Kong, whose "membership" in the movement of the squares has been "validated" by activists in other countries, are not covered in this book simply due to issues of convenience. Other movements, such as Euromaidan, the Argentinian *cacerolazo*, the *forconi*, and the Five Star Movement, while sharing some elements of the movement of the squares, especially at the level of tactics, and in the adoption of a populist discourse had—to different degrees—a more conservative slant, and as such appeared beyond the remit of this study.

Cycles of struggle tend to be associated with an iconic start date and location. In the case of the anti-globalisation movement, it was the 1994 Zapatista uprising in south-eastern Mexico, or the anti-WTO protests in Seattle in November 1999,[5] one of the first strong demonstrations of rising global discontent about free trade agreements in the West. In the case of the movement of the squares, some people have identified its origins in the 2009–11 Icelandic "saucepan" revolution or the UK student protests of 2010, some of the first protests against the financial crisis that had international resonance.[6] However, the more commonly accepted starting point is the moment the Arab Spring exploded in several Middle East and North African countries between the end of 2010 and the beginning of 2011.

MOVEMENTS IN THE CRISIS OF NEOLIBERALISM

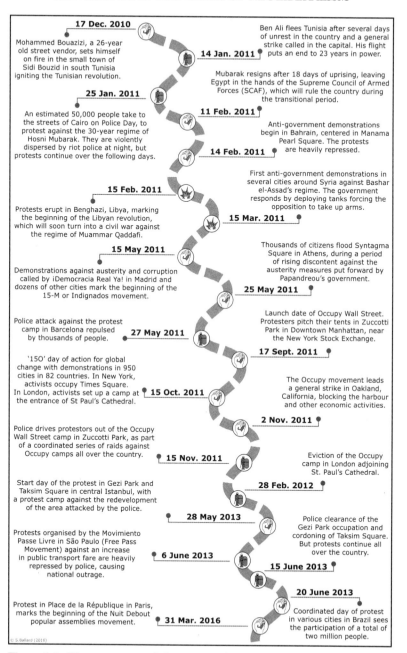

17 Dec. 2010

Mohammed Bouazizi, a 26-year old street vendor, sets himself on fire in the small town of Sidi Bouzid in south Tunisia igniting the Tunisian revolution.

Ben Ali flees Tunisia after several days of unrest in the country and a general strike called in the capital. His flight puts an end to 23 years in power.

14 Jan. 2011

25 Jan. 2011

An estimated 50,000 people take to the streets of Cairo on Police Day, to protest against the 30-year regime of Hosni Mubarak. They are violently dispersed by riot police at night, but protests continue over the following days.

Mubarak resigns after 18 days of uprising, leaving Egypt in the hands of the Supreme Council of Armed Forces (SCAF), which will rule the country during the transitional period.

11 Feb. 2011

Anti-government demonstrations begin in Bahrain, centered in Manama Pearl Square. The protests are heavily repressed.

14 Feb. 2011

First anti-government demonstrations in several cities around Syria against Bashar el-Assad's regime. The government responds by deploying tanks forcing the opposition to take up arms.

15 Feb. 2011

Protests erupt in Benghazi, Libya, marking the beginning of the Libyan revolution, which will soon turn into a civil war against the regime of Muammar Qaddafi.

15 Mar. 2011

Thousands of citizens flood Syntagma Square in Athens, during a period of rising discontent against the austerity measures put forward by Papandreou's government.

15 May 2011

Demonstrations against austerity and corruption called by iDemocracia Real Ya! in Madrid and dozens of other cities mark the beginning of the 15-M or Indignados movement.

25 May 2011

Launch date of Occupy Wall Street. Protesters pitch their tents in Zuccotti Park in Downtown Manhattan, near the New York Stock Exchange.

Police attack against the protest camp in Barcelona repulsed by thousands of people.

27 May 2011

17 Sept. 2011

'15O' day of action for global change with demonstrations in 950 cities in 82 countries. In New York, activists occupy Times Square. In London, activists set up a camp at the entrance of St Paul's Cathedral.

15 Oct. 2011

The Occupy movement leads a general strike in Oakland, California, blocking the harbour and other economic activities.

2 Nov. 2011

Police drives protestors out of the Occupy Wall Street camp in Zuccotti Park, as part of a coordinated series of raids against Occupy camps all over the country.

15 Nov. 2011

Eviction of the Occupy camp in London adjoining St. Paul's Cathedral.

Start day of the protest in Gezi Park and Taksim Square in central Istanbul, with a protest camp against the redevelopment of the area attacked by the police.

28 Feb. 2012

28 May 2013

Protests organised by the Movimiento Passe Livre in São Paulo (Free Pass Movement) against an increase in public transport fare are heavily repressed by police, causing national outrage.

Police clearance of the Gezi Park occupation and cordoning of Taksim Square. But protests continue all over the country.

6 June 2013

15 June 2013

Protest in Place de la République in Paris, marks the beginning of the Nuit Debout popular assemblies movement.

20 June 2013

31 Mar. 2016

Coordinated day of protest in various cities in Brazil sees the participation of a total of two million people.

© S.Ballard (2016)

Figure 1.1: The movement of the squares: key events in the 2011–16 protest wave

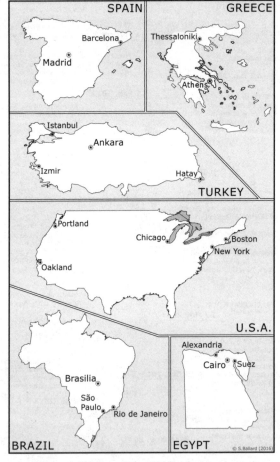

Figure 1.2: Map of the 2011–16 protest wave

The protests in Tunisia started in December 2010 after the self-immolation of street seller Mohammed Bouazizi, and in the public imagination came to be seen as the "spark that lit the prairie fire":[7] the one event that came to precipitate an entire protest wave. The death of Bouazizi, in fact just one of many suicides due to harsh living conditions in Tunisia, managed to generate a wave of outrage in a country blighted by economic hardship, corruption, and violations of human rights, and humiliated by thirty years under the rule of Zine El Abedine Ben Ali. On 14 January 2011, after extended fighting between demonstrators and police and a general strike, the president escaped to Saudi Arabia. The Tunisian uprising, and its ultimate victory, set in motion a process of emulation that soon swept a number of Arab countries, starting with the most populous one: Egypt.[8]

On 25 January 2011 thousands of Egyptians responded to a call for protest that had originally been launched through the Facebook page Kullena Khaled Said [We are all Khaled Said] and supported by the 6 April Youth Movement.[9] While originally largely dominated by the middle and upper middle class, the movement eventually managed to mobilise the masses of the poor, who flooded the streets of Cairo, Alexandria, Suez and several other Egyptian cities on the "Friday of Anger," 28 January 2011. Tahrir Square was seized by protesters, tens of police stations across the country were torched and security forces retreated from the streets, though they would be immediately substituted in the evening by the tanks of the Egyptian army, in what constituted a *de facto* military coup. The battle between protesters, the police, and pro-regime thugs continued in the following days, seriously testing the mettle of the pro-democracy movement. Eventually, on 11 February 2011, dubbed by protesters the "Friday of Departure," Hosni Mubarak announced his resignation, and a military junta, the Supreme Council of the Armed Forces (SCAF), took power promising to supervise a peaceful transition to democracy. This passage would however prove highly tortuous, and the first democratically elected president of Egypt, the Muslim Brotherhood's Mohamed Morsi, was eventually deposed by an army coup d'état on 3 July 2013 led by his minister of defence, General Abdel-Fattah el-Sisi, in the aftermath of large anti-government protests on 30 June.[10]

The heroic example of the Tunisian and Egyptian revolutions along with other uprisings in Libya, Syria, Yemen, and Bahrain were the inspiration for the birth of new protest movements in the West, where the severe social distress caused by the effects of the financial crisis of 2008 had not yet been met with mass protest, except for isolated events like the Greek riots of 2008, the London anti-G20 protests of 2009, and the 2010 student protests in the UK. Yet the events taking place in the Arab World—widely televised, live-streamed and tweeted the world over—ignited a sense of possibility about a revolutionary transformation of society away from extreme inequality and the gutting of democratic structures. From the Indignados in Spain and the Aganaktismenoi in

Greece, to Occupy Wall Street in the US, a Western protest wave followed in the footsteps of the Arab Spring, trying to adapt to local circumstances the blueprint of popular protest displayed in Tahrir Square in Egypt, Manama Square in Bahrain and the rebel neighbourhoods of Damascus and Aleppo in Syria.

The Western country which first attempted to import the "Tahrir model" of protest with an all-out occupation of a central square was Spain, one of the European nations worst hit by the effects of the financial crisis of 2008. 15 May 2011 (leading to the movement being dubbed "15-M"), the day of the protest called by the newly formed group ¡Democracia Real Ya! [Real Democracy Now!], marked the beginning of an intense mobilisation that saw the participation of millions of Spaniards and forced the Socialist government of José Luis Rodríguez Zapatero to call snap elections. Taking inspiration from the book *Indignez-vous!* by French nonagenarian *résistant* Stéphane Hessel,[11] the press called the protesters "Indignados," that is, those who are outraged at the economic crisis and the behaviour of politicians, accused of being in cahoots with bankers. Protesters set up over a hundred protest camps all over the country, the biggest and most visible in Madrid (Puerta del Sol) and Barcelona (Plaça de Catalunya). After the main occupations were evicted in June 2011, the 15-M movement changed its strategy. It moved to the neighbourhoods, where thousands of local assemblies were organised and mobilised around single-issue campaigns, known as the colour-coded *"mareas ciudadanas"* [civic tides] and focusing on specific issues, such as the green tide for education, the white for health and the black in mourning at public spending cuts.

The rise of the Indignados in Spain had immediate reverberations in Greece, a country facing even worse economic conditions. Spanish protesters had in fact explicitly launched an invitation to their Greek brothers and sisters to join the struggle, expressed in the ironic slogan, "Ssshhh... do not wake up the Greeks!" It took a Facebook page set up by a Greek teenager and an initial protest was organised in Syntagma [Constitution] Square in Athens in front of the parliament building on 25. It soon became an occupation that lasted until the summer, joined by tens of other occupations and assemblies all over the country invoking to the spirit of ancient Athenian democracy. Translating the Indignados to the local vernacular, the movement was named the Aganaktismenoi Polites [indignant citizens] or in short Aganaktismenoi [indignants]. The broad-based and largely peaceful revolt deeply dented the credibility of the government headed by Socialist Prime Minister George Papandreou, who would eventually resign in November 2011, handing the reins to a technocratic government led by economist Lucas Papademos, widely seen as a representative of the Troika.

After the Arab Spring and Mediterranean Summer, it was the turn of the American Autumn, marked by the appearance of Occupy Wall Street in the US, a country suffering from the worst economic downturn since the Great Depression. In imitation of Tahrir and Puerta del Sol, starting on 17 September 2011 activists occupied Zuccotti Park, soon renamed "Liberty Plaza" by activists, a small privately-owned public space close to the New York Stock Exchange on Wall Street. The call for protest was originally launched by the Canadian countercultural magazine *Adbusters*, in an article that questioned whether "America's Tahrir moment" had arrived, and it was supported by a series of organising assemblies in New York over the summer.

Initially public reception was rather lukewarm and it was only after two weeks of occupation, and a streak of episodes of police repression, including a mass arrest on the Brooklyn Bridge,[12] that the movement managed to attract the attention of the news media and to capture the public imagination. Hundreds of small encampments sprung up in the US and abroad, involving people of different backgrounds who shared dismay at the bleak economic situation. Protesters cast blame not at "Big Government", or irresponsible poor people applying for a mortgage, as had been the sentiments of the Tea Party movement in previous years, but rather at large investment banks like Goldman Sachs and JP Morgan, their lobbies, and their political allies.

The movement developed a resonant populist discourse epitomised by the slogan "We Are The 99 Percent", and a series of iconic tactics such as the "people's mic", with participants collectively repeating the words of the speaker to make up for the lack of amplifiers. However, a concerted wave of evictions in mid-November 2011 that targeted the camps in New York, Denver, Portland, Oakland, and other cities proved a deathblow for the movement, which would never regain momentum.

Where 2011 had seen protest movements on the offensive virtually all over the world, leading to *Time* magazine celebrating it as "the year of the protester," 2012 proved a year of retreat on the protest front. In the Arab World, protest movements were either forced to demobilise due to political pacification imposed during the transition, as happened in Egypt or Tunisia, or were forced to fight bloody civil wars as happened in Libya and Syria.

In Mediterranean Europe both the Indignados and the Aganaktismenoi saw their assemblies and occupations progressively shrinking, after their peak in the late spring and summer of 2011. However, they managed to evolve into new forms by transforming into solidarity movements in the case of Greece or single-issue civic campaigns in the case of Spain. In the US, the decline of the movement was the sharpest, with the May Day 2012 protests failing to reignite the movement, and a number of Occupy reboot attempts misfiring. The exhilarating sense of momentum experienced between the spring and the autumn of 2011 seemed to have vanished into thin air.

2013 seemed, however, to give new impetus to the protest wave, with the emergence of two new mass movements that bore strong similarities to the 2011 movements: the Gezi Park protests, beginning in Turkey in May 2011, and the almost contemporaneous Movimento de Junho [June Movement] in Brazil. While specific to their own national circumstances these protests echoed many themes of the movement of the squares, including the popular discontent against corrupt political and economic elites and the suspicion towards large-scale, faceless institutions; and utilised similar tactics, such as using social media platforms, occupying public squares and streets, and creating assemblies.

In Turkey the protests were ignited by a controversial renovation project of the highly symbolic Taksim Square in Istanbul, where the adjoining Gezi Park was set to be demolished to erect a shopping mall built in neo-Ottoman architectural style. The resistance against the incoming bulldozers and police managed to transform what was initially a local and single-issue environmental movement into the biggest protest movement in Turkey since the 2002 rise to power of Prime Minister Recep Tayyip Erdoğan's Islamist Justice and Development Party (AKP). For eleven days Taksim Square was turned into a police-free commune in which disparate political groups and ordinary citizens organised collectively in popular assemblies. Demonstrations and occupations also arose in several other major Turkish cities including Ankara, İzmir, Hatay and Bursa, panicking the government and leading to a wave of repression. Although by mid-June the police had managed to regain control and had enforced a ban on demonstrations in Taksim Square, the movement continued at a lower scale in the following months, fuelled by outrage at revelations from corruption cases involving government officials and at growing censorship.

The protests in Brazil began just a few days after the beginning of the Turkish movement. Lacking a single recognised collective name, the mobilisation was attributed different labels, including Movimento de Junho [June Movement], stemming from the month in which most protests took place, "V de Vinagre" [V for Vinegar], given the use of vinegar against teargas and in reference to *V for Vendetta*, or the Salad Revolt, because of the association of vinegar with salad. Also in this case the protests developed out of a single-issue campaign, the Movimento Passe Livre [Free Fare Movement],[13] calling for free public transport. The mobilisation began in response to the decision taken by the mayoralty of São Paulo to increase ticket prices by 20 cents,[14] a relatively small amount, but one many felt was the proverbial straw that broke the camel's back, given the high price and bad quality of public transport, in common with many other public services.

The protests, starting on 6 June 2013, initially mobilised only a few thousand people, but they quickly escalated due to heavy police repression against both protesters and journalists covering the event. A wave of public outrage motivated hundreds of thousands of people all over Brazil to join demonstrations in the ensuing days. As the movement grew, coinciding with the Football Confederations Cup of June 2013, a logistical rehearsal for the Football World Cup scheduled for the following year, it came to encompass a greater variety of issues than the question of transportation, including the vexing question of public corruption, criticism of "mega-events" like the World Cup and the 2016 Rio de Janeiro Olympic Games, and demands for better health and education services. Despite their initial success, the movements in Brazil and Turkey also experienced the same rapid fizzling-out as their predecessors.

The final movement discussed in this book is Nuit Debout in France. Literally translated as "Up all Night," Nuit Debout, a reference to its evening assemblies, is a protest movement that emerged in France on 31 March 2016. The mobilisation was sparked by the new labour law drafted by Minister Myriam el-Khomri, which gave companies more flexibility in hiring and firing workers. Initially launched by the radical Left coalition Convergence des Luttes, the movement was influenced by a number of Marxist intellectuals such as the journalist and film-maker

François Ruffin and the economist Frédéric Lordon. Similarly to Occupy and the 15-M movement, Nuit Debout organised daily assemblies held firstly in Place de la République in central Paris, close to the locations of the terrorist attacks of 13 November 2015, and then also in hundreds of other locations all over the country. Unlike other movements of the squares, protesters for the most part did not erect a fixed protest camp, but set up small tents for working groups and committees on a daily basis. In late May and June 2016, Nuit Debout mobilised in support of a general strike against the labour law called by the main trade union CGT (Confédération générale du travail), blocking refineries and nuclear power stations. The movement's assemblies disappeared, however, by the end of June, as the strikes came to a halt and the el-Khomri Law was eventually approved but in diluted form.

As we have seen, the phenomena covered under the umbrella term "movement of the squares" display both common elements and noteworthy differences in their composition, their aims, their interaction with institutions and existing organisations, and their evolution. They varied by degree of intensity, ranging from a full-fledged revolution as in the case of Egypt, to far more moderate and non-violent contestations of the existing political order. Most of them confronted centre-left social-democratic governments of varying hues (in the US, Spain, Brazil, Greece, and France), whose right-wing policies and corruption alienated some of their traditional bases of support. Others were posed against right-wing or authoritarian governments (such as the UK and Turkey). All of them but Brazil shared common protest tactics, particularly in their use of protest encampments and general assemblies. They did vary to some degree in their focus. Some movements such as Occupy Wall Street, and to a lesser extent the Indignados and Aganaktismenoi, were most concerned with the economy. Others, such as the movements in Egypt, Brazil, and Turkey, mostly raised political grievances. With regard to the Arab Spring, due to its obvious peculiarities—the movement being in opposition to a dictatorship, experiencing high levels of violence, and with a revolutionary character in that it aimed for the overthrow of the existing political regime—it would be better understood as a prologue to the movement of the squares.

Notwithstanding these differences, and the limits to any totalising interpretation, these mobilisations can all be considered in a broad sense as part of a common movement of the squares, due to the way in which they have made reference to a shared constellation of symbols, discourses, and practices. This common culture has been epitomised by the ubiquity of the Guy Fawkes mask, borrowed from the blockbuster movie *V for Vendetta*, and by their use of a number of shared tactics, such as the use of social media as an organising platform, of protest camps, and of popular assemblies. Furthermore, protesters across all these countries have consistently expressed mutual solidarity by celebrating each other's victories, protesting against the repression of mobilisations abroad, by waving other movements' national flags in the squares, sending delegations to visit each other, and voicing the belief that their local mobilisations were the manifestations of a shared global struggle, or "global revolution", against economic and political tyranny, and for real democracy. These commonalities, which manifest the emergence of the common protest culture of citizenism, in turn rest on the presence of common structural conditions: the economic crisis of 2008 and the political crisis of neoliberal post-democracy.

In the shadow of the Great Recession

The scale and intensity of the movement of the squares reflects the tremendous shock of the 2007–08 financial crisis and the ensuing Great Recession, a term which carries ominous echoes of the catastrophic Great Depression of the early 1930s, which destabilised the world economy for almost twenty years. This period of prolonged economic decline ignited by the burst of the housing bubble, with depressed demand and rising levels of unemployment and indebtedness, generated growing inequality, widespread economic hardship, and social distress, which taken together have greatly contributed in opening a space for the emergence of the movement of the squares (Figures 1.3, 1.4, 1.5).

The burst of the US housing bubble in the summer of 2007 unleashed a domino effect, as trillions of dollars invested in risky derivatives—securities backed by home mortgages—evaporated in a few days. The behemoth of investment banking, Lehman Brothers, a symbol of the smugness of the financial elite, was forced to declare bankruptcy, while other financial giants such as AIG, Fannie Mae and Freddie Mac, along with Northern Rock and the Royal Bank of Scotland in the UK, were saved only by government intervention. The world economy ground to a halt, as a "credit crunch" froze inter-bank lending and made it more

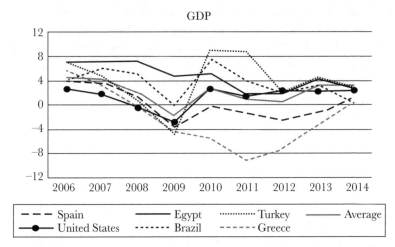

Figure 1.3: The onset of the Great Recession: GDP growth (%), 2006–14[15]

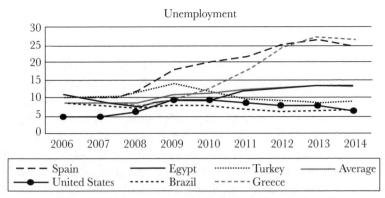

Figure 1.4: Unemployment 2006–14 (% of labour force)[16]

difficult for companies to secure loans. Of course, the real victims of the crisis were ordinary people, who first had to foot the bill for banking bailouts and then had to bear the brunt of stringent austerity policies which, by further depressing demand, made millions unemployed and shut down countless small firms.

The financial crash needs to be understood as the climactic moment of a neoliberal era that is deemed to have started between the 1970s and the 1980s and which led to abandonment of the post-war compromise

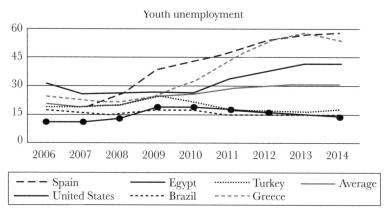

Figure 1.5: Youth unemployment 2006–14 (% of labour force aged 15–24)[17]

between labour and capital and an erosion of the social-democratic welfare state.[18] Neoliberalism's free-market ideology can be summed up in two clauses, both originating from former British Prime Minister Margaret Thatcher, one of its main political champions: "There is no alternative [to neoliberal capitalism]" (also known by the acronym TINA); and "*There is no such thing as society*. There are *individual* men and women, and there are families" [author's emphasis]. This ideology, which has been shaped by Friedrich von Hayek, Milton Friedman and the Chicago tradition of neoclassical economics, has attacked social-democracy and the welfare state as wasteful and a constraint on people's freedom.[19] Its hegemony and adoption by both centre-right and centre-left parties has resulted in policies of free trade, privatisation, de-regulation of the financial market, the curtailing of the welfare state, and the weakening of trade unions.

The Great Recession has laid bare the calamitous results of neoliberal economics, which has created an uncontrolled (and uncontrollable) financial system and skyrocketing levels of economic inequality, the likes of which had not been seen since the 1920s.[20] The 2008 crash and the ensuing recession have gravely affected the living conditions of dozens of millions in Europe and North America, with the lower and middle classes hit by unemployment, falling wages, labour insecurity, indebtedness, rising taxes, and shrinking public services. Unemployment suddenly doubled to over 10% in countries with historically low unemployment such as the US, and over 20% in southern European economies like Spain and Greece. Young people have suffered disproportionately from the Great Recession, with youth unemployment skyrocketing everywhere, reaching levels of over 50% in Greece and Spain, and 40% in Italy. The crisis has also adversely affected those in employment, with salary cuts or freezes for both public and private sector workers and a further precarisation of the workforce, with increased casualisation of jobs (e.g. the zero-hour contract) and growing incidence of part-time work, leading to discussions about the emergence of a new class of precarious workers dubbed the "precariat."[21]

Furthermore, the economic crisis has seriously damaged public finances and led to cuts in public services. Growing government debt, provoked by government bailouts of bankrupt banks and companies (the so-called "socialism for the rich") in addition to falling receipts and growing social spending during a recession served as justification for austerity policies, with cuts on public spending and privatisation of state assets. The so-called European sovereign debt crisis of 2010–11 saw countries like Spain and Greece forced to accept bailout programmes offered by the Troika, the triumvirate formed by representatives of the European Central Bank, the European Commission and the IMF. In return for EU loans, the levers of national economic policy were effectively put in the hands of Brussels and Frankfurt.

While the causes of the Arab Spring rest largely with the political exhaustion of ageing dictatorships, they also stem from deep-rooted economic imbalances that have been exacerbated by the onset of the global economic crisis. Egypt had experienced steady economic growth during the late 1990s and 2000s, but this did not translate into substantial improvement for the great masses of the poor. Rampant inequality was exacerbated by a "youth bulge," a demographic situation in which the share of young people is significantly larger than other age groups, well known to be conducive to social unrest, especially when, as in the case of Egypt, there were (and remain) insufficient jobs for the nation's youth. The financial crisis of 2008 added further tension, leading to a slowdown of economic growth, which halved between 2008 and 2009, and a 20 per cent drop in revenues for the tourism sector, pushing up unemployment. A further factor for instability was the peak of global food prices in 2011, which led to food riots and is widely considered to have been a trigger for the Arab Spring.

In southern Europe, Spain and Greece experienced severe economic distress. Greece has become a "poster child" for the deleterious effects of the economic crisis and austerity policies, with the economy shrinking by about one quarter since the beginning of the crisis. Unemployment has skyrocketed, reaching a peak of 24.2% in 2012, with the youth unemployment rate at a staggering 55.3% the same year. Lack of job opportunities and falling wages have produced widespread poverty and despair, with a severe rise in child malnutrition and a 35% increase in suicides during the first two years of the austerity programmes.[22] Spain has suffered a similar course. The Iberian economy, heavily dependent on tourism and the construction sector, experienced a deep downturn after the crisis of 2007–08 and had been almost continuously in recession between 2009 and 2013. Levels of unemployment have touched similar peaks to those experienced in Greece, with general unemployment at an incredible 25%, and youth unemployment at 53.2% in 2012, forcing many young people to emigrate in search of employment. Public services have been cut to the bone in many sectors in a flawed attempt to stem the growth of public debt that has more than doubled since 2007.

While not as heavily affected as Spain and Greece, France's economy has also suffered in the aftermath of the 2008 financial crash. In 2009 GDP growth shrank by 2.9% and has remained stagnant since. Headline unemployment has grown to around 10%—around twice that of Germany—and around a quarter of France's youth are unemployed, with the rest facing an increase in short-term and precarious contracts. Austerity policies had not initially been as aggressive as in other European countries. At the outset of the Nuit Debout protests in 2016, France was still the developed country with the largest public sector, totalling 57% of GDP, and with relatively high welfare provisions. However, eventually France's economy policy veered towards austerity after the appointment of Manuel Valls, the second prime minister of Francois Hollande's presidency, with cuts on public spending and an attack on workers' rights, culminating in the Loi Travail [Labour Act] drafted by minister Myriam el-Khomri, which made it easier for employers to lay off workers and extend or reduce working hours at their whim. In the UK the crisis produced widespread distress. The economy lost 4.2% of GDP in 2009, before slowly returning to growth. Unemployment almost doubled (compared to pre-crisis figures) in 2012 to 8% with youth unemployment at 21.4% the same year. Furthermore, the victory of the

Conservative Party in 2010 led to harsh austerity policies imposed by the Chancellor George Osborne, who delivered tens of billions of pounds of cuts, tripled student university fees, deprived 150,000 elderly people of care services, and forced thousands to resort to food banks to feed their families, without however managing to achieve his stated aim of lowering the budget deficit.[23]

In the US the evolution of the crisis was less brutal than in Europe, due to the fiscal stimulus adopted by the Obama administration. However, the downturn still hurt many, with the most severe effects impacting upon those in lower income brackets. The worst years for the US economy were 2008 and 2009, when GDP contracted by 3% from pre-crisis levels. Several major companies, including the insurance corporation AIG and vehicle manufacturing giant GM, had to be bailed out by the government. Social distress produced by the economic crisis seeped into the fabric of American society. The unemployment rate peaked at 9.6% in 2010 before decreasing, and the youth unemployment rate almost doubled during the recession, hitting a peak of 18.4% in 2010. What might seem a less dramatic picture when compared with other countries, needs to be understood in the context of the traditional upward mobility of the United States where young people, unlike their European counterparts, had no experience of being unemployed after college and being forced to return to the parental home due to their inability to support themselves. The absence of strong social safety nets in the US has made the impact of the crisis all the more ravaging: a survey calculated by AP/GFK found that 80% of American adults face unemployment and near-poverty at some point in their life.[24] Although the recent union campaigns for living wages in the fast-food industry and a hike in the mandatory minimum wage have tried to redress US wage inequality, income distribution has become even more skewed, especially due to the stellar salaries awarded to executives in recent years.

The thesis of economic causation gets more complicated when we move from southern Europe and North America to Turkey and Brazil, two emerging economies which, prior to the crisis, had experienced a period of sustained economic growth, which had led to the emergence of a new middle class and earned praise from neoliberal economists. The economic crisis of 2008 nevertheless resulted in a substantial slowdown in these countries also, from which they have yet to recover. If anything their economic prospects, and in particular those of Brazil, have further worsened since the 2013 protests.

Under the premiership of Recep Tayyip Erdoğan, in government with his Islamist AK Party since 2003, Turkey experienced an "economic miracle" with GDP growth accelerating in the late 2000s. However, the country felt the impact of the financial crisis and growth decelerated to a puny 2.2 per cent in 2012. The strongly pro-business agenda of the Erdoğan government did not manage to address high levels of unemployment among Turkey's urban youth and poverty in rural areas.

Brazil, part of the so-called BRIC group of emerging economies, experienced a period of strong economic growth in 2000s, known journalistically as the *decada de oro* [golden decade] under the government of Luiz Inácio Lula da Silva (more commonly known as Lula) of the PT (Partido dos Trabalhadores, or Workers' Party), profiting from the 2000s cycle of high commodity prices which favoured the extractive sector that has traditionally been central to Brazil's economy. These governments heralded in clear socio-economic improvements for the poor through a series of socially progressive policies, such as a rise in the minimum wage and the *bolsa família*, a vast government social welfare programme against poverty that, as of 2011, covered 26 per cent of Brazilian families. However, under the PT's watch, economic policy by and large failed to move the country away from the extractivist model, leaving the economy in a very fragile position.

The Great Recession has thus brought income and wealth inequality to grotesque extremes, thereby completing the neoliberal reversal of the redistributive policies that had been pursued by social democracies in the post-war period. In a dire assessment of the state of economic injustice at the beginning of the twenty-first century, an Oxfam report found that 50 per cent of the world's wealth was in the hands of 1 per cent of the population.[25] This situation has led some to speak of a "second gilded age":[26] the current conjuncture has uncanny parallels with the US at the end of the nineteenth century, when so-called "robber barons" oversaw the rise of monopoly capitalism, provoking the birth of the left-populist People's Party.[27] Some even speak of "capitalist neo-feudalism" to express the rentier nature of the contemporary economy.[28] At this conjuncture the majority of the population, including the middle class, has been made to suffer from economic decline and escalating uncertainty, leading to widespread discontent and dissatisfaction with the economic system, and especially undermining the argument for neoliberalism and its cult of a self-regulating market. This grim economic situation and the way it has affected sections of society, like the (hitherto supportive of neoliberal-

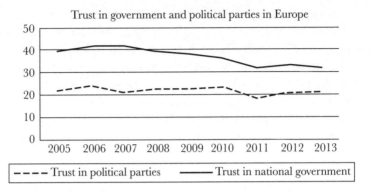

Figure 1.6: Trust in government and political parties in Europe[29]

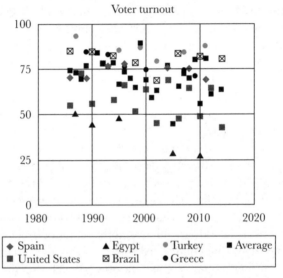

Figure 1.7: Voter turnout in parliamentary elections[30]

ism) middle class, goes a long a way towards explaining the large-scale level of support enjoyed by the movement of the squares.

The crisis of neoliberal "post-democracy"

However, the root cause of the movement of the squares is not simply economic. A key factor is the crisis of political legitimacy—the acute distrust felt for political institutions and parties—that has been brewing for years in several countries and which has been pushed to boiling point by the economic crisis. This condition comes close to what Antonio Gramsci called an "organic crisis," in which the political order of society is shaken, and the representational linkages between various organisations and institutions and their social bases become wobbly. The symptoms of this condition can be identified through a number of measurable indicators—trust in government, parliament and parties and rates of voter abstention—which in their sum signal a far-reaching political discontent.

Confidence in government has experienced a spectacular drop since the economic crisis (Figure 1.6). The record belongs to Greece with trust in government at an abysmal 13% of the population in 2012. In Spain and the US the advent of the Great Recession has seriously dented the confidence of the populace in their elected leaders, with 34% in the former, and 35% in the latter in 2012.[31] According to the Edelman Trust Barometer, in 2012 Brazil experienced a 53% plunge in the level of trust in government, the deepest drop in trust across the countries surveyed,[32] a predictable result of intensifying corruption scandals around construction projects for the 2014 World Cup and the 2016 Olympics. Similarly, France saw a substantial drop in confidence in the aftermath of the economic crisis, dropping from 34% to 28% in 2012 and further receding in 2014. Further evidence for the crisis of legitimacy is provided by the downward trend in voter turnout. This has been especially evident in European countries, which have seen an average drop of around 10 percentage points in voter participation in the second half of the twentieth century, with a steady decline over the last forty years in established democracies, revealing the disillusion of voters about an increasingly closed-off political process.[33] Finally, across most countries there has been a shrinking share of the vote going to mainstream parties, opening the way for new political formations, including many right-wing populist groups.[34]

This crisis of trust can be understood as reflecting popular discontent with "post-democracy": the trend towards the "gutting" of democratic participation that has accompanied the rise of the neoliberal ideology. Political theorist Colin Crouch describes post-democracy as a condition in which the formal institutions of democracy, such as elections and a free press, are maintained, yet the substance of democracy is betrayed, given that "politics and government are increasingly slipping back into the control of privileged elites in the manner characteristic of pre-democratic times."[35] Wolfgang Streeck has argued that we are witnessing a crisis of "democratic capitalism," in which international financial markets have taken sovereignty away from voters through exploiting their grip on state debt.[36] Similarly, French philosopher Jacques Rancière has denounced contemporary electoral democracies marked by the "monopolising of *la chose publique* by a solid alliance of state oligarchy and economic oligarchy," which undermines the foundations of a functioning democracy, starting with the principle of popular sovereignty and the participatory rights attached to citizenship. Presenting economic globalisation as a fact of nature, governments proclaim that they are "simply administrating the local consequences of global historical necessity."[37] In this context, all attempts to reinsert popular participation in political decision-making are scoffed at by neoliberal elites as manifestations of "populism," a convenient term used to "lump together all forms of dissent in relation to the prevailing consensus."[38]

This crisis of democracy crucially involves an erosion of citizenship: the basic structure of democracy and the necessary link between individual members of the community and the institutions governing over them. Wendy Brown in fact argues that neoliberalism has brought about a process of "de-democratisation": an "undoing of the demos" which involves the substitution of the participatory ethos of citizenship with the subjectivity of the *homo economicus*, governed solely by the profit motive, as seen in the neoliberal glorification of the entrepreneur.[39] In this context citizenship itself becomes privatised, due to "an effort to reorganise the relationship between the state and the citizenry from non-contractual rights and obligations to the practices of quid-pro-quo market exchanges," as explained by Margaret Somers and Erik Olin Wright.[40] Instead of being a universal right, the status of "citizen" becomes a privilege for those the market considers deserving of the title.

The post-democratic trend and the doing away of citizenship rights have been arguably most evident in the European context: in the transferring of sovereignty and decision-making away from elected national governments and to supranational institutions such as the European Union; in the disregard for popular votes in individual EU member states, as happened with the EU constitutional referenda in France and Ireland, which had to be re-run because the people did not select the response the elites wanted; in the application of highly unpopular austerity measures dictated by economists, firmly at odds with the opinion of the majority of the population; in the installation of unelected technocratic governments in Italy and Greece after the crisis; and in the European fiscal compact, obliging countries to enshrine budget-balancing edicts into their constitutions.

Additionally, it is significant that many of these movements have been motivated by outrage at decisions in other policy areas, further displaying the contempt of ruling elites for the opinions of ordinary citizens, as in the case of transportation or construction projects pursued without any concern for the views of those affected. This was seen in Turkey, with the Taksim protests initially instigated by a controversial renovation project that would have destroyed one of the few green areas in central Istanbul, and in Brazil, where building infrastructure and facilities for the World Cup and the Olympics displaced many impoverished communities. Such machinations have laid bare the intensely anti-democratic spirit that lies at the heart of contemporary politics and neoliberal ideology, and its disregard for the opinion of ordinary citizens.

One of the most notorious reasons for citizens' growing distrust of politicians was the surge in political corruption. In Tunisia and Egypt, indignation at glaring instances of embezzlement implicating Ben Ali, Mubarak, and their families contributed to motivating the population to mobilise. In Greece, a number of revelations documented the mishandling of funds for public works, misallocations from foreign aid money, and nepotistic hiring practices for public sector workers. In Spain a number of corruption cases, many connected with real estate projects, have involved the two historically dominant parties, the PSOE and the PP, and have even stained the image of the Royal Family, with the daughter of King Juan Carlos on trial for tax fraud and money laundering. In Brazil, analysts estimate the costs of corruption at a staggering $53 billion a year,[41] and a number of investigations have seriously damaged the reputation of the governing PT, leading to the impeachment of President Dilma Rousseff in the spring of 2016. In Turkey, a corruption probe on alleged bribes paid by Halkbank to several AKP politicians caused widespread anger. Finally in the US, the debate about the influence of money in politics, and about lobbying as a form of legalised bribery, has intensified, as seen in the debate over the Citizens United v. Federal Election Commission [2012] Supreme Court case[42] and the controversy surrounding the publication of the memoir of former lobbyist Jack Abramoff.[43]

A further blow to the political system's legitimacy has come from the frequent recourse to heavy-handed repressive measures against protesters. The Arab Spring was largely motivated by the authoritarianism of entrenched dictatorships and their record of human rights violations. Furthermore, it is significant that many of these protest movements surged in the aftermath of highly publicised cases of police violence against protesters, as happened after the mass arrest of Occupy Wall Street activists on Brooklyn Bridge on 1 October 2011, the police attack on Gezi Park in Turkey, and the brutal intervention of military police against protesters in São Paulo in mid-June 2013, which also resulted in severe injuries for a number of journalists.[44] These episodes contributed towards painting a picture of the contemporary state as a new Orwellian regime that sees protest as a public order problem to be solved. Feeding into this narrative, there is also a growing awareness of the expanding surveillance apparatus the state uses to pursue activists, including via data harvested on social media, as was first revealed by Wikileaks and further confirmed by the revelations of US information analyst Edward Snowden in 2013.[45]

The crisis of legitimacy has not just engulfed state institutions, but also civil society, broadly defined, including parties, trade unions, and NGOs, as well as the established news media. The movement of the squares expressed ardent distrust towards parties which—deprived of the mass membership base they enjoyed in the industrial era—were seen as having developed into self-perpetuating electoral committees through which different factions of the national elite battle for political supremacy. This distrust affects parties of the Right and of the Left, perceived as having betrayed their commitment to social democracy and largely converted to the market theology of neoliberalism. Furthermore, it also impacts upon the parties of the radical Left that have made themselves irrelevant by clinging to the orthodoxy of communism.

This is why, with the notable exception of Syriza in Greece, which underwent a process of re-foundation in 2013 and came to power by winning the general elections of 2015, leftist parties which pre-dated 2011 have not enjoyed significant electoral gains in the wake of the mobilisations. Possibly even more startling is the extent of the distrust nurtured by many participants in these movements towards civil society organisations, such as trade unions and NGOs, which enjoyed much higher trust among activists during the era of the anti-globalisation movement.[46] Specifically trade unions have been repeatedly accused by protesters of being complicit with neoliberal policies, and of simply pursuing the corporatist interests of their ageing members, while at the same time neglecting the general interest of society and an increasingly precarious workforce.

Lastly, distrust also affects the mainstream news media, a fundamental component in the liberal-democratic public sphere that has often been accused of exhibiting a servile attitude towards economic and political oligarchies—not least because of its reliance on corporate advertisements—and of self-censorship. One of the most vivid manifestations of this tendency was surely the decision of the Turkish news channel CNN Turk to broadcast a long documentary about penguins at the moment of one of the most intense clashes between protesters and police in Taksim Square, which attracted widespread derision on social media.

In conclusion, governments, political parties, civil society organisations and the news media have all seen their confidence levels dropping, in a demonstration of the growing gap between ordinary citizens and those supposed to represent them and voice their concerns in the public sphere and political institutions alike. It is precisely from these growing ranks of "unrepresented," of citizens who feel frustrated at the lack of representation of their views and demands, that the movement of the squares recruited its supporters.

A new popular alliance

The movement of the squares was impressive in its ability to tap into the brewing discontent generated by a sense of economic destitution and political disenfranchisement, each reinforcing the other. Its ability to mobilise millions of people and capture the sympathy of many more at home constituted a major distinguishing feature of this cycle of protest vis-à-vis other recent movements, which enjoyed far more limited and less heterogeneous support, with most of the protesters who comprised the post-'68 new social movements coming from the urban middle class youth.[47] Breaking out of these protest heartlands, the various movements of the squares were "catch-all movements,"[48] able to command the support of people with lower levels of politicisation, from older age brackets and poorer backgrounds, and with more diverse social and political backgrounds than those that formed many post-industrial movements. The impressively large and heterogeneous public backing was evident both in the direct physical participation in protest camps and demonstrations, and in the levels of public approval as measured by opinion polls.

One of the images that will be forever associated with the movement is that of teeming crowds filling large public spaces to capacity, as repeatedly seen in Tahrir Square in Cairo, Puerta del Sol in Madrid, and many other iconic occupied squares. These huge gatherings provide a visual representation of the staggering volume of people that were mobilised, often numbering in the millions. In Egypt, up to one million gathered in Cairo alone on the 1 February protests in one of many aptly named "million man marches" [*milioneya*].[49] In the case of the Indignados movement, it has been estimated that up to 6 million people, out of a total population of 46 million, participated in the movement in one way or another.[50] Similarly, of the 80 million-strong Turkish population, between 3.5 and 7 million actively took part in the protests.[51] In Greece, a country of just over 10 million people, up to a third were said to have participated in the Aganaktismenoi movement.[52] In Brazil over one million people joined one of the biggest demonstrations on 20 June 2013.[53] In France, 30,000 people participated in the 9 April 2016 protests against the labour reform, called by Nuit Debout, and many more joined the strikes in May and June of the same year.[54] Even in countries such as the US, where recent years have seen a paucity of mass protest events, Occupy Wall Street managed to organise smaller but still significantly-sized protests, as demonstrated on 15 October 2011, when at least 5,000 people blockaded Times Square in central Manhattan.[55]

It is true that these are not all-time records. The 15 February 2003 global demonstrations against the impending war on Iraq are estimated to have numbered 12 million participants in 60 countries worldwide.[56] Furthermore, the anti-globalisation movement also saw some large demonstrations during counter-summit protests, with hundreds of thousands taking to the streets in Genoa in 2001 against the G8, and in 2003 against the EU summit in Barcelona. However these protests, in both the anti-war and anti-globalisation movements, were ephemeral events lasting for one or a few days. On the contrary, the various movements of the squares lasted for protracted periods of time, often several weeks or months.

Besides the scale of protest participation, also notable was the diversity of the protesters. While young, urban, and highly educated middle class people—the bulk of contemporary protesters in post-industrial societies—no doubt comprised the lion's share of overall participants, protest camps and demonstrations saw the participation of a highly diverse cross-section of society. The diversity of participants was frequently celebrated as a demonstration of the popular and broad-based character of the movement. The catalogue of unlikely participants related by the author's interviewees included "old ladies," "poor people," "religious people," "people dressed in suit and tie," "shop-keepers," and "my auntie who never before went to a protest." Elizabeth, a lecturer and a participant in Occupy Wall Street in New York, asserted that the protests were "representative of the broad spectrum of humanity. It's incredible how diverse it is." Selyne, a 32-year-old participant in Nuit Debout in Paris recounts that the assemblies comprised besides students and young people many unemployed and pensioners. José Ordóñez, a 37-year-old self-employed worker and Indignados participant, asserted that, "there were people of all kinds, of all social, cultural, and intellectual levels, and of all ages." During the fieldwork conducted for this book, this diversity of participation was epitomised by the case of Angelos, an interviewee in Syntagma Square, who was a 46-year-old businessman in the hospitality sector, currently unemployed, and who had been an activist for the right-wing New Democracy party in his youth—a profile I had never previously encountered in anti-globalisation protests. As Julian, an Occupy activist, sums up, protests were far from the stereotype of the "anarchist hippies" associated with previous movements.

The 2010s occupation movements also commanded an impressive degree of public support, as testified by a number of opinion polls. In June 2011 an *El País* poll recorded 66% of Spaniards as sympathising with the Indignados, with 81% agreeing with the reasons for the protests.[57] Such levels of support continued in the following months, topping 68% in a new poll conducted on the occasion of the first anniversary of the movement, and even rising to 78% on the second anniversary.[58] Similar or even higher levels of support were also seen for other movements of the squares such as the Aganaktismenoi in Greece, where according to a poll by Public Issue for broadcaster Skai over 80% of respondents supported the movement.[59] In Brazil at the end of June 2013, the poll institute Datafolha gave 8 in 10 Brazilians supporting the protests.[60] Also in Turkey the Taksim protest enjoyed near-majoritarian support, with a Pew poll asserting that 49% of Turks supported the movement, while 40% opposed it.[61] The support enjoyed by Occupy Wall Street in the US was considerably lower, probably due to its more overtly anarchist and countercultural inspiration, but still greater than what was seen during the anti-globalisation movement. In mid-October

2011 a *New York Times* poll gave 46% of US citizens as agreeing with OWS, though support decreased steadily in the ensuing months, as a result of a number of controversies surrounding the movement.[62] Finally, the French Nuit Debout also enjoyed majoritarian support in the country, with 60% of French citizens supporting the movement, according to an Odoxa poll for the TV channel ITele.[63]

These figures demonstrate that these movements managed to harness a majoritarian or quasi-majoritarian popular alliance, comprising demographics which had not been seen mobilising together for many decades, especially in the West. Within this highly diverse social coalition we can identify three main "social forces"—at the intersection between class, generational and educational factors: "the lost generation," "the squeezed middle" and "the new poor." These social categories were also themes of activist discourse and came to be used in public discussion about the crisis in the news media and therefore provide a convenient shorthand to capture the social composition of this protest wave.

The "lost generation" is one of the many terms used to describe the condition of young people disproportionately affected by the consequences of the economic crisis: the "youth without a future, without a job, without home, without fear" as described by the Spanish group Juventud sin Futuro [Youth Without a Future] that was among the forerunners of the Indignados movement. The movement of the squares saw significant participation from among the so-called "Generation Y," or Millennials, those born in the 1980s and 1990s, and in particular from those who were university educated and middle class. These are the members of the best-educated generation in recent history, a cohort highly skilled in the use of information technology, often speaking more languages than previous generations, and more well-travelled than their parents. Yet it is a generation, termed the "graduates without future" by Paul Mason,[64] that has disproportionately suffered the effects of the economic crisis and for whom high cultural capital often does not translate into opportunities for employment. Some of them belong to the category of the NEETs (Not in Employment, Education or Training), with severe negative consequences for their long-term prospects. The lost generation is a victim of intergenerational inequity, in which precarious young people are facing shrinking welfare provisions and rising cost of living compared to their parents. While the youth—or at least those who are in employment—are contributing to comparatively gen-

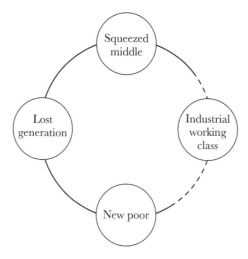

Figure 1.8: The social base of the movement of the squares

erous pensions for the elderly, they are destined to receive a meagre pension, if any, for themselves. Finally, they are a generation confronting a cost of living crisis; the "generation rent" that is less likely to get on the housing ladder, forcing many young people to live with their parents well into their thirties.

The "squeezed middle" is a term used to describe the hardships of the middle class, and in particular of middle-aged and older people who see their own living standards, and the prospects of their children, experiencing a severe drop. One of the social consequences of the Great Recession has been the "proletarianisation of the middle class," a trend of inverse social mobility for those on middle incomes, who had long been considered a beacon of social and political stability, and a base of support for neoliberal policies.[65] In a world marked by falling wages, rising levels of indebtedness, and cuts to public services, large sectors of the middle class found themselves struggling to maintain their living standards. Furthermore, small entrepreneurs and shopkeepers were badly affected by the economic downturn, and many of them came to harbour anger toward banks refusing to provide them with credit, and toward the state and its taxation agencies offering no reprieve despite the difficult economic situation. This economic condition, alongside a general feeling of disaffection from mainstream politics, motivated many middle-class people to join the movement of the squares, as seen in the considerable numbers of office workers both in the private and public sector, professionals and other members of the so-called new middle class, but also shop-keepers, self-employed and small entrepreneurs in protest camps and demonstrations.

The *nouveaux pauvres* is possibly the most contentious term here, given that references to the "new poor" have been found in public discourse, but not with the same prominence as the "lost generation" and the "squeezed middle."[66] This term is used to comprise those people that have been severely impoverished by the economic crisis, including the long-term unemployed and the homeless, but also the so-called "working poor", people for whom employment does not ensure a decent standard of living.[67] The participation of poor people has been quantitatively the most significant in developing countries. In Egypt, people coming from the poorer neighbourhoods of Cairo, Alexandria and other cities played a crucial role in defying the repressive apparatus of the regime on 28 January. In Turkey, poor working people were an important section of the movement, as shown by the contribution of football fans and "ultras". In Brazil, favela inhabitants (sometimes pejoratively referred to as *favelados*) were significant participants in the Movimento de Junho. In other countries such as the US, Spain, France and Greece, the poor appeared in the guise of the unemployed and others bearing the brunt of the economic downturn, and homeless people that flocked to protest camps in search of shelter and food.

The notable absentee in the coalition brought together by the movement of the squares was the organised industrial working class. Clearly this is not to say that, individually, workers did not participate in these movements, but rather that the level of participation of the industrial working class was very low and not collectively organised by unions. Except for Occupy Wall Street and Nuit Debout, most of these movements had a problematic relationship with trade unions, suspected of defending only their corporate interests while betraying those of ordinary citizens. In both Spain and, to a lesser extent, Greece, unions have been criticised by protesters for not having produced a sufficiently strong response to the economic crisis and the politics of austerity. In other cases, where protesters were initially keen to see the participation of trade unions, there has been a sense of disappointment at their lukewarm mobilisations, as seen in the failed general strike organised by Turkish trade unions during the Taksim uprising in June 2013. This situation reflects the degree to which the industrial working class, which Karl Marx considered the quintessential revolutionary class, found itself in a rather conservative position, partly because, contrary to other sections of society, it mostly continued to feel that its interests were represented by trade unions and social-democratic parties.

These different social forces participated with different degrees of intensity in the movement of the squares. The lost generation no doubt constituted the hegemonic force in this popular alliance, and its members were not only numerically the largest social component, but also the most active section of the movement. As will emerge from the empirical research presented in this study, the overwhelming majority of the organisers, both digital activists and ground co-ordinators, of this movement hailed from the ranks of the lost generation. One could thus argue that the lost generation has become a sort of new "universal class,"[68] whose conditions epitomise the worst of the present conjuncture and in which other sections of society can more easily identify their interests. This is why in the following chapters, it is mostly their voices we will hear.

2

ANARCHISM, POPULISM, DEMOCRACY

The people want the downfall of the regime.

Egyptian revolution slogan

They call it democracy and it is not.

Indignados slogan

A just government receives its power from the people.

Occupy Wall Street

"I love you democracy because it is as though you are absent." The expression used by the Spanish Indignados, in an ironic twist on a famous poem by Pablo Neruda,[1] similar to the *"Démocratie t'es ou?"* [Democracy, where are you?] banner used by Nuit Debout protesters (Image 2.1), spells out the centrality of the question of democracy for the 2011–16 uprisings. Democracy was the all-important issue in this protest wave, to the point that some analysts described them as "pro-democracy" movements, and some protest groups used such language in their own names. This concern with democracy stemmed from the diagnosis of a degeneration of liberal democracy reigning over an ever more unequal society. Seeing the founding spirit of democracy betrayed by their governments, protestors engaged in a number of alternative democratic practices, starting with the popular assemblies celebrated in the occupied squares, one of the most famous practices of this protest wave. What is the vision of democracy put forward by the movement of the squares? And how does it respond to the challenges of the present era?

The pursuit of radical democracy is certainly not something unique to the movement of the squares. Democracy was a key issue for many historical protest movements, from the Levellers to the Chartists, the French Revolution to the 1848 national insurrections, the Suffragettes to the Civil Rights movement, right up until the 1989 anti-communist protests and the anti-globalisation movement. Protest movements have been fundamental drivers of democratisation: they have forced governments to introduce democratic institutions, and act to hold elites to account.[2] The movement of the squares needs to be understood as a new chapter in this long-running struggle for democracy from below, where the question of democracy has acquired a new centrality at a time of "post-democracy"[3] or "de-democratisation"[4], and the erosion of basic citizenship rights under neoliberalism.

We can approach the demand for democracy, or rather for "real democracy," as expressed by the Spanish protest group ¡Democracia Real Ya! [Real Democracy Now!], as the nodal point of the citizenist ideology of the movement of the squares. To speak of ideology might sound incongruous, as many activists and commentators have insisted that the movement of the squares—just like politics more generally these days—was "non-ideological" or "post-ideological."[5] Bracketing the complex debate about ideology,[6] and simply taking this notion in its simplest and most neutral sense, as a "system of ideas," it is easy to see that these movements had an ideology: one centred around the slogan "real democracy", and branching out into many connected ideas—participation, horizontality, sovereignty, citizenship, and so on.

Driven by the perception of a democratic deficit and the rise of oligarchic power—the unholy alliance of the "financial dictatorship" of bankers and a self-serving "political caste"[7]—these movements saw, in the restoration and bottom-up expansion of citizenship, the way to "democratise democracy;"[8] to reconstruct democracy through the empowerment of individual citizens and their engagement in the most basic of political acts, such as assembling in public space and discussing political issues face-to-face. A restored citizenship was seen as the condition that made possible a real democracy, because of the perception that the roots of the present democratic crisis originate in the way in which individual citizens have been reduced to a condition of passivity and apathy. This vision of a politics of radical citizenship has encompassed elements from the anarchist and the populist traditions and their conflicting views of direct democracy:

Image 2.1: Nuit Debout banner in Place de la République asking, "Democracy, where are you?" [*Démocratie t'es ou?*] (Paolo Gerbaudo)

participatory and deliberative in the anarchist case, plebiscitary in the populist one.[9] Protestors have combined the method of *horizontality*[10], aimed at making movements a level playing field in which each person may participate as an equal, with the demand for *popular sovereignty* as the government of and by the people, enshrined in all democratic constitutions, yet too often betrayed by the oligarchic distortions of existing democracies.

The encounter between these two visions has raised obvious contradictions. Where the principle of sovereignty aligns with the vision of mass- or macro-democracy, of the sovereign people, united in the act of decision-making and self-government, the anarchist vision is a sort of micro-democracy, embedded in face-to-face communities and aiming at achieving a consensus among all those involved. Where horizontality affirms the idea of participation among equal and leaderless individuals, sovereignty expresses the vertical necessity of the unity of the people and their control over the state, and by the state. Where anarchism understands democracy as a process of grassroots action, which involves the assertion of the autonomy of individuals and communities from large, oppressive entities, populism's democratic vision is customarily concerned with big collectives, with the People, with a capital P, often in connection with the State, seen as the necessary instrument to exercise the People's Will. The vision of an anti-oligarchic reclamation of citizenship rights has provided the movement with a way to articulate these conflicting sensibilities.

In a world marked by extreme levels of economic and political inequality, the movement of the squares has identified the central conflict of society as that between the citizenry and the oligarchy, understood as the concentrated power of economic and political elites, responsible for depriving democracy of its substance. To overcome the present state of injustice, the movement of the squares proposed the notion of "real democracy" as an inclusive term for a project of radical re-democratisation of society from the bottom up, encompassing both alternative practices of grassroots decision-making, and the ambition of a restoration and expansion of existing democratic institutions. To this end they brought together the deliberative and participatory functions of assemblies and spokescouncils, and the plebiscitary and radical democratic objective of a reclamation of state institutions as a means of re-asserting citizens' participation in politics.[11] The encounter between notions of horizontality and sovereignty has also bred a new organisational culture, informed by a logic of "participatory mass action" that has mixed the mass ambition of populist politics with a libertarian emphasis on self-organisation and horizontality, inspiring the flexible and inclusive "liquid organising" practices seen both on social media and in the occupied squares.[12]

The neo-anarchist influence: horizontality and autonomy

The movement of the squares bears the mark of "neo-anarchism," the resurgence of anarchist politics that, dating from the 1970s, has gone on to inspire many protest movements.[13] For a number of decades now, theorists have noticed how the social transformation of society away from the Fordist mass production paradigm and towards a post-industrial service economy, as well as the defeats of the Soviet socialist project and of the labour movements in the West, precipitated a revival of typical anarchist themes—freedom, equality, rejection of hierarchy, anti-statism—within protest movements. The spirit of anarchism—the nineteenth-century ideology of Proudhon, Bakunin, and Kropotkin calling for a society without the state, and based on freedom of expression, voluntary self-organisation, mutualism and federalism[14]—was awakened and adapted to present circumstances, featuring prominently in the wave of "new social movements"[15] that emerged in the 1970s and 1980s: environmentalism, squatters' movements, Marxist autonomism, and later the anti-globalisation movement, precarious workers struggles, and hacker groups.

Authors such as David Graeber[16] and Raúl Zibechi[17] in fact argue that the movement of the squares should be considered anarchist, as we saw in the Introduction. Such an impression was also shared by many of my interviewees. For example Orsan, a Turkish activist, contended that the movement was anarchist in the same sense that the internet is, "anarchism more as a practice than as an idea", while Mahmoud Salem, an Egyptian activist, declared that the Tahrir movement was "anarchist without knowing it is anarchist." These assertions reflect the presence of a neo-anarchist sensibility in the 2011 protest movements, visible in their suspicion of large organisations and hierarchy, and their connected belief in spontaneous self-organisation. However, as we shall see, the movement of the squares had a complex and often conflictual relationship with neo-anarchist culture, and in particular with its notion of "autonomy".

To understand neo-anarchism's influence on the movement of the squares it is necessary to briefly delve into its history and the vision of direct democracy it developed in contradistinction to liberal-democracy, which it considered "pseudo-democracy" as it limits participation to the mere casting of a ballot during infrequent elections, dominated by candidates with similar policy platforms. As Graeber has argued, "anarchism does not mean the negation of democracy [...] Rather anarchism is a matter of taking [...] core democratic principles to their logical conclusions."[18] Democracy has been a paramount concern for neo-anarchist movements, as seen in the development of many alternative practices of participation and deliberation: assemblies, affinity groups, spokescouncils, collectives, and other forms of organisation that embodied the principles of participatory direct democracy, and were underpinned by a criticism of the authoritarianism and centralism of communism and social-democracy alike.

The American and European New Left, though still deeply influenced by Marxist doctrine and Leninist organisational models, espoused many classic anarchist ideas such as workers' control, de-centralisation and direct action. The student protests of May 1968 tilted toward typical anarchist themes in calling for self-management (autogestion), and criticising the bureaucratism of trade unions and socialist and communist parties. Leading figures of the movement made explicit declarations of sympathy towards anarchism. "Danny the Red", the famous leader of the Sorbonne occupation Daniel Cohn-Bendit, would call himself "a Marxist in the way Bakunin was", while his German counterpart, the beloved student leader Rudi Dutschke, presented himself as "both an anarchist and a Marxist."[19]

The shift to a post-industrial society in the 1970s and 1980s, marked by a weakening of the industrial working class, the expansion of the service sector, and the rise of a new middle class of social and cultural workers,[20] created propitious conditions for these ideas to develop into a fully-fledged political culture. If nineteenth-century anarchism had found its strongest appeal in such strata of the population as the independent-minded watchmakers of the Jura Federation in Switzerland, neo-anarchism found it with university students, and the creative class of a service and knowledge-driven economy. Neo-anarchism soon became a dominant influence upon urban struggles, student mobilisations, feminist movements and environmental campaigns, all calling in different ways for self-management and grassroots participation vis-à-vis closed-off bureaucracies. Furthermore, it intermixed with the various countercultures emerging around the time, such as hippies and punks. Eschewing the socialist Left's imperative of the taking of state power, and informed by revulsion toward a "totally administered society" or "one-dimensional society" as described by Frankfurt School thinkers Theodor Adorno and Herbert Marcuse,[21] it developed a politics of refusal and "exodus."[22] This was most clearly seen in the creation of alternative communities: communes, squats, eco-villages and alternative neighbourhoods; "liberated spaces" adhering to alternative lifestyles in terms of gender roles, sexual morality, and work ethics, where one could escape from the system's "colonisation" of everyday life.[23]

This libertarian turn in the radical Left in protest movements, which was paralleled by the rise of left-libertarian Green and New Left parties,[24] affected groups well beyond those self-identifying as anarchists. Most notably it left its mark with Marxist autonomism,[25] a movement which had strong roots in Italy, Germany, and elsewhere during the 1970s, and which asserted the need for workers to self-organise outside of the structures of trade unions and leftist parties. Autonomists had important differences from anarchists; they were Marxists and neo-Leninists in many of their organisational practices, and autonomist authors such as Hardt and Negri have often explicitly rejected the moniker "anarchist."[26] However, they came to adhere to similar left-libertarian worldviews in their belief in self-organisation and spontaneity. This turn stemmed from their analyses of post-industrial society as moving away from the hierarchical Fordist system of production, and ushering in a more molecular social structure, in which vertical forms of organisation could not work and more "rhizomatic"[27] ones would have to be developed.[28] This often conflictual convergence between neo-anarchism and Marxist autonomists led to a common political stream, sometimes described as "anarcho-autonomism,"[29] which held sway with one of the most important sectors of the anti-globalisation movement.

The anti-globalisation movement was the point of culmination of this neo-anarchist lineage.[30] Naturally, this movement was far broader than anarchist and autonomist groups alone. It also encompassed a motley and often discordant crew of trade unions; civic campaigns such as the Association for the Taxation of Financial Transactions and Citizen's Action (French acronym ATTAC); grassroots organisations of the Global South such as Via Campesina and the Movimento Sem Terra; NGOs such as Oxfam and ActionAid; various Trotskyist groups; and leftist parties.[31] Yet, within this "movement of movements," neo-anarchism constituted the hegemonic political culture, especially among younger protesters. It would suffice to search online for the most striking images associated with this protest wave, and one could see that almost all of them stemmed from this political school of thought: creative direct actions against the "red zone" of global summits, hacktivist meetings in social centres and squats, the militant actions of the Black Bloc, the councils of the Zapatistas in south-eastern Mexico, or the political theatre of the Clown Army.

Neo-anarchism has provided a response to the perceived detachment between everyday life and institutional politics, and catered to the new desire for individual self-determination emerging in a complex and highly diversified post-industrial society. However, the implications of neo-anarchism have sometimes been problematic because of its warped reflection of the individualism of neoliberal ideology.[32] Similarly to neo-liberalism, neo-anarchism has tended to value freedom and spontaneity against all forms of institutionalisation and formalisation, perceived to be inauthentic and alienating. This inadvertent complicity between neo-anarchism and neoliberalism, built upon their shared individualism and anti-statism, has appeared particularly problematic in the aftermath of the Great Recession, leading protesters to forgo some typical neo-anarchist orientations.

From this neo-anarchist stream originate two ideas key to understanding the culture and organisational forms of the movement of the squares: autonomy and horizontality.

Autonomy can be defined as the self-determination of individuals, groups and local communities against the encroachment of larger entities.[33] The idea of autonomy—a modern update on the classical anarchist preoccupation with freedom—has a storied pedigree in the anti-authoritarian Left. Already in the 1960s Cornelius Castoriadis, the philosopher of the libertarian socialist group "Socialisme ou Barbarie," had emphasised the notion of autonomy as the faculty to be governed by one's own moral norms.[34] Furthermore, as argued by Alain Touraine and colleagues, the "new social movements": feminism, environmentalism, the anti-nuclear movement, and regionalist movements that emerged in the aftermath of the student protests of the 1960s, all focused on the "demand for *autonomy* against the State and big organisations."[35]

Marxist autonomist movements in Italy and Germany in the 1970s and 1980s argued for the autonomy of the urban proletariat from unions and parties, and the constituent power of social struggles.[36] The women's movement also struggled for autonomy, in demanding control over women's bodies against attempts by the state and men to meddle with domains of intimacy, and asserting that the personal, the most fundamental sphere of autonomy, was political.[37] Lastly, the environmental movement's belief in autonomy was connected to its vision of a society of small, autonomous and self-reliant communities, independent from large-scale structures of production and consumption, connected with the idea that "small is beautiful."[38] In more recent years the principle of autonomy was a key trend in the anti-globalisation movement, as seen in its investment in "autonomous spaces"—from Zapatista villages, squats, hacker groups, social centres and rural communes—conceived of as liberated areas, outside the control of the state and capital.[39]

Horizontality is closely linked to autonomy, both sharing a suspicion of bureaucracy and large-scale organisation, but approaches from a different angle. Its focus is not on the relationship with other actors, but on the internal organisation of a given actor, which—as the term suggests—has to be "horizontal" rather than hierarchical or vertical. On the basis of this libertarian and radically egalitarian principle protest movements are required to create a "horizontal space" to allow for authentic grass-roots participation. As Marina Sitrin, an activist and author who popularised the term in academic and activist debates, argues, horizontality is "a social relationship that implies, as its name suggests, a flat plane upon which to communicate" as well as "the use of direct democracy and striving for consensus: processes in which attempts are made so that everyone is heard and new relationships are created."[40]

The term originated from the Argentinian revolt of December 2001, in which protesters were united by the cry *"Que se vayan todos"*[41] ["They should all go"] against impoverishment wrought by a financial crash, itself in turn caused by the irresponsible behaviour of bankers and politicians. However, its roots can be found in the long-standing tradition of direct democracy and non-hierarchical organising of the New Left and in its "prefigurative politics". As described by Wini Breines, this culture "was hostile to bureaucracy, hierarchy and leadership" and aimed "to create and sustain within the live practice of the movement, relationships and political forms that 'prefigured' and embodied the desired society."[42] This anti-hierarchical and pre-figurative trend was heavily developed in the context of the anti-globalisation movement. David Graeber, in describing anti-globalisation activists as the "new anarchists", asserted that they were involved in "creating and enacting horizontal networks instead of top-down structures like states, parties or corporations; networks based on principles of de-centralised, non-hierarchical consensus democracy."[43]

The 2011 and post-2011 occupation movements were selective in their inheritance of the legacy of neo-anarchism, and in particular in respect to the notion of autonomy. While retaining some of the elements of autonomy, such as the idea of independence of social movements from political parties and formalised organisations, as well as the view of social movements as carriers of constituent power, capable of creating new institutions beyond the existing ones,[44] activists progressively veered towards a reclamation of the principle of popular sovereignty, stemming from the tradition of democratic populism, with its unifying and expansive imaginary of the sovereign People. Autonomy's imaginary of a molecular politics of self-managed communities appeared unsuitable to meet the requirements of an era of widespread popular discontent, in which the possibility of a generalisation of struggle was concrete and the option of constructing autonomous spaces in capitalism, and pursuing an exodus from the system, irrelevant and self-defeating.

What the occupation movements instead transplanted more completely from the neo-anarchist stream was horizontality. Many interviewees frequently used the idea of horizontality, alongside other terms such as "organic" and "leaderless", as a shorthand to describe their participatory forms of organising, and their suspicion of personality-driven politics. Thus, for example Loubna, a member of the action commission of Nuit Debout in Paris, asserts that "the main idea of the movement was horizontality, this criticism of the vertical structures of traditional organisations." Similarly Bernardo Gutierrez, a Spanish journalist and activist based in Brazil who witnessed the development of this protest wave across different countries, states that what these movements had in common was "the idea of horizontality, the rejection of leaders, and personality politics." This horizontalist and anti-leader orientation is ultimately implicit in the very symbology of the Guy Fawkes mask, and the way in which concealing the identity of protesters was supposed to make everybody equal and prevent the presence of a recognisable leader, since everybody is Guy Fawkes and hence everybody and nobody is a leader. As we will see in the course of the book, the principle of horizontality heavily shaped the practices of these movements, in their adoption of consensus-based methods in assemblies, the design of protest camps as participatory spaces, and the use of social media as arenas for open discussion and interaction. But it also created serious problems due to a tendency to deny the existence of informal leadership, and a suspicion towards the new organisations that organically emerged out of the squares.

The democratic populist revival: sovereignty and citizenship

The novelty of the 2011 upheaval's protest culture can only be understood by taking into account the unexpected populist turn, which constitutes the real emergent phenomenon of this protest wave, and which has overlapped with and sometimes overruled pre-existing neo-anarchist motives. Populism, understood in a general sense as the "ideology of the People," designates a politics which, as Daniele Albertazzi and Duncan McDonnell put it, "pits a virtuous and homogeneous people against a set of elites and dangerous 'others' who were together depicted as depriving (or attempting to deprive) the sovereign people of their rights, values, prosperity, identity, and voice."[45] As we shall see in the ensuing empirical chapters, this orientation has been evident throughout the wave of public square occupations as seen in their appeal to the People, the Citizens, and the majority, echoed in Occupy Wall Street's "We Are The 99 Percent" slogan, as well as in the demand for a restoration of democracy, sovereignty and citizenship against the power of finance and corrupt politicians.

The populist character of the movement of the squares, on which this author has previously written,[46] has become increasingly apparent to a number of scholars, initially in the US, where the term "populism" does not carry all the negative connotations it does in the old continent. For example, the historian of populism Charles Postel has argued that, "the Occupy movement resembles nineteenth-century American populism in its anger at the avarice of bankers and financiers and in its notions of majoritarian democracy."[47] Similarly, Joe Lowndes and Dorian Warren have proposed that Occupy Wall Street has "antecedents in the late nineteenth and early twentieth centuries, when populists framed their struggle as one of the common people against a tiny moneyed elite."[48] Íñigo Errejón—a political scientist and the second-in-command of the new left-wing populist party Podemos—as well as Lasse Thomassen and Alexandros Kioupkiolis have identified such populist elements in the Spanish Indignados and the Greek Aganaktismenoi, as seen in each movement's discourse of the people and the citizen.[49]

Describing the movement of the squares as "populist" may appear demeaning, given the pejorative connotations the term has accrued in recent decades. In European debates this notion has been used to cover all manifestations of a perceived "democratic disease,"[50] seen in the rise of xenophobic right-wing parties such as the FPÖ in Austria, Geert Wilders' Party for Freedom in Holland, Lega Nord in Italy, and the Front National in France.[51] Furthermore, it has been utilised to describe the demagogic behaviour of centre-left and centre-right politicians alike, in a time of mediatised politics that favours a direct contact between the charismatic leader and the electorate. The pejorative use of the term and its association with "pathological" phenomena is however highly problematic. On the one hand, it reflects the suspicion of liberal elites toward all political phenomena that mobilise the popular masses without their mediation.[52] On the other hand, it ignores the fact that the genealogy of populism stems not from the Right, but from the revolutionary and progressive left-wing movements of the eighteenth and nineteenth centuries.

The first use of the term "populist" was in fact associated with two nineteenth-century democratic movements: the Russian Narodniks, and the US People's Party. The Russian *narodniki* [literally: populists], were a nineteenth-century democratic movement that was a forerunner of the socialist movement.[53] Inspired by Rousseau's doctrine of the *volonté géné-rale* [general will] and by the French Revolution, the Narodnik move-ment—mostly composed of middle class intellectuals—called for the emancipation of the peasantry and the overthrow of the Tsar. Following the slogan, "Go to the people", activists went to the countryside to agi-tate the peasantry, but were not well received, and were often denounced by the rural population. Despite their failure, the Narodniks were to inspire the politics of revolutionary socialism, with pre-eminent anarchist Mikhail Bakunin having been a member of the movement.

Equally concerned with the emancipation of the People and the extension of basic political rights was the Chartist movement in the UK, which took its name from the People's Charter of 1838. In demanding a "just representation of the people," the movement has also been described as "populist."[54] The US People's Party,[55] who introduced the term "populist" to the English language, had a rather different story to both the Chartists and the Narodniks. Its main targets were economic actors, the robber barons of the Gilded Age: bankers, railroad tycoons, and the industrialists of the steel and oil trusts. Against these economic forces the People's Party united a coalition of peasants and trade unions and called for the abandonment of the restrictive monetary policies of the gold standard. Aside from movements explicitly considered "popu-lists", a populist element was present in many others, certainly including the French Revolution of 1789 with its appeal to popular sovereignty, the 1848 uprisings calling for the end of autocratic rule and for popular government, and the early anarchist movement as seen in the writings of Bakunin and Kropotkin, who mostly referred to "the people", rather than the working class, or the workers, as the revolutionary subject.[56]

While the nineteenth century simmered with the populist ambition of constructing a "people's power", the twentieth century saw a retreat of democratic populist politics. The 1930s popular fronts, established in different Western countries like France, Spain and the US, used populist themes to halt the rise of fascism.[57] But for the most part, the social-democratic and communist Left adopted the Marxist paradigm of class struggle rather than the more unifying notion of popular struggle.[58] Fascist movements in Italy and Germany fused the idea of the People with the idea of the Nation, and of race. The retreat of democratic populism continued in the aftermath of the Second World War, when, as argued by Michael Kazin, "populism began a migration to the Right", in which "the vocabulary of grassroots rebellion served to thwart and reverse social and cultural change rather than to promote it."[59] In the US, right-wing figures like the segregationist governor of Alabama, George Wallace, claimed the mantle of populism in the late 1960s and 1970s. In Europe a similar process was visible in the 1990s, with the rise of right-wing xenophobic parties adopting the discourse of the people and of popular sovereignty. Thus, with few exceptions, notably the way in which the New Left initially adopted some anti-elitist populist themes,[60] the Left lost its erstwhile ownership of populist ideology.

The beginning of the third millennium has, however, signalled a possible change in this trend and a return of populism to more progressive shores. A number of protest movements, anti-corruption drives, environmental campaigns and civic initiatives have in recent years reclaimed the idea of the people, or its more libertarian version: the citizenry. The most well-known example of this revival of progressive "neo-populism" has been the so-called pink wave of Latin American socialist populism, as manifested in the electoral victories of Hugo Chávez in Venezuela and Evo Morales in Bolivia.[61] Taking power on the back of powerful popular campaigns that united the poor, the workers, and sectors of the middle class, these leaders presented themselves—in typical populist manner— as champions of the people against national elites and the imperialist interference of the US. Once in government they implemented a raft of measures to further social and economic equality, but also drafted new constitutions aimed at ensuring more popular participation in democratic life. This political stream—which has, however, now entered a phase of crisis and authoritarianism—constituted one of several populist inspirations for the movement of the squares.[62]

As we have seen, populism is a political tendency that has historically manifested itself on both the Left and the Right of the political spectrum, a feature that has led to much confusion regarding the nature of this ideology. To explain this eccentric character of populism, some scholars argue that populism is not a self-standing ideology but rather a discursive form that can complement and accommodate different political contents. Representative of this position is political philosopher Ernesto Laclau, who has theorised populism as a discursive logic that revolves around rhetorical appeals to "the People", intended as the totality of the political community of a given country, against a common enemy, mostly identified in unresponsive institutions.[63] Populist discourse thus generates what Laclau calls a "chain of equivalence"—as opposed to a logic of difference—that unites different sectors of society and their respective demands.[64] In a similar vein, Michael Kazin has described populism as, "a persistent yet mutable style of political rhetoric with roots deep in the nineteenth century."[65]

The problem with these definitions of populism as simply a style or a form, is that they neglect the fact that populism does carry its own substantive content. The kernel of populism, be it right-wing or left-wing, is the principle of "popular sovereignty,"[66] according to which the People are the source of power, and government should act in the People's interest. The intellectual history of popular sovereignty is associated with social contract theorists and in particular with Jean-Jacques Rousseau, who in *The Social Contract*—a work which directly inspired eighteenth-century American and French revolutionaries and the ensuing republican constitutions—argued that in the People, as the collectivity of all citizens of a given city or nation, rather than the King, was to be found the legitimate depository for sovereignty, traditionally understood as the right to govern a country without the interference of any external power.[67]

Popular sovereignty is a principle which populism shares with republicanism, but for which the former goes to far more uncompromising ends than the latter. As John McCormick has argued, republicanism sees the popular will as having to be carefully sifted through the guarantees of rule of law and a system of mixed government, with its inherent checks and balances. Populism sees popular sovereignty as a principle that needs to assert itself as much as possible without institutional and organisational mediations, and expresses an attitude of mistrust and distaste towards the elites that purport to represent the people's will.[68] This difference between republican and populist views of popular sovereignty can be appreciated by looking at three issues: majority rule, representation and citizenship.

Popular sovereignty, according to Rousseau, should be informed by a general will [*volonté générale*] which had to be indivisible—akin to an individual, with a single will. Given that, in a world of plural and competing interests, it is impossible to reach unanimity on any given issue, popular sovereignty has been associated with the doctrine of "majority rule,"[69] where the majority of citizens are considered a proxy for the *volonté générale*.

This was already apparent to Alexis de Tocqueville when he argued that, "it is the very essence of democratic government that the power of the majority should be absolute, for in democracies nothing outside the majority can keep it in check."[70] Majority rule has however been often criticised for clashing with minority rights and democratic pluralism, including by republican theorists like Philip Pettit.[71] As such, popular sovereignty and majority rule have often been looked upon with suspicion by the radical Left and protest movements, who, rather than taking the side of the majority and the People, often preferred to identify themselves with oppressed minorities, as we will see in the next chapter.

Rousseau vociferously opposed the doctrine of majority rule and the connected notion of representation, which he considered a violation of popular sovereignty. Inspired by the political model of his town of birth, Geneva, which at the time was a city-state, and the democratic system of the Roman Republic, Rousseau devised a participatory of popular assemblies, open to all citizens, which would possess legislative power. Elected magistrates would be responsible for governance, but in strict accordance with the people's laws.[72] However, representative government is the arrangement that has prevailed within contemporary democracies,[73] in which parliaments and parties act as mediators between the people's will and power. Furthermore, within this system, the people's representatives are not seen as people's delegates having to uphold a binding mandate from their electorate, but are instead considered to possess their own autonomy in law-making, a principle that was famously defended by the English conservative politician and philosopher Edmund Burke.[74] Democracy has thus mostly become, as Joseph Schumpeter argued, a procedure for choosing among competing elites.[75] Rather than a true "democracy," what we see in these political systems is a "polyarchy", as expressed by Robert Dahl: an oligarchic form of government in which the elites exercise power under the dubious pretext that they are doing so in the people's name.[76]

Democratic populism has often denounced representative democracy for betraying the democratic promise of direct participation in self-government. As John P. McCormick has argued, "populism [...] is modern, representative democracy's 'cry of pain.' [...] an occurrence in regimes that adhere to democratic principles, but where, in fact, the people do not rule."[77] As described by Yves Mény and Yves Surel, many populist movements, such as the People's Party in the US, campaigned for the institution of plebiscitary forms of direct democracy, including referenda and popular initiatives, as means of asserting the sovereignty of the conjunct will of the People.[78] Alternatively, they have seen in maverick and charismatic politicians a more direct form of mediation between popular will and power than the one offered by parties and parliament, as seen in the profusion of populist leaders from Peron to Chávez.[79] Thus, far from being a "disease" of democracy, populism is also an attempt to reclaim its founding principle of "people's power". Like anarchism it makes claim to direct democracy, though not in the participatory form of assemblies and collectives, but more frequently through the "verticality" of plebiscitary democracy, charismatic leaders, or anti-establishment parties.

The reclaiming of popular sovereignty, a notion which had long seemed out of fashion with protest movements, constituted a central theme for the movement of the squares. It was thematised in the Arab revolutions through the famous slogan: "The people want to bring down the regime," along with many other "the people want..." variants.[80] Furthermore, it was seen in Occupy Wall Street, whose assembly resolutions often alluded to the "We the People...", the wording of the preamble of the US constitution, and again in the "We Are the 99 Percent" slogan, an evident assertion of majority—or better supermajority—rule, that is strongly in line with the populist view of an unmediated sovereignty.

The peculiarity of citizenism, vis-à-vis other forms of populism, is its libertarian twist. The reclaiming of popular sovereignty is enforced in a bottom-up manner starting at the individual level through the re-appropriation of citizenship, reflecting the legacy of neo-anarchism and its intermixing with populist themes, and more generally the individualising tendencies of contemporary society, in which, as argued by Alberto Melucci, the individual is conceived of as the basic unit of social organisation.[81] Citizenship, usually understood as a bundle of rights and responsibilities that derive from one's own membership in a political community, is a concept that carries a complex history and heavy luggage, as it has been shaped by a number of traditions including liberalism, with its focus on personal rights, civic-republicanism, with its focus on political participation, and social-democracy, with its focus on the material basis of citizenship.[82]

The view of citizenship proposed by the movement of the squares encompassed elements from these different traditions and in particular the civic-republican one. Citizenship rights were reclaimed due to the perception that they could constitute a weapon against the oligarchic usurpation of power by non-elected and self-serving elites; they were seen as a means to achieve a better balance of forces in the confrontation between citizenry and oligarchy. The occupation movements, however, did not just demand participation in existing institutions. They also involved an element of "democratic invention": a claim to new rights and to new institutions, which came close to the "insurrectional model of citizenship" proposed by Étienne Balibar, according to which "insurrection [...] is the active modality of citizenship". As we shall see this demand for a restoration and expansion of citizenship and democracy was key in these movements' view of a world beyond the neoliberal order.

Citizenry vs. Oligarchy

French sociologist Alain Touraine claimed that all historical eras are marked by a central conflict around which the main antagonism in society is organised, and whose results come to define the key values and meanings of society.[83] Following this theory it can be argued that for the movement of the squares, the central conflict of contemporary society has been the one between the citizens and oligarchies.[84] The citizenist worldview counter-poses the citizens, as the individual members of the sovereign people, with the concentrated forms of economic and political power—the financial dictatorship and the political caste—by whom the former feel victimised: corrupt politicians, the Troika, Goldman Sachs, JP Morgan, and so forth.[85] Echoing the discourse of the movement of the squares, in his best-selling book *The Establishment* Owen Jones describes the oligarchy as an array of "powerful groups that need to protect their position in a democracy in which almost the entire adult population has the right to vote," and which includes "politicians who make laws; media barons who set the terms of debate; business and financiers who run the economy; police forces that enforce a law which is rigged in favour of the powerful."[86] The oligarchy stands accused of depriving citizens of democracy, their right to collective self-determination, and forcing them into a situation of gross economic inequality that diminishes their liberty and dignity, as expressed in Occupy's juxtaposition of the 99 per cent and the 1 per cent. The citizenry is instead viewed as a redemptive force, a type of new revolutionary subject which pursues collective control over society from below, starting with the self-organising capacity of individuals and their aggregation in online discussions and in the occupied squares.

This framing of contemporary conflict differs starkly from that proposed by the labour movement and post-industrial new social movements, which Touraine had analysed. The labour movement focused on the material conflict between capital and labour, and the post-industrial new social movements instead drew attention to the emerging confrontation between the technocratic power of a "programmed society,"[87] and an emerging class of cultural and social workers, but also to the generational conflict between the free-minded baby boomers and their conservative parents.[88] The opposition between citizens and the oligarchy does not focus on the materialist question of exploitation, nor upon the post-materialist question of cultural alienation, but on the decline of citizenship and popular sovereignty, wrought by the rise of oligarchic power. It thus frames the extreme inequality that has emerged in neoliberal societies not just as an economic but chiefly a political question, seeing economic inequality as resulting from the violation of the principle of political equality that is inherent in the notion of citizenship.

This conception of contemporary conflict is not just a translation of anarchist themes into an accessible language, as runs the argument of Mark Bray,[89] but rather a transition from the neo-anarchist narrative of contestation of the State and all large-scale institutions to a denunciation of the elites perverting them. It results in a re-organisation of the "topology" of political conflicts, substituting the Left/Right or socialism/capitalism binary oppositions with the opposition of bottom versus top; the ordinary people against oligarchic power.

Table 2.1: Transition from anarchist to populist beliefs

	Anarchism	Populism
Economic conflict	Anti-capitalism	"Down with the banks!", anti-finance and anti-plutocratic attitude
Political conflict	Anti-State	Anti-elitism, anti-corporatism, anti-cronyism

Two main enemies have been elided under the umbrella of the Oligarchy, targeted by the 2010s upheavals: bankers and politicians, as summed up in ¡Democracia Real Ya!'s slogan: "We are not goods in the hands of politicians and bankers" [*No somos mercancías en manos de políticos ni banqueros*].

From Spain to Greece and the United States, bankers, a blanket term used to attack the financial sector in its multiple manifestations, were among the most hated oligarchs targeted by protesters. Slogans included, "jail the bankers" and, "people need to be bailed out and bankers foreclosed,"[90] and the quip "banksters" (combining bankers and gangsters) entered the lexicon. Reflecting the depth of popular discontent ignited by the financial crisis of 2008, protesters took aim at the "super-rich": those with large fortunes that have been growing apace under neoliberalism, and their coterie of brokers, financial advisors, analysts, economists and lobbyists, held responsible for the financial crash of 2008, and more generally for supporting an economic model making "the rich richer and the poor poorer".

In movement discourse, bankers were depicted not just as a greedy self-serving elite, but also as an arrogant one, a "business class", that after having caused the deepest economic downturn since the end of the Second World War has unashamedly pled for public aid, only to soon return to reap rich bonuses. Take for example the Declaration of the Occupation of New York City, possibly the most programmatic text produced by Occupy Wall Street. It describes bankers as those who "have taken our houses through an illegal foreclosure process, despite not having the original mortgage," those "who have taken bailouts from taxpayers with impunity, and continue to give executives exorbitant bonuses", and those who "have held students hostage with tens of thousands of dollars of debt on education, which is itself a human right".[91] Additionally, bankers are accused of having cynically used the crisis as an opportunity to force in yet more neoliberal measures, a thesis advanced by Naomi Klein in her "shock doctrine" argument,[92] and expressed in the oft-repeated slogan of anti-austerity movements: "This is not a crisis, it is a fraud."

This "anti-bank" attitude foregrounds a different type of economic enemy than that of the anti-globalisation movement, whose favourite targets were corporations such as Nike, Gap and McDonald's; companies producing consumer goods like clothing and food and accused, from a moral standpoint, of running an unethical "sweatshop" production model in Third World countries, and of exacting a negative toll upon the environment and human health.[93] The movement of the squares' criticism focused instead on banks as actors that negatively affect the everyday life of many people "here at home", as most clearly experienced by those affected by rising levels of indebtedness, foreclosures, and spiralling student loans.

What was most striking about this anti-bankers discourse is that it was, to a great extent, not anti-capitalist, as one would see with global justice activists, but rather "anti-plutocratic."[94] Protesters were not primarily concerned with the nature of bankers as agents of exploitation and capitalist accumulation, but rather with the way in which the financialisation of the economy had become a tool of autocratic political power. This is evidenced in the frequent references to the idea of a "financial dictatorship". Bankers were criticised for having underhandedly acquired unofficial political power, by means of which unelected and private organisations, such as banks, meddle with the functioning of society and impose an economic system which leads to "inequality, tension and injustice [...] in a growing spiral that consumes itself by enriching a few and sending into poverty the rest," as argued by ¡Democracia Real Ya![95]

This anti-plutocratic discourse, strikingly reminiscent of the US People's Party tirades against robber barons during the Gilded Age at the end of the nineteenth century,[96] proposes a reversal of the anarchist position of Emma Goldman, who argued that political oppression was the by-product of economic exploitation.[97] It alerts us to the way in which economic inequality is the result of policies pursued by the ruling elites through exploiting the growing democratic deficit: the gap between governments and their citizens. This claim is reflected in a passage of the Occupy Wall Street Declaration where it affirms that, "corporations do not seek consent to extract wealth from the people and the Earth," and that, "no true democracy is attainable when the process is determined by economic power." On this theme, an Indignados slogan pointedly asked: "Why do the markets rule, if I have not voted for them?"

Politicians featured as regularly as the hated bankers among the "enemies of the People" targeted by the movement of the squares. They were accused of being part of a self-serving political class or "caste," a term used by parties such as the Five Star Movement in Italy and Podemos in Spain, to describe elites separated by hundreds of miles from the experiences and problems of ordinary citizens; or even a "regime," an autocratic political Establishment that frustrated people's thirst for democracy. As with bankers, "politicians," a term repeated with scorn in protest manifestos or assembly resolutions, is an umbrella term, one that stands to metonymically evoke a coterie of figures held responsible for the hollowing out of democracy: political leaders, congressmen, party apparatchiks, public functionaries, state technocrats, and even sometimes trade unionists and members of other "intermediary bodies" of civil society, accused of sacrificing the general interest and instead beholden to the corporate interests of their members and to political opportunism.

Unsurprisingly, the staunchest attack against the incumbent political class came from the Arab Spring, in which the suffering wrought by decades of dictatorship, even if recently guised in farcical pseudo-democratic garb, had bred a deep-seated hatred for the ruler as individual, and for the regime supporting him. This sentiment was at the root of well-known revolutionary rallying cries such as the Tunisian French slogan "*dégage*", the Arabic "*erhal*" [both translating as "leave"], or the pan-Arab slogan, "*El-sha'ab yurid isqat el-nizam*" ["The people want the downfall of the regime"]. Obviously the political conflict waged by the movements outside the Arab World was radically different due to their operating in the context of liberal democracy. Nonetheless it is remarkable the extent to which the anti-dictatorship struggle of the Arab Spring urged people in other countries to question the reality of their own democracy, leading many to recognise in the West and elsewhere a "post-democratic" situation, in which formal democratic mechanisms continued to exist even as their application was rendered less and less meaningful.[98]

In the other movements, from Spain to Brazil, politicians were often represented as corrupt, self-serving and opportunistic, likened to the unscrupulous characters of the American TV drama *House of Cards*.[99] This accusation was echoed in slogans such as the Greek "I vote, You vote, He votes, She votes, We vote, You vote, They steal" and in the 27 May 2011 declaration of Syntagma Square, demanding that "any corrupt politician should either be sent home or to jail". A similar anger was thematised in the Spanish protesters' description of politicians as "*chorizo*", a term used to indicate a corrupt individual, or in the rhetoric of the pre-Occupy group, US Day of Rage, who focused on the way in which moneyed interests "corrupt our political parties, our elections, and the institutions of government."[100] Accusations that politicians were all corrupt also proliferated in the movements in Turkey and Brazil.

The diagnosis that informed these attacks was that of a "cartelisation" of mainstream parties in which, despite their nominal ideological differences, such as that between Left and Right, they were ultimately united by allegiance to corporate interests of a common "political class", at odds with popular interests.[101] This idea was captured in the Spanish *"PSOE y PP la misma mierda es"* [PSOE and PP are the same shit], or in the acronym PPSOE, merging the two, a criticism of the two-party system (*bipartidisimo*) and its alternation between dominant parties (*turnismo*) with no substantial change in policy. In Italy, the Five Star Movement similarly quipped that Italian politics was all about PDL—Berlusconi's People of Freedom Party [Popolo della libertà]—and PD without L—the Democratic Party [Partito Democratico]—the assonance between the two betraying their true identity.

The essence of this discourse was thus the assertion of a betrayal on the part of politicians, and a usurpation of popular sovereignty as expressed in the Indignados slogans: "Error 404. Democracy not found" and *"Lo llaman democracia y no lo es"* [They call it democracy and it is not]; laments for a lost democracy. This problem is also thematised in a passage of the manifesto of ¡Democracia Real Ya!:

> In Spain most of the political class does not even listen to us. Politicians should be bringing our voices to the institutions, facilitating the political participation of citizens through direct channels that provide the greatest benefit to the wider society, not getting rich and prospering at our expense, attending only to the dictatorship of major economic powers and holding them in power.[102]

In a similar vein, the first resolution of the Syntagma assembly on 27 May 2011 asserted that, "for a long time decisions have been made for us, without consulting us", a reference to the many unpopular decisions taken by Greek politicians in the advent of the protests, including the decision of George Papandreou's government to accept the highly unpopular bailout package, imposed by the Troika to "rescue" the country from the risk of bankruptcy, and deny the Greek people a referendum on the issue. Given this dire view of the political class, it should not come as a surprise that the direct messages sent to politicians from protesters have often taken the trenchant form of an insult or an ultimatum, as in the Greek "Thieves!", the Arab "Leave", the Spanish quip "Politicians: We're your bosses and this is a layoff plan", or the Argentinian 2001 slogan, in vogue again in 2011: *"Que se vayan todos!"*—"They should all go!"

Some of this anti-oligarchic discourse bore resemblance to conspiracy theories, including narratives about the Illuminati, the Bilderberg

Group,[103] and the ideas of the Zeitgeist Movement. These are phenomena that have become highly influential in recent years[104] and their presence was visible at these movements' fringes, where, as with many protest movements, lunatics abounded. Yet, there were two major differences. Firstly, for these movements the conspiracy was not hidden in a Swiss hotel, or in a secret bunker, but out for everyone to see. Secondly, ordinary citizens were not framed as hapless victims, but as a force able to stop this "business as usual" from devouring the entrails of society. This was exemplified by the text of the global Day of Action, 15 October 2011, where it boldly stated: "No longer will banks take our homes. No longer will banks rob students of our future. No longer will banks destroy the environment. No longer will banks fund the misery of war." The text resonates with the message of a famous speech by US populist presidential candidate William Jennings Bryan: "We shall answer their demands for a gold standard by saying to them, you shall not press down upon the brow of labor this crown of thorns. You shall not crucify mankind upon a cross of gold."[105]

The pragmatic utopia of "real democracy"

The ideology of the movement of the squares did not propose only a trenchant criticism of "actually existing democracy." It also contained a redemptive element: the vision of what a "real democracy" should look like, after "they all go." Against the depiction of a society plagued by oligarchic power and a democratic deficit, the occupation movements saw in a democratic "regime change," and a restoration and bottom-up expansion of democratic space, the road toward reconquering people-power and addressing the manifold problems of a neoliberal and elitist society, marked by grotesque inequality.

The notion of "real democracy," a term coined by ¡Democracia Real Ya! [Real Democracy Now!] in Spain and then adopted in other countries, has been criticised by some activists for its vagueness. For example, in the Greek context, activists tended to prefer more explicit references to direct democracy, mostly understood in this context in the anarchist sense. However, the value of the phrase was precisely its indeterminacy,[106] and its ability to evoke an inclusive platform of democratic overhaul, which, besides the construction of grassroots forms of direct democracy, also encompassed the restoration and expansion of state democracy.

The more radical component of this project of democratic overhaul were the popular assemblies, seen in the occupied squares of 2011–13 and strongly reminiscent of those devised by Jean-Jacques Rousseau in *The Social Contract.*[107] The declaration of Occupy Wall Street in New York City, for example, invited people to gather in public space and start a process of collective deliberation to assert people's power: "Exercise your right to peaceably assemble; occupy public space; create a process to address the problems we face, and generate solutions accessible to everyone."[108] Similarly, the 27 May 2011 communiqué of the Syntagma assembly contrasted the "pseudo-democracy" inside the parliament building to the authentic democracy performed in the squares, saying "When we, the people, start discussions without fear, fear grips them inside the parliament building."[109] Here we find an anarchist-inspired view of what a "real democracy" means: a face-to-face democracy exercised in the "authentic" space of public squares and streets, away from the perceived artificiality of institutional politics.

These movements' political investment in direct and participatory democracy did not equate to a wholesale rejection of representative democracy. "They don't represent us" only in part means "No to representative democracy."[110] Contrary to such an argument, advanced by Sitrin and Azzellini, this battle cry should also be read as expressing a demand for better, and more direct and participatory representation to overcome the current "misrepresentation" of the people's will. This more nuanced view is reflected in the "official" documents produced by these movements, the manifestos of protest groups, and the declarations and resolutions of popular assemblies. Reading them it is clear that the protesters did not mostly see "horizontal democracy" as substitutive of "vertical democracy," but rather demanded (extremely vocally) a reclamation of institutional democracy, its restoration to its founding values, and its update in consideration of present social conditions, including via forms of online democracy. The paradox here is that while the assemblies that produced these documents mostly followed neo-anarchist consensus procedures, the content of their deliberations was adamantly populist, demanding a restoration of popular sovereignty and an opening-up of the state. Neo-anarchist methods ended up delivering populist results.

This pragmatic approach towards the state and representative democracy is reflected in the manifesto of ¡Democracia Real Ya! where it declared: "Democracy belongs to the people (demos = people, krátos =

government) which means that government is made of every one of us."[111] Similarly the Occupy Wall Street declaration asserted that "a democratic government derives its just power from the people,"[112] only to immediately add that in present circumstances, this principle is precluded by the interference of corporate interests. The very idea that there can be such a thing as "just government power" stands truly remote from the anarchist mission of eliminating government in all its forms. The root problem in this context—in contrast to the customary anarchist or revolutionary socialist position—was identified not in the existence of state democratic institutions as such, but in their distortion by corrupt elites occupying them and foreclosing it to any form of popular intervention.

To overcome the present corruption of state democracy, protesters envisioned a radical refoundation of public institutions to restore them to their core democratic principles, a stance which, as Hannah Arendt has shown, is a component of many revolutions.[113] Interestingly, a previous draft of the aforementioned Occupy Wall Street Declaration appealed to the right of citizen rebellion, as accorded by the US Declaration of Independence's words: "We hold it as self-evident ... that whenever any Form of Government becomes destructive of these ends [Life, Liberty, and the Pursuit of Happiness], it is the Right of the People to alter or abolish it." In this context, protest is framed not merely as an act of contestation of the institutions, but also as a constituent moment, that may construct new institutions in place of the old ones, and thus contribute to regenerating society.

In line with this vision, activists called for a democratisation of the state and a reassertion of citizenship rights, as seen in a number of concrete demands discussed by popular assemblies and by key protest organisations. In fact, far from the stereotype of lacking clear demands, the movements of the squares were also "proposal movements" that did not shy away from fleshing out their desired policies:

- A guarantee of the rights to privacy, freedom of expression and freedom of assembly
- Reforms of the political system to guarantee enhanced participation of the citizenry, including direct democracy via referenda and online voting
- Reforms of the financial sectors to stop the "financial dictatorship"
- Public services and welfare provisions, housing, health, and education, to guarantee the dignity of all citizens

- Measures against political corruption[114]

   This platform laid claim to elements coming from different visions of citizenship: from liberal citizenship, in the re-assertion of freedom of expression and protection from police brutality; from social citizenship in the demand for the restoration of material rights that were previously guaranteed by social-democracy, such as the right to housing, health and education; and more evidently also from the civic-republican platform, with its emphasis on active citizenship and civic virtue, as seen in the demand for new democratic institutions such as referenda and online voting. Indeed the participatory element, most closely associated with the civic-republican tradition is the one that emerges most strongly from the demands put forward by the movement of the squares. It is true that, as evidenced in the list above, the assemblies also demanded economic rights and public provisions, and a check against the financial system. However their view of citizenship was political before being social or economic. These movements often displayed a strong suspicion towards what they perceived as the passivity and bureaucratism of social-democracy, and sought to remedy these tendencies in the pursuit of grassroots participation. Building on the spirit of popular democracy and the "reclaim the state"[115] strategy of previous protest movements, such as the practices of participatory budgeting in Porto Alegre in Brazil that attracted much attention during the anti-globalisation movement, protesters proposed the creation of various forms of direct democracy through which ordinary citizens could have a say on all important decisions otherwise controlled by political elites.

   What is apparent is that despite its revolutionary imaginary, citizenism was (and is) not a revolutionary ideology in the traditional sense of violent struggle and totalising political change. These movements, including the more anarchist-inspired ones such as Occupy Wall Street, did not posit a total break with representative democracy and state institutions. Rather they called for a radical but peaceful overhaul of the economic and political systems, leading to the ouster of the oligarchies that have perverted them, the restoration of the founding principles of democracy, and the reclamation of citizenship, through such measures as electoral reform, the introduction of referenda and popular initiatives, and a redirection of the state's role to become a guarantor of a minimum condition of social dignity.

ANARCHISM, POPULISM, DEMOCRACY

The organisational logic of participatory mass action

The crossover between anarchism and populism in the emerging culture of citizenism also led to the development of a new organisational culture combining principles of inclusivity and flexibility around the logic I describe as "participatory mass action." This organisational blueprint combined two distinct logics of action: the logic of participatory action and the logic of mass action.

The logic of participatory action lays emphasis on the centrality of participation as a process of creative involvement and intervention. This logic has been at the heart of anti-authoritarian and anarchist movements due to their criticism of hierarchy and bureaucracy, and their valuing of creativity and active intervention of individuals in collective action. The logic of mass action, associated with populist and revolutionary movements, instead puts an emphasis on the power of numbers as an incarnation of the general will of the sovereign people, and on the importance of unity among all those involved. It is the logic that has been at the heart of many democratic populist movements, with their ambition of constructing a popular politics against the establishment.

Combining these anarchist and populist logics of action, the movement of the squares was capable of mobilising the masses without resorting to formal mass membership organisations. This trend was displayed in different domains of these protest movements' activity, including their forms of communication, their protest tactics, and their forms of decision-making, which will be examined in the ensuing empirical chapters. The use of social media as a means of mobilisation resulted from both the populist desire to use the people's platforms, due to their high level of penetration among the population, and the anarchist intention of making use of their participatory and supposedly horizontal affordances. The occupation of protest camps on the one hand reflected the neo-anarchist tradition of direct action, and the attempt to create a horizontal and participatory space, but on the other was also imbued with the centralising narrative of popular sovereignty and unity. Finally, the creation of popular assemblies reflected these movements' political investment in horizontality and consensus-based decision-making, but it also manifested the "popular spirit" and the reassertion of strong collective unity.

As we shall see in the coming chapters, this hybrid organisational culture provided protest movements with a powerful way to structure collective action in accordance with the narrative of a self-organised citizenry fighting against the oligarchy. But it also led to some significant quandaries that bespeak the more general contradiction between the libertarian and populist orientations of citizenism, as well as the internal clashes between the more anarchist and populist inclined wings of the movement.

3

THE 99 PER CENT AND THE INDIGNANT CITIZEN

We are the 99 percent. We are getting kicked out of our homes. We are forced to choose between groceries and rent. We are denied quality medical care. We are suffering from environmental pollution. We are working long hours for little pay and no rights, if we're working at all. We are getting nothing while the other 1 per cent is getting everything. We are the 99 percent.

"We Are the 99 Percent" Tumblr blog[1]

The movement of the squares was pervaded by a highly inclusive form of collective identity, evidenced by the profusion of different slogans all sharing the same message: "We Are the 99 Percent", "we are many", "we are the majority", "we are more", "we are normal, common people", and "we are ordinary citizens". These expressions reintroduced a majoritarian ambition to protest politics—most evident in Occupy Wall Street's "99 Percent" motto—that had long been considered out of place within progressive movements, in a postmodern and "post-ideological" world. The anti-globalisation movement, as it strove to cope with the shock of the fall of the Soviet bloc and the demise of the labour movement in the West, and to connect the multiple subjectivities and fragmented identities of a defeated and marginalised Left, preferred to stay away from such majoritarian and unifying notions. It opted for more plural and "rhizomatic" identities such as the notion of "multitude," proposed by Antonio Negri and Michael Hardt as an alternative to the idea of the People.[2] By the same token, terms such as the People and the Citizen were thus assumed to belong exclusively to the lexicon of the populist Right, from the Front National Front to the American Tea Party. Why, then, have such expansive notions of collectivity, sometimes described as the "Big We", been resurfacing in contemporary protest politics? And what have their consequences been for the attitudes, language and aesthetics of the movement?

The resurgence of a discourse of "the people", especially in its variants "the citizen" and "citizenry", signalled the unexpected revival of inclusive and syncretic "popular identities,"[3] which appeal to the virtual totality of the political community of a given country, or to "anybody and everybody,"[4] to use the terms of French philosopher Jacques Rancière. This form of collective identification reflected the intention to overcome the situation of fragmentation and atomisation that stymies dissent in neoliberal society, and the emphasis on sectional divisions—based on gender, age, class, ethnicity—that had been starting points for the neo-anarchist and "identity movements"[5] of the 1970s and onwards, including movements associated with environmentalism, squatters' rights, feminism, and queer liberation. It sought to make a common front against a common enemy: the oligarchy, the alliance between political and economic elites that was discussed in the previous chapter. Protesters thus reclaimed an imaginary of popular protest that harks back to the French Revolution, the anti-fascist popular fronts of the 1930s in Spain and France, Salvador Allende's Unidad Popular [Popular Unity], and the "pink wave" of Latin American left-populism in the late 1990s and 2000s. However, as we shall see, they also tried to adapt it to the individualisation and liquidity of contemporary digital societies by foregrounding the notion of citizens and citizenry, with their emphasis on the individual and the grassroots over the notion of the People.

The adoption of popular identities marked a rupture with the forms of subjectivity and political imaginary of the anti-globalisation movement. Where the anti-globalisation movement conceived of itself as a minority, or rather as an alliance of minorities, hence the notion of "multitude,"[6] the movement of the squares saw itself as a popular movement, whose cause was the cause of the majority of the population, whose enemies were the enemies of the people, and whose hopes were those of the common people. Where the global justice movement adopted a countercultural discourse geared against mainstream corporate culture and were often happy to present themselves as exceptional rebels and heroes, the movement of the squares laid claim once again to normalcy and ordinariness, espousing pragmatism and common sense. Finally, where the anti-globalisation protests connected traditional political identities together in a rainbow coalition, the movement of the squares was vocal in its rejection of pre-existing political symbols, and put forward movement-wide collective identities exemplified by mass names like Occupy, Indignados, 15-M and Aganaktismenoi.

Table 3.1: Collective identities in comparison

	Anti-globalisation movement	*Movement of the squares*
Appeal	Minoritarianism Multitude We are the 1 per cent	Majoritarianism Citizenry We are the 99 per cent
Ideal subject	The rebel, the squatter, the migrant, the indigene	The indignant citizen
Cultural orientation	Countercultural contestation of majority views and mainstream culture	Common sense, search for respectability and normalcy
Collective identifiers	Colour-coded political identities (green, black, red, pink) clustered in a coalition	Mass names (Indignados, Occupy, Anonymous) acting as fusion-identities

However, the popular identity mobilised by the movement of the squares was not a mere repetition of the modernist discourse of the "sovereign People" mobilised by traditional revolutionary and populist movements. In their reference to the citizens and the Citizenry, the movement of the squares reflected its indebtedness to the libertarian spirit of neo-anarchist movements, and its adoption of a vision of the universal subject as something that emerges organically from individuals and their personal networks rather than being imposed from above. This adoption of popular identity, though in its libertarian variation as the Citizenry, was instrumental in the ability of these movements to mobilise millions of participants and capture the public imagination. Thus, if Deleuze and Guattari famously proclaimed in the 1980s that "the people are missing,"[7]—meaning that "the People" as the foundation of republican democratic politics no longer constituted a credible political category in a society of increasing complexity, and that the only possibility was a "minority" politics—the political upheavals of 2011–13 stand as proof that the People are back, and with a vengeance, in the guise of the self-organised Citizenry, the revolutionary subject for times of profound social crisis and digital connectivity.

The multitude as an alliance of minorities

No other idea better captured the political imaginary of the anarcho-autonomist segment of the anti-globalisation movement than the concept of the "multitude". This term, put forward by movement intellectuals Michael Hardt and Antonio Negri—who constituted a major source of inspiration for anti-globalisation activists—was conceived precisely in opposition to the notion of the People, considered too homogenising and potentially authoritarian:

> The multitude is a multiplicity, a plane of singularities, an open set of relations, which is not homogeneous or identical with itself and bears an indistinct, inclusive relation to those outside of it. The people, in contrast, tends toward identity and homogeneity internally while posing its difference from and excluding what remains outside of it. Whereas the multitude is an inconclusive constituent relation, the people is a constituted synthesis that is prepared for sovereignty. The people provides a single will and action that is independent of and often in conflict with the various wills and actions of the multitude.[8]

Albeit sharing some features in its all-inclusivity, the Multitude is in many respects the opposite of the People. While the People is united, the Multitude is irreconcilably diversified, a multi-headed hydra. Where the People is One, composed of many, the Multitude is a many that remains many, without fusing into One. Furthermore, while the People aspires to be a majority, the Multitude contents itself with being a minority.

Cohering with the idea of the multitude, the anti-globalisation movement was conceived as a space of convergence for disparate marginal groupings, an alliance of minorities, that together could face up to the pressure of the majority, seen as necessarily malign. Nowhere was such minoritarian orientation more explicitly fleshed out than in the writings of Subcomandante Marcos, the leader of the Zapatista insurgent army in south-eastern Mexico, which, since its emergence onto the public scene on 1 January 1994, provided a powerful inspiration for activists the world over. In what amounts to one of his most evocative political texts, Marcos, a *nom de guerre* that, together with the use of a ski mask, stood to evoke the anonymity and collectivity of resistance, thusly described his own identity:

> Marcos is gay in San Francisco, black in South Africa, an Asian in Europe, a Chicano in San Ysidro, an anarchist in Spain, a Palestinian in Israel, a Mayan Indian in the streets of San Cristobal, a Jew in Germany, a Gypsy in Poland, a Mohawk in Quebec, a pacifist in Bosnia, a single woman on the Metro at 10pm, a peasant without land, a gang member in the slums, an unemployed worker, an unhappy student and, of course, a Zapatista in the mountains. Marcos is all the exploited, marginalised, oppressed minorities resisting and saying 'Enough'.[9]

Indigenous people, lesbians and gays, precarious workers and students, single women and slum dwellers: these were representatives of the "exploited", "marginalised", "oppressed", and "resisting" minorities which anti-globalisation activists hoped to mobilise. This vision of the movement as a champion for the rights of minorities was accompanied by a moral value ascribed to "every minority who is now beginning to speak," as opposed to "every majority that must shut up and listen."[10] This assertion reflects a refusal to constitute oneself (or one's movement) as a majority: a key theme for the anti-globalisation movement.

To be fair, the anti-globalisation movement was not completely tied to this minoritarian worldview. Inklings of a possible majoritarian turn in the movement's discourse could be read in assertions like, "You G8, We 6 Billion", seen during protest events in Prague, Genoa, and Rostock, and the depiction of the rulers of the "Great 8" as a small elite standing against the interests of the overwhelming majority of the world's population. Majoritarian precepts were especially evident in the squares flooded by the 2003 anti-war movement all across Western cities. Furthermore, they could be seen in slogans such as "We are everywhere", and in the plebeian imaginary evoked in activist texts such as "From The Multitudes of Europe,"[11] written by Italian literary collective Wu Ming in preparation for the Genoa protests, and in which a number of historical popular movements were invoked including the peasant rebellion of the Jacquerie, the Ciompi of Florence, and the peasant army of Thomas Müntzer. Yet, these majoritarian tendencies were never fully realised in the anti-globalisation movement. To a large extent this shortfall was due to structural conditions. The anti-globalisation movement emerged at a time of almost uncontested dominance for neoliberal ideology, where to claim to be representing the majority would have sounded laughable. But it also stemmed from the radical Left's longstanding disdain for the majority and main-stream society, often suspected of complicity with neoliberal capitalism due to its political apathy and rampant consumerism.

The panegyric on minorities proposed by "El Sup" Marcos,[12] and subscribed to by many anti-globalisation activists, was actually the latest chapter in a long radical Left and anti-authoritarian tradition: the deep-seated distrust of the majority and the associated faith in the dogged determination of a small minority of rebels. Exemplary of this attitude is the essay "Majorities versus Minorities" written by anarchist Emma Goldman, herself a very influential reference point for contemporary anarchists and anti-globalisation activists. In the text, the Russian-American agitator lambasted the masses and the majority as manifesta-tions of an era obsessed with quantity and uniformity, at the expense of quality and creativity. For Goldman, "the majority represents a mass of cowards, willing to accept him who mirrors its own soul and mind pov-erty."[13] Again and again in history, argued Goldman, rebel movements lost their radical edge once they grew from small groups of committed people to large movements with mass followings, as happened to Jesus and Martin Luther, among others. Such anti-populist suspicion of the majority, and of "majority taste"—reminiscent of Mark Twain's famous advice that "whenever you find yourself on the side of the majority, it is time to pause and reflect"—resurfaced in the thinking of many far-left groups in the 1970s and 1980s, providing a rationalisation of, and con-solation for, their repeated defeats.

It is true that initially the New Left had hegemonic majoritarian ambi-tions and a populist discourse critiquing the elites, as seen in C. Wright Mills' *The Power Elite*.[14] However, faced with the objective impossibility of winning majority support, largely due to the conservative sentiments of the older generations who had fought in the Second World War, mostly inimical to political destabilisation and worried about the "Red threat", the tendency resigned itself to a minoritarian orientation and a counter-cultural politics of resistance. As Theodore Roszak, the famous chroni-cler of the 1960s movements put it, "the students may rock their societies; but without the support of adult social forces, they cannot overturn the established order. And that support would seem to be nowhere in sight."[15] Despairing at the inability to win the consent of the majority, post-1968 protest movements abided by a countercultural loathing for mainstream culture, and progressively adopted the "marginal" as a prototype of the subject of resistance. This position was most explicitly formulated in Germany by the Autonomen,[16] whose name had been styled after their Italian "Autonomia" comrades, and who engaged from the 1970s in the so-called *Randgruppenstrategie* [marginal groups strategy], that identified revolutionary potential in marginalised sectors—unemployed, drop-outs, drug addicts and small criminals—the groups Marx had disapprovingly described as the *Lumpenproletariat*.[17] Other groups moved from political commitment to self-absorption, from "slogans to mantras,"[18] as the great wave of 1960s and 1970s radical politics was followed by the phenomena of spiritual movements such as the "New Age" and Western Buddhism.[19]

The rejection of the majority was also a key element in the "identity politics" of the 1970s and 1980s, from the Black Panther Party, representing ghettoised people of colour, to various forms of gender politics geared against the oppression of patriarchal society, and the protests of ACT UP, waged by people suffering from HIV/AIDS. In affirming foundational identities, based on race, class, gender, or cultural preferences, these movements implicitly or explicitly positioned themselves against the majority, and particularly Richard Nixon's "silent majority,"[20] searching for a cultural "recognition" of their unique identity, while at the same time mostly forsaking the struggle for systemic change. This attitude went hand in hand with the pursuit of a small group politics, in which activists abandoned the ambition for mass mobilisation since, as explained by Marina, a German veteran of the Autonomen and the anti-globalisation movement, "we didn't care how many we were, because we were more of a subculture, and you do not recruit people to a subculture".

In a telling celebration of this minoritarian and inward looking regression of the radical Left and protest movements, in a famous 1969 song French anarchist folk singer Léo Ferré celebrated the stubborn if numerically negligible resistance of anarchists who, "might not even comprise 1 per cent, but yet they do exist."[21] Four decades later the punk group Green Day, who influenced protest movements in the US and beyond, would propose a similar eulogy of the political underdog in the chart-topping song "Minority".

In conclusion, as reflected in these exhibits of counterculture from the 1960s through the 2000s, for large sections of the radical Left being the minority, against the majority, constituted the default ethical and political position. Quite a contrast with contemporary movements claiming to represent the 99 per cent.

"We are more than them and we will win"

No message coming from within the squares' movements resonated more powerfully in the public imagination than the famous slogan, "We Are the 99 Percent", launched by Occupy Wall Street during the first days of the occupation. This slogan originated from an article by Joseph Stiglitz, in which the Nobel Prize economist referred to the fact that 1 per cent of the American population controlled almost a quarter of the national income, and cautioned that even the super-rich would come to regret this situation, since "their fate is bound up with how the other 99 per cent live."[22] This phrase captured the widespread anger at the situation of economic inequality and political disenfranchisement under neoliberalism that had become more apparent since the beginning of the Great Recession. Marxist commentators have sometimes termed this slogan a vulgar expression of class consciousness. However, it can be better understood as the manifestation of a popular identity sustaining the construction of a "politics of everybody and anyone," that is, a politics aiming at winning the hearts and minds of the majority of the population. After a period marked by the assertion of the moral superiority of the minority, the movement of the squares reclaimed the majority for their own side, and regained faith in the power of mass collective action.

With its suggestive mathematic metaphor contrasting an overwhelming majority and a minuscule minority, Occupy's "We Are the 99 Percent" slogan is merely the most famous expression of a new protest lexicon that has constantly laid claim to the People and the majority.[23] In Spain protesters presented themselves as "common people" fighting against self-serving elites and proclaimed: "We are more than them, let's change the world" [*Somos mas que ellos, cambiemos el mundo*]. Their Greek comrades, the "indignant citizens," described themselves as the "majority of the people" against the "profit of the few." Indications of this popular imaginary were found in the references to "the many," as in the expressions "we are many," used in the title of a famous activist text about Occupy,[24] "we are many, we are right and we will win," the slogan of the Greek Solidarity for All network, "they have billions, we are millions" used in the Nuit Debout protests in France,[25] or even in the motto "We are legion," used by hacker group Anonymous, which evokes the vastness of internet user support for online attacks against companies and state agencies.[26] These different expressions thematised that most classic of political conflicts: the "hoi polloi," the many, as the protagonists of democracy, versus the "hoi oligoi," the few, the oligarchic power structures always intent on preserving the status quo; the plebs versus the Senate, the People against the Oligarchy.[27] Similar phrases were seen in Egypt, Turkey and Brazil where protesters used terms broadly translating to "people": "*shaab*", "*povo*", "*gente*" and "*halk*", to express the popular and broad-based character of these movements.

The adoption of this discourse, with its references to the People and the majority was a reflection of this protest wave's reclamation of a "popular" identity, as a sort of paradoxical or "anti-identitarian" form of collective identity that appealed to the totality of the population, instead of addressing specific categories of society defined by their gender, class, ethnicity, or life-style grouping. Presenting oneself as part of "the People" is different from calling oneself "middle class" or "working class", young or old, man or woman, conservative or progressive, left-wing or right-wing, atheist or religious: exclusive identifications that have been widely adopted in many recent protest movements bearing the moniker of their collective identities, as students, women, squatters, the poor, or people of colour. To refer to the idea of "intersectionality" that has become increasingly popular in activist discourse to describe a politics of alliance across different gender, race and class-based movements,[28] one can say that the populist discourse of citizenism is not precisely intersectional, but trans-sectional, because it aims to transcend rather than simply ally diversity.

Popular identity necessarily transcends specific social categories; it ideally appeals to all, irrespective of class, gender, or race. But since no movement can ever really represent the totality of the population, populist discourse often resorts to the majority as a practical approximation for the ideal of the People. This logic is most evident in the references to the 99 per cent—that is, all but the 1 per cent. In this context the 1 per cent takes the role of the "constitutive outside": an Other, an enemy against which the coherence of the People, otherwise uncertain, can be asserted.[29] The movement of the squares thus derived its legitimacy from its numerical superiority vis-à-vis its opponents, the neoliberal oligarchy of a self-serving, super-rich 1 per cent and their political allies, a claim that has in fact been supported by their ability to mobilise millions to take part in protest.

Possibly the best literary representation of this political imaginary can be found in Percy Bysshe Shelley's famous poem "The Masque of Anarchy," often quoted by activists in the movement of the squares. The poem was written in the aftermath of the Peterloo Massacre of 1819, so named as to invoke an ironic comparison with the Battle of Waterloo, in which the British cavalry attacked a gathering of 80,000 people calling for parliamentary reform in St. Peter's Field, Manchester. Depicting the event that inspired the rise of the Chartist movement, the poem encouraged the people to rise against an oppressive regime, reassuring them of their numerical strength and valour:

Rise, like lions after slumber
In unvanquishable number!
Shake your chains to earth like dew
Which in sleep had fallen on you:
Ye are many—they are few![30]

In line with Shelley's exhortation to rise in "unvanquishable number," contemporary protesters became once again convinced that thanks to their numerical superiority the people would prevail over the oligarchs, because "we are more."

The assertion of numerical superiority of the People versus the Oligarchy and the connected imaginary of the mass echoed in Shelley's poem strongly informed the visual culture of the protest wave. Reflecting its reclamation of more expansive and totalising modernist dreams, the movement of the squares departed from the postmodern prejudice against the crowd, and reasserted a positive vision of mass action in public space. Indeed, the imaginary of the crowd was ubiquitous in the visual culture of the 2011 upheavals, which constantly celebrated the power of mass action. It was seen in the frequent citations of the Wachowski brothers' movie *V for Vendetta*, which acquired cult status among movement participants. At first sight the popularity of this movie could just be read as a popular fascination with the heroic figure of a revolutionary vigilante fighting single-handedly against the state, reminiscent of Hobsbawm's primitive rebels.[31] Yet, a crucial element in the success of the comic and the movie consists in the story's evocation of a sense of possibility for mass rebellion.

It is not by chance that the most popular sequence is the final revolution scene, an almost hypnotic act, in which a mass of people wearing Guy Fawkes masks and costumes floods the streets of London, converging on the Houses of Parliament to overthrow the regime of the fascist Norsefire party. Here, we witness thousands of individuals becoming a crowd, symbolised by one individual—not an indistinct mass, but a personality and a face, the smiling and moustachioed features of V. We also encounter this theme of the overflowing crowd in the famous "Tank Man" poster, produced by Occupy Wall Street in New York to publicise a "mass non-violent direct action" on 17 November 2011.[32] The poster takes inspiration from the famous scene in Beijing's Tiananmen Square during the 1989 insurrection, where a solitary man in white shirt and a plastic bag was seen trying to block the path of a column of tanks. However, in contrast to that iconic display of individual heroism, in this case the man is not alone. Behind him appears a compact mass of identical men in white shirts, who seem certain to overwhelm the tanks due to their superiority in numbers.

A further example comes from a YouTube video produced by ¡Democracia Real Ya! in advance of the 15 May 2011 protests that would kickstart the Indignados movement (Image 3.2).[33] The sequence represents the fight between people and oligarchies in the form of a chess match. The People, playing white, have a double set of pawns, but no bishops, rooks, horses, king, nor queen. Conversely, the Oligarchy, playing black, only has the set of "mounted" pieces representing the nobility; it has no pawns. As the match starts the mass of white pawns quickly overwhelms the black mounted pieces, signifying the fact that the numerical inferiority of the oligarchies will mean their defeat, despite all the resources they might have at their disposal. The scene is accompanied by the caption, "Because we are more humane. Because we are more decent. Because we are more respectable. Because we are more"; an explicit claim to the numerical, hence moral, superiority.

Image 3.1: *V for Vendetta* final revolution scene

Image 3.2: Screenshot of ¡Democracia Real Ya! agitprop video *Porque Somos Mas* [Because We Are More]

Saying "we are more" as the movement of the squares did is an implicit acceptance of the principle of majority rule, or better "supermajority rule," as encapsulated by the 99 per cent motif. It entails positing that one's side is at some point bound to prevail, because the numerical strength is so overwhelming that the financial and political class will need to eventually come out of the bunker in which it has been besieged. This assertion of numerical superiority is the key to understanding the new sense of possibility, opened by the succession of mass uprisings around the world. On the other hand, saying "we are more" also entails a moral judgement—it means that the people carry greater moral weight than the elites in power, and that the needs of the many are more important than the needs of few. As a handmade sign at Zuccotti Park read, "The people are too big to fail", not the banks. Reflecting its embrace of a populist spirit, the movement has shifted from a standpoint of upholding the dignity of minorities to a standpoint of advancing the legitimate power of the majority. This imaginary has proven well suited to riding the wave of widespread indignation at rampant inequality.

The Citizenry as a leaderless People

Unsurprisingly, this turn from minoritarianism to majoritarianism raised hackles among some, especially older activists who came from the neo-anarchist and autonomist sector of the anti-globalisation movement. Some criticised the tendency to uniformity, the elision of difference, and the scarce regard for the needs of minorities in this populist discourse. For example, Jeffrey Juris and other scholars have attacked what they call "Occupy's homogenizing discourse and practice," that according to them has led "to a difficulty recognizing and addressing internal specificity and difference."[34] Some have gone so far as to see in the 99 per cent versus 1 per cent discourse traces of a "colonial mentality."[35]

In the Spanish context, the most famous manifestations for this contradiction between principles of unity and of diversity was an incident that took place in Puerta del Sol during one of the first days of the occupation, when a feminist banner was removed because it was felt to be too factional and not in keeping with the "ecumenical" spirit of the camp. While feminist activists saw the movement as a space for different identities, the majority of the activists in the square at that moment, including those who eventually removed the banner, saw the movement as a unitary effort and were determined to keep more disparate demands at bay. Similar frictions happened inside Occupy Wall Street. In October 2011, the People of Color Working Group contested a draft declaration of the Zuccotti Park assembly—the initial version of that quoted at the beginning of the chapter—where it described participants as "one people, formerly divided by the color of our skin, gender, sexual orientation, religion, or lack thereof, political party and cultural background."

As these conflicts demonstrate there is an evident trade-off between popular identity and more minoritarian factional identities: appealing to the former tends to imply demoting the latter. However, the choice to opt for a popular identity over sectional identities was a sensible response to the change in the economic and political conditions that emerged in the aftermath of the 2008 economic crisis and the new political opportunities it opened for protest action. This shift in collective identity stemmed from a desire to mobilise all the categories that are at disadvantage in the present predicament, and is informed by a deep-seated criticism, including self-criticism, of the practices of previous movements and their "self-ghettoisation"; the way in which they ended up accepting marginal positions, contenting themselves to act within a small activist scene with little consequences on the larger political arena. In adopting a popular identity, protesters tried to reverse the divisive effects of identity politics and to reinsert a necessary sense of collective unity and strength, as well as to construct an expansive politics capable of engaging with ordinary citizens.

While the character of the movement of the squares could be described as a type of popular identity, due to its inclusivity and emphasis on popular unity, it was nonetheless different from more traditional notions, informed by the modernist conception of the People as a homogeneous, totalising, and almost divine subject, as invoked in many revolutions and populist movements of the past. It was a popular identity which, reflecting its indebtedness to anti-authoritarian movements, acknowledged the importance of diversity and individuality. Protestors saw the collectivity of the People as an emergent phenomenon, growing out of the progressive aggregation of individual citizens. Furthermore, it was a collective identity that matched the nature of social experience in a society dominated by individualism, as described by sociologists including Ulrich Beck and Zygmunt Bauman, in which any assertion of collectivity needs to start from personal experience if it has to have any appeal.[36]

This attempt to articulate unity and diversity can be seen in the discourse of the "citizen" and the "citizenry" which pervaded these movements. In Egypt, the revolutionary movement was often referred to as a "citizen revolution" [*thawra el-muwatineen*]. In Spain, many of my interviewees insisted on the civic nature of these movements, with Aitor Tinoco, a 28-year-old unemployed graduate living in Barcelona, arguing that, "15-M is a citizen movement, not a social movement", one which sought to "mobilise the entirety of the citizenry and not just activists", while Indignados activist Fabio Gándara argues that, "15-M was the citizenry organising itself." Similar references to the citizenry abounded in the discourse of the Greek movement, the Aganaktismenoi Polites, which translates to "indignant citizens." Nikos, a 32-year-old Greek activist explains, "The general impression was that we are the people, we are the citizens [...] and we have to unite together." Similarly David, a 25-year-old participant of Nuit Debout, argues that, "all the participants, regardless of who they were shared the fact that they were supposed to be citizens. Citizenship was their common denominator". In the absence of strong class identities, citizenship as a "lack," something that is missing, provided a common ground for the identification of atomised individuals into a collectivity.

This primacy of the citizen over the People also reflects the perception of a new capacity for self-organisation of individuals, facilitated by digital communication technologies. Thus for example Caiti, a 22-year-old university student and Occupy participant, commented, "All you have is people's power, everything is what you can do yourself. Nobody is going to do anything for you. Nothing is going to happen unless you make it happen. There's really only us." In this context, the universal subject of the People does not emerge from a top-down leadership directive, as proposed by Gustave Le Bon in his analysis of the crowd as a temporary aggregation made possible by the charismatic power of the leader. Rather the People, in its variation as the Citizenry, coalesces from a bottom-up call to arms (*auto-convocatoria*) relying on the active participation and continued contribution of thousands of individual citizens who offer the movement not just cumulative resources, such as their physical presence in protest events, but also qualitative and incalculable "assets" such as their dedication, their personal networks, their digital connectivity, or their reputation.

Thus the notion of Citizenry that has widely been adopted as a collective identity of the movement of the squares lies in-between the extreme multiplicity of the Multitude, and the total unity of the People; it designates a collective subject that, while emerging from the multiplicity of individual actions, nevertheless aims to achieve a common unity. If citizenism is a libertarian populism, the Citizenry is a libertarian variation on the notion of the People.

In search of common sense

One of the timeless lessons of democratic populist movements is that in order to mobilise the people one not only has "to go the people"—the famous maxim of the Russian Narodniks—but also speak "the language of the people", that is to present oneself in such a way as to be understood, recognised and trusted by the majority of the population. Breaking with the militant and antagonistic discursive style of neo-anarchist activism, and with the intellectualist jargon of the radical Left, protesters from Tahrir to Taksim put great effort into dispelling the customary association of protest with unreasonable demands and self-righteous, often violent, rebellion. They tried to couch protest movements in the language of common sense,[37] normality, reasonability, and respectability, often making more militant activists cringe at what they saw as a glorification of petty-bourgeois decorum.

While neo-anarchist activists often indulged in the language of provocation and subversion, the movement of the squares was adamant in its espousal of moderation and civility, and its insistence on the unquestionable rectitude of the grievances raised. For example, during the protests in Turkey one famous tweet read "we are so right that I am going to lose my mind because of righteousness"[38] while a banner proclaimed: "the first day we were terrorists, the second day provocateurs, the third day protesters, and the fourth day we became the people."[39] As Selçuk, a 34-year-old Turkish activist explains, protesting in Gezi Park "was an issue of almost public decency, of common sense—to be against the destruction of the park—that it almost didn't feel political to most people." People were called to mobilise not because of their subjective or partisan dislike of Erdoğan's regime but due to an overriding sense of being affected by his irresponsible actions. Spanish Indignados activists similarly proclaimed that "*no somos anti-sistema, es el sistema que es anti-nosostros*" [we are not against the system, it is the system that is anti-us]. The slogan alludes to the way in which news media in Spain represented activists, such as those involved in anti-globalisation campaigns, as "anti-system". This is a term conveying a sense of unreasonableness and extremism, coherent with the dominant popular perception of activists as drop-outs, marginal punks, or hippies, who should "get a life" or "get a job"—demands often shouted by passers-by during protests. By saying that they were not against the system, but it was the system that was against them, Indignados activists turned the reactionary media discourse on its head, laying emphasis on the fact that they were acting out of self-defence against the attack of an unequal and predatory system that gave them no other options.

Normalcy, ordinariness, averageness, which constituted typical demons in the imaginary of post-1968 anti-authoritarian movements, preoccupied about the homogenising and "normalising" tendencies of mass consumer society, were thereby reclaimed as a point of pride; a rhetorical means to capture an emerging common sense, in which being against the system is not an expression of mindless rebelliousness and antagonism, but an attestation of political sanity and human dignity. For instance, the manifesto of ¡Democracia Real Ya!, the leading organisation in the Spanish movement of 2011, describes protesters as "normal and common people", people just "like you":

> We are normal, common people. We are like you: people who get up every morning to study, work or find a job, people who have family and friends. People who work hard every day to provide a better future for those around us. Some of us consider ourselves progressive, others conservative. Some of us are believers, some not. Some of us have clearly defined ideologies, others

are apolitical, but we are all concerned and angry about the political, economic, and social outlook we see around us. This situation has become normal, a daily suffering, without hope. But if we join forces, we can change it. It's time to change things, time to build another world.

The insistence on the populist imaginary of the "common man" or "average man" as a silent hero of society, the person whose largely invisible toil keeps things going, constitutes a veritable break from the dominant attitudes of previous neo-anarchist movements. Struggles of the post-industrial era, such as the squatters' movement, the ecologist movement, the feminist movement, and the LGBT movement, have often made of difference, exceptionality and abnormality values in their own right, to counter dominant homogenising "normativities" of gender, race, work ethic and consumerism. It is therefore truly remarkable that the movement of the squares not only abandoned this dominant attitude, but in fact adopted the reverse logic. However, it should be noted that this "search for normality" did not entail an elision, but a transcending of diversity, the search for a "unity in diversity" that might unite an otherwise excessively fragmented social base. Protestors yearned for a minimum common ground across very different sectors of society, as the means to unite against common enemies.

This populist conversion of the discourse and aesthetic of the movement of the squares did not mean it completely lost a countercultural edge and taste for provocation with a neo-anarchist flavour. Rather it utilised typical neo-anarchist rhetoric more as a means to expand popular common sense. This tendency could be seen in the Turkish Gezi movement's appropriation of the word "*çapulcu*", or "thugs", which became prominent in the protests. Erdoğan, then prime minister, directed the term at protesters in a rambling speech, upon which activists humourously adopted it in a spectacular feat of cultural reappropriation. Many activists changed their Twitter username to include the name *çapulcu* and even jokingly coined a new verb "*çapulling*", which roughly translates to "fighting for one's rights." In a similar vein came the term "*yayoflautas*", used by a group of senior activists in Spain connected with the Indignados movement. The portmanteau includes the words "oldie" [*yayo*] and "flute," in an ironic twist on the term "*perroflauta*" [literally "dog and flute"], originally used to refer to homeless beggars playing the flute and carrying a dog, and by extension to protesters, portraying them as good-for-nothing marginal kooks. While retaining an element of self-conscious irreverence, reminiscent of countercultural politics, these expressions also reflected the turn towards a popular identity as they were aimed at demonstrating the patent unreasonableness of power-holders and their collaborators in the news media, ridiculing the latter's attempts at demonising ordinary citizens with legitimate demands.

The search for normalcy and common sense was reflected in the adoption of non-violent tactics and self-imposed strictures in protest camps. These movements in fact often adopted internal rules about acceptable behaviour within protest camps, that besides "safe space" policies on sexual harassment and aggressive behaviour also included prohibitions on the consumption of alcohol and drugs. These policies provoked angry reactions among some participants, who saw them as facets of a "normalising" petty-bourgeois mentality, in thrall to decorum and order. However, they reflected these movements' attempts to cast themselves as legitimate actors representing the interests of the majority, including people who would be alienated by militant tactics and a self-indulgent protester lifestyle.

Similar in purpose was the adherence to non-violent tactics within these movements, which reduced confrontations with the police to a minimum. In the Arab Spring "*selmiya*" ["peaceful"] was a chant frequently used by protesters, calling upon participants to adhere to a non-violent code of conduct, and in countries like Spain and Greece the protest movement was, in the main, remarkably consistent in its use of non-violent tactics. Brazil, Turkey and France were somewhat different, since some confrontations with police and sections of the movement did take place. However, also in these cases violence was relatively mild compared with the era of the anti-globalisation movement, which witnessed militant black bloc tactics of confrontation with the police and property destruction. As Sarphan Uzunoğlu, a Turkish activist, noted at the time, "these protests are among the most peaceful that I have ever attended". In Brazil, middle class protest participants, disparagingly called "*coxinhas*" [a Brazilian snack associated with the petty-bourgeois], also brought white flags to the squares to express their demand for non-violence.

The adoption of non-violent tactics—which marked another break with the stance of the anti-globalisation movement and previous anti-authoritarian movements—constituted an important factor in these movements' legitimacy. They reflected the idea proposed by Leonidas Martin, a 40-year-old Spanish activist and political artist, that "nowadays being radical is not burning or destroying things, but rather protecting our society and the only world we have from the destruction of capitalism". Activists wanted to demonstrate their intention to be positive agents of social change and a means for the active construction of another future, but also a preservation of those parts of society that were worth defending against the brutal onslaught of financial markets. In fact, the surfacing of episodes of violence in these movements, from the involvement of Occupy Oakland in violent confrontations with police, to the emergence of a Black Bloc in the Brazilian protests, were widely held as key factors in these movements' loss of a broad, popular consensus.

These shifts in practice responded to the overarching aim of breaking with previous movements' frequent tendency towards self-induced isolation. The movement's ambition was to construct, instead of a "politics of autonomy," a "politics of citizenship," which would necessarily have to situate itself as part of the dominant "common sense" if it was to win people's hearts and minds, rather than simply affirming absolute values and pursuing a politics of testimony.

Unifying signifiers for a phantom people

Popular identity does not just involve a discourse of the People and the majority but also a quest for popular unity, often thematised in populist movements, and celebrated in the famous Chilean song first recorded by Quilapayún, "*El pueblo unido jamas sera vencido*" ["The people united will never be defeated"]. This pursuit of unity suffused the expressions adopted in this protest wave. Egyptian revolutionaries described the People as one hand composed of many fingers, yet united around a common palm. Furthermore they often made references to the idea of togetherness as exemplified by the text of a Revolutionary Youth Coalition communiqué in April 2011 that proclaimed, "Together with resolve, so that the revolution isn't stolen from us... Together... One hand, always and forever." Similarly in the US, "together" and "united" were among the most frequent terms in protest discourse, as seen in the name of the activist website Occupy Together; in a poster by visual artist Miss Brainwash, styled after the logo of Solidarność [the iconic Polish trade union, Solidarity], with the name substituted by the word "Together", and the flag by "99 per cent";[40] or in the text of the Declaration of the Occupation of New York City, where protesters described themselves as "one people, united". Interestingly, in the aftermath of the protests the idea of "popular unity" was commandeered by various activist groups and political parties, such as the Greek party Popular Unity (Laïkí Enótita), which split from Syriza after Tsipras' capitulation to the finance ministers of the Eurozone, and Podemos, which called itself a party of "civic and popular unity".

To sustain this push for popular unity, the movement of the squares adopted an array of unifying symbols including popular icons like the *V for Vendetta* mask, national flags, as well as "mass names" such as Occupy, Indignados, or Aganaktismenoi. The process of identification that accompanies the use of these symbols abandons the "networking" and "convergence" logic of the anti-globalisation movement, pursuing instead a logic of mass aggregation and fusion of atomised individuals around a unifying popular identity.

Coherently with the imaginary of the multitude and its irreducible multiplicity, the anti-globalisation movement was conceived of as a space in which pre-existing Left identities, often associated with a certain political colour—the red of socialism, the black of anarchism, the green of environmentalism, and the pink of feminism and queer politics, as described by Milanese activist Alex Foti, the organiser of the EuroMayDay movement against labour precarity—could converge in a common struggle against neoliberalism.[41] As Rodrigo Nunes, a 37-year-old Brazilian activist and political philosopher puts it, "the anti-globalisation movement was about pre-existing political identities of the Left, already identified as being Left, coming together". This act of convergence allowed forms of cross-pollination between these identities and their respective political cultures. However, the convergence did not result in the formation of an altogether new collective identity. The anti-globalisation movement resembled, as argued by Graeme Chesters and Ian Welsh,[42] a "parallelogram of forces": a sort of rainbow identity in which different forces would enter a common coalition but without ever renouncing their own specificity and autonomy. This reluctance to unite around a common identity was also reflected by the fact that while naming the enemy (neoliberalism), the movement never adopted a name for itself; the expression "anti-globalisation movement" became prevalent in news media coverage, but was detested by many activists who preferred more edifying but academic sounding monikers like the "global justice", or "alter-globalisation", movement.

Counter to such postmodern *bricolage* logic, patching pre-existing group identities, the movement of the squares was imbued with a neo-modernist spirit, forging new schemes of collective identification. On the one hand, these shied away from all associations with pre-existing political identities and ideologies, and on the other hand belied the ambition of acting as all-encompassing and movement-wide reference points; practical implementations of the unity of the phantom People. Where the anti-globalisation movement followed a strategy of "Left unity", aimed at "organising the organised" and bringing together pre-existing Left forces to remedy their age-old tendency towards division, the movement of the squares pursued a logic of "organising the disorganised": mobilising all those who did not feel represented by any social or political group. Where the anti-globalisation movement appealed to specific groups, collectives, movements, associations, and to their individual members, the movement of the squares appealed directly to individuals qua citizens, regardless of their various affiliations or precisely by virtue of their non-affiliation. As Petros, a 34-year-old Greek activist based in Athens recounts, "people believed that Syntagma [Square] was a collaboration of individuals, not a union of different political groups," to the point that people recognised as affiliated with political groups were looked at with suspicion. The movement attempted to eliminate all forms of intermediation between individual citizens and the collective People, seeing, in typical Rousseauian fashion, organised political groups as endangering the unity of the People.

This fusion-logic of collective identification is premised on an iconoclastic moment; a dismissal of all pre-existing leftist identities and a bonfire of their worn-out iconographies, the hammer and sickles, the circled "A"s, and the red flags that dominated the aesthetic of previous protest waves, and which were often banned in the 2011 demonstrations and protest camps because of their sectarian implications. The precept originated from the Arab Spring where protesters were instructed from the start to leave all factional symbols at home and embrace the national flag as a symbol of popular unity. In Spain, from the start of the 15-M movement the intention was to "leav[e] flags and ideologies behind, and to discuss specific problems in order to mobilise the whole population", as retold by Aitor, an activist based in Barcelona. In Greece the first call for the Syntagma protest, launched on Facebook by an 18-year-old student, explicitly asked participants not to bring any political symbol to the square. In Turkey, where political symbols were initially present in the protests, there was a lot of unease at this, especially from younger protesters. The last assembly before the eviction of the square resolved to set aside all political symbols, allowing only the Turkish flag as a symbol of popular unity.

To fill the symbolic void created by this necessary iconoclastic moment, the 2011 upheavals adopted a series of new unifying symbols for the entire movement. Most notable among these phenomena was the creation of various "mass names": Indignados, Aganaktismenoi, Occupy Wall Street, or Nuit Debout, used as labels of convenience for the movement. These mass names can be understood as "empty signifiers", inclusive symbols that encompass masses of atomised individuals in search of a collective reintegration, rather than clusters of pre-existing groups as it was the case with anti-globalisation protests. An "empty signifier", argued Ernesto Laclau, is a "signifier without signified", a name or symbol deprived of substantive meaning, and which, precisely because of this lack of clear determination, can come to capture that nebulous entity which goes under the name of the People. This semantic emptiness allows the unfolding of an "equivalential chain", a process by means of which different sections of society come to see their disparate demands as equivalent to and connected with each other, and realise the need for making common cause.[43] It is this emptiness, in the sense of a certain degree of symbolic indeterminacy, which made collective identifiers like Occupy and Indignados extremely inclusive, allowing them to appeal to people who while objectively sharing a condition marked by economic and political injustice were not necessarily politicised, or may even have had conservative beliefs distant from the average activist's worldview.

Occupy, Indignados, Aganaktismenoi, and similar terms did not possess inherent meaning in isolation. Their nature was performative and contextual, since their meaning depended on the actual circumstances in which they were utilised and on what protest participants made of them in any specific event. They were not assertive and descriptive terms that explained what a certain movement was protesting against, as in the various "anti-" expressions used in social movements, or by demands they put forward, as with feminism, environmentalism, or pacifism, but rather acted as pliable and inclusive referents for collective identification, well suited to encompassing the highly heterogeneous constituency that was mobilised in 2011.[44]

Possibly the most emblematic example of this tendency is the multi-faceted nature of the identifier "Occupy", which, as Joan Donovan, a Los Angeles-based Occupy activist, argues, reflected the combinatory logic and proverbial adaptability of the internet. It was reported that up to 100,000 Occupy themed hashtags were used during the protests. The expression Occupy was not just used in the naming of local protest chapters (Occupy Philly, Occupy Portland, Occupy Oakland), but also to label specific initiatives pursued by the movement or its spin-offs (Occupy Congress, Occupy Sandy, Occupy the Hood), and in humorous expressions like "Occupy—(add something here)", seen on a signpost at an Occupy demonstration in New York. Occupy's naming logic resembled that of a franchise company, whose brand, while utilised in thousands of different localities, and hundreds of activities, retained the basic format of action, whose essence revolved precisely around a narrative of physical "occupation".

In adopting these mass names—by saying phrases such as "I am an Indignado" or "I support Occupy" often found in social media conversations—participants were not expected to adhere to a systematic teleological view of society and progress, as was prescribed by many twentieth century ideologies, and socialist ideologies in particular, but instead alluded to a more pragmatic and modest desire of democratic social change to which many people could easily relate. As Isham Christie, a 34-year-old Occupy organiser notices, "When people were signing up to Occupy Wall Street, they were not signing up to much. They were simply saying that they were against Wall Street and they were available to camp in protest". Similarly, according to Fabio Gandara, 27-year-old lawyer and organiser in ¡Democracia Real Ya!, "anybody could identify with the 15-M movement, anybody who shared that very basic sense of indignation for what was going on". A similar process was at play in the frequent "We are all…" expressions encountered in these movements, as in the case of the Facebook page, *Kullena Khaled Said* [We are all Khaled Said], or the rise of specific ordinary individuals to become symbols of the movement, as was the case in Brazil with Amarildo, a protester living in a favela, who disappeared after a protest in what was suspected to be a police killing, or with Mohammed Bouazizi in Tunisia. The only requirement was one's agreement with the diagnosis—that there existed a situation of social emergency—and one's availability to enter a collective process to identify the right solutions, with no pre-ordained plan established at the outset.

The underside of this extreme inclusivity is a certain degree of indeterminacy and impermanence that pervades contemporary protest.
Firstly, while claiming to represent everybody, or almost everybody, these
mass names and the connected popular identities ran the risk of not
representing anyone in particular. They were very effective in gathering
the collective body of a citizenry, diagnosed as having become too fragmented and helplessly divided along single-issue and identity lines, but
did not offer a long-term and stable source of identification. Secondly,
these identities were ad hoc and event-specific, and therefore provisional.
They were associated with moments of enthusiastic mobilisation that
were necessarily temporally limited, as most clearly seen in the term
15-M, used as an alternate name by Indignados activists, and referring
to the date when the protests started.

Thus, mass names and similar unifying symbols used by the movement
of the squares, such as the Guy Fawkes mask, were a reflection of the
powerful and inclusive, but often evanescent, character of contemporary
protest movements. They reflected the way in which the 2011 protests
acted as moments of social re-composition for infusing a syncretic feeling
of collective solidarity, capable of transcending the many social, cultural
and political cleavages that divide us from one another in complex, diversified and fragmented post-industrial societies; but they also betrayed the fact
that this syncretic moment was a necessarily temporary and exceptional
rendezvous. In fact, as we shall in Chapter 8 when looking at the aftermath
of the occupations, within the unifying popular horizon opened by the
movement of the squares, a more diverse set of identities arose to support
various civil society campaigns and parties that have pursued variant direc-
tions, some at odds with the movement's founding mission.

4

FROM THE GLOBAL TO THE NATIONAL

The giant [Brazil] *woke up.*
Slogan of the 2013 Brazil protest movement

Proud to be Egyptian.
Frequent message on social media and hand-made
signs during the 2011 revolution

Greece belongs to the Greeks.
Slogan from Syntagma Square during the 2011 protests

Nobody expects the Spanish revolution.
Slogan in Puerta del Sol, May 2011

One of the most surprising and revealing features of the movement of
the squares has been its reclaiming of the nation as a central battleground and source of identity. The 2011 generation overturned the idea
behind the anti-globalisation movement, which postulated that in a globally interconnected world nation-states had lost their erstwhile centrality,
and the only scale at which the power of capital could be confronted was
the global.[1] Counter to this narrative the movement of the squares demonstrated the continuing importance of national space, and the way in
which it continues to demarcate the confines of everyday experience for
the majority of people in the world. Mobilisations often appealed to a
sense of national identity and solidarity against external forces, and in
particular against the global power of finance.[2]

This reclaiming of the nation was on display in a number of different contexts: the adoption of national flags and various forms of national symbologies and imaginaries; the nationally coordinated character of the mobilisations; their attuning to the rhythms of national politics; and their capacity to penetrate the entirety of the national territory, from the metropolitan to the hinterland. These movements were obviously not limited to the national level, as demonstrated by the robust transnational connections they built and the sense of mutual solidarity they constructed. However, they did so from the starting point of the nation, seen as the necessary principal battlefield for the struggle between citizens and oligarchies.

This return of the national, which generated deep unease among many leftist activists due to the customary association of "the nation" with right-wing politics, reflected the influence of left-wing populism, an ideological orientation that sees the nation as the necessary source of identity for the People, and so pursues a democratic and progressive patriotism, profoundly different from xenophobic nationalism. Claiming the imaginary of the nation allowed these movements to address a broader constituency than their predecessors, including moderate and conservative people that were previously seen as out of the reach of radical protest movements. This was seen, for example, in the way Occupy Wall Street managed to garner support among sectors of the population that previously supported the Tea Party. However, there was obviously also a worrying element to this return to the nation, in its mirroring of a right-wing nationalist return, seen in the "Brexit" referendum in Britain, in the rise of xenophobic populist movements all over Europe, and in the election of Donald Trump, an overtly racist presidential candidate, in the US. Furthermore, as I will argue, there is an issue of political efficacy in this trend, due to the way in which the economy continues to be managed largely at a supranational level,[3] making an excessive emphasis on national space potentially self-defeating.

The twilight of the Global

"Our resistance will be as transnational as capital"—so proclaimed a famous anti-globalisation slogan often found daubed on walls and written on protest banners during counter-summit demonstrations. This protest mantra, alongside more famous rallying cries like the World

Social Forum's motto "Another World is Possible," or the Zapatista slogan "A World Where Many Worlds Fit," condensed the spatial imaginary of the great mobilisations against corporations and global financial and trade institutions around the turn of the millennium. In defining globalisation as the main ideological terrain of struggle, the anti-globalisation movement positioned itself in the emerging space of global interconnectedness,[4] seen in the flow of goods and proliferation of internationally recognised brands, and new waves of migration in the 1990s that marked what is sometimes described as the second era of globalisation, the first having begun at the turn of the twentieth century. The anti-globalisation movement was an attempt to confront the new challenges and political opportunities of this emerging global and post-national world.

If the "anti-globalisation movement" was indeed a bit of a misnomer, leading to the coining of alternate names such as the "global justice movement," or the "alter-globalisation movement", it was because activists, far from rejecting globalisation as such, saw in globalisation not just an inevitable structural process, but also a precious opportunity for the development of a new emancipatory politics no longer restrained by what they saw as arbitrary and fictitious national borders. Globalisation meant not only the rise of multinational corporations like Coca Cola, Monsanto, and McDonald's, and unaccountable institutions like the WTO or the IMF, which would become the most typical targets of anti-globalisation protests, but also the withering away of the nation-state, a longstanding figure of hate for radical leftists, whether communist or anarchist. The opening of this global space seemed to offer activists the opportunity to construct a cosmopolitan politics that, in transcending national borders, could realise the utopia of a politics embracing the totality of humankind, irrespective of ethnicity, religion, or cultural identity. The mirror image of the monstrous global empire of capital was the international, multi-racial and cross-cultural global multitude,[5] a formless yet powerful entity whose arms would span across all continents, with the same fluidity and flexibility as capital flows, but with its political charge the polar opposite.

Manifestations of this anti-globalisation imaginary were the heroic feats pulled off at counter-summit protests, in particular those in Seattle in 1999, Prague in 2000 and Genoa in 2001, epic street battles in which participants directly and often physically confronted the institutions of global capitalism at the height of neoliberal hegemony. These events were the building blocks of a largely unprecedented global mobilisation, in which the global elites were countered by an equally global protest movement, advancing across borders to participate in protest actions. Counter-summits were remarkably multinational in their composition; there amassed a global revolutionary army whose recruits were drawn from countries the world over, starting with the most economically advanced, with high levels of participation from the US, Italy, Spain, Greece, France, Canada, Belgium, and the Netherlands, along with many from emerging countries in Latin America, particularly Brazil, Mexico, and Argentina, lending some credence to the activist slogan, "We are everywhere". Coming together during different counter-summits, protesters were immersed in a cosmopolitan collective, many activists being polyglots and passionately international in outlook. In protest camps activists could experience the mixing of cultural references in a global political soup, where divisions had more to do with different political allegiances within the radical Left than with nationality. Many of them stemmed from an emerging global "precarious class," who often felt they had more in common with their fellow "precarians"[6] around the world than with the rest of the population of their own countries.

A similar spirit informed various protest movement gatherings for debate and discussion, starting with the Zapatista "Intergalactic Meetings" (*Encuentros Intergalacticos*) in Chiapas, Mexico, and continuing through the 2001 establishment of the World Social Forum in Porto Alegre, Brazil, from which sprung the continental social forums formed in the following years, starting with the European Social Forum in Florence in 2002. Counter-summit protests and global gatherings gave the movement the semblance of a global travelling circus, accompanied by a global touring crew, benefiting from the relative laxness of border controls for Western citizens, and the advent of low-cost aviation through the rise of companies such as Ryanair and EasyJet.

Obviously the anti-globalisation movement was not reducible to these global gatherings and the cosmopolitan constituency that gathered there. Its deeper roots lay in a multitude of local campaigns and activist groups. In the Global South these local roots were epitomised by peasant movements like La Vía Campesina and the landless movement Movimento Sem Terra. In the Global North they had their bases in the urban anarchist and autonomist scenes located in the countercultural neighbourhoods of metropolitan areas, such as San Lorenzo and Pigneto in Rome,

Kreuzberg and Friedrichshain in Berlin, Exarchia in Athens, Christiania and Nørrebro in Copenhagen, and Hackney, Whitechapel, and Brixton in London. These local hotspots were the islands of a "rebel archipelago,"[7] not a continuous territory, but rather a federation of liberated spaces; a latter-day "Hanseatic League," to use the expression of Italian activist Alex Foti in interventions in the activist mailing list Net-Time,[8] made of squats, social centres, community projects, eco-villages, and other alternative spaces—acting as caravan stations for the nomadic multitude—but also ephemeral events, occupations, raves, and parades, akin to Hakim Bey's Temporary Autonomous Zones or TAZs,[9] all fighting against the irreducible enemies of Capital and the State. It was within this translocal texture, knitted around more or less stable oases of resistance where one could seek refuge in a soulless neoliberal world, that the "latent networks" of the anti-globalisation movement nested themselves, and continued to silently operate even in times of relatively low activity at the global level.

The anti-globalisation movement thus embraced both the global and the local space. It combined local attachments to alternative communities in which people tried to live an alternative lifestyle and fight against the local manifestations of capital in its various forms—gentrification, precarisation of labour, environmental destruction—while ever mindful of the global horizon of political conflict, in a way redolent of the once fashionable idea of the "glocal," as a fusion of the global and the local, and the motto "think globally, act locally". Yet something seemed to be amiss in this political space. Despite spanning across an extensive local rebel archipelago of occupied spaces and global protest events, the movement appeared largely incapable of interpellating all those who fell in-between these far-flung scales. Making "participation" in the movement premised on physical engagement in the everyday life of the movement scene, and on the costly and risky attendance of global counter-summits, the movement ultimately proved exclusionary towards all those who neither resided in alternative communities nor participated in protest events. This high barrier to entry contributed to a problematic tendency towards self-ghettoisation and marginalisation—one that the movement of the squares actively sought to overcome in their own protest praxis.

The protest space constructed by the movement of the squares differed radically from that proposed by the anti-globalisation movement in one deceptively simple, yet ultimately fundamental, regard. While the anti-globalisation movement constructed a global space of action, the movements of the squares were rooted in national space. They mostly cast themselves as national movements, their aims being largely domestic and also involving a reclaiming of national sovereignty from those global political and economic forces that had deprived citizens of control over their common life. It is true that these movements were often described as part of a "global revolution", as celebrated in activist hashtags such as #GlobRev. Yet, quite unlike what happened with the anti-globalisation movement the movements of the squares turned the national space into a real centre of mobilisation, reclaiming the nation both as a space of contestation between the people and the oligarchy, and as a space of belonging, that is, a space within which the otherwise nebulous idea of the people could be given a more concrete anchoring. As Rodrigo Nunes, an academic and activist, rightly summarises, "the antiglobalisation movement was about the global as such, about taking on the organisms of global governance, whereas now it is much more about the nation-state, about democratic responses and some kind of reform that would bring more representativity".

Flying the national flag

The return of the nation as central to protest is reflected in a deep change in the culture, language and imaginary of protest movements, which shifted away from the global and cosmopolitan framework that held sway among anti-globalisation protesters, and back to the national symbology that was the hallmark of revolutionary upheavals in the nineteenth and twentieth centuries. Protesters in the movements of the squares often presented themselves as defenders of the national community against both local overlords and global forces and mobilised a sense of national identity and a popular attachment to the history, symbols and customs of the nation. The clearest manifestation of this return of the nation and the national at the centre of protest culture was the frequent appearance of national flags and similar national symbols in the occupied squares, and the way in which it provided a backdrop to their appeal to popular unity against common enemies.

National flags were wildly popular in the Arab Spring revolutions of 2011, where in Tunisia, Egypt, Syria, Bahrain, and Yemen the emblem of the country became a symbol of the revolutionary forces that wanted to reclaim its "true" spirit and tradition against the governing elites who had stained it through corruption and repression. Thus, for example, in preparation for the Egyptian 25 January protests people were told to carry only the national flag, and to leave any political symbols that might have been divisive at home. Indeed, protestors were stopped by police and arrested for the mere fact of carrying the flag. In the course of the revolution and its aftermath, the red, white and black of the Egyptian flag became a recognised symbol for revolutionaries, which would festoon Tahrir Square during big demonstrations and adorn the houses of supporters and veterans of the revolution. Interestingly, in the cases of Libya and Syria protesters used different flags from those officially sanctioned, in the first case reclaiming the flag of the Kingdom of Libya, which had been discarded by Qaddafi, and in the second case utilising a modified version of the 1932 independence flag, as if to signify that the nation they appealed to was not the same as that ruled by the dictatorship. This prominence of national emblems was the most perceptible manifestation of the wave of patriotic fervour and national pride which animated the protests, expressed in oft-

Image 4.1: Protester fixing the Egyptian and Syrian revolutionary flags to a lamppost in Tahrir Square, Cairo, November 2011 (Courtesy Lara Pelaez Madrid)

Image 4.2: Protesters flying the Turkish flag in Taksim Square, June 2013 (Paolo Gerbaudo)

repeated slogans like the "Proud to be Egyptian" found on banners throughout Tahrir Square, or the chanting of "Libya in our hearts, Libya we will die for you" by anti-Qaddafi protesters.

In the other movements of the 2010s wave, the recourse to national symbology was understandably much more subdued given a number of factors, including the lower intensity of the conflict protesters waged against power-holders, and the stronger influence of anti-nationalist sentiment. Yet compared with previous protest movements, and in particular with anti-globalisation protests where the presence of national flags would have been considered tantamount to a desecration of the cosmopolitan spirit of the movement, the extent to which national symbology became part and parcel of these mobilisations is remarkable.

Among Western countries, the use of national symbology was arguably most evident in Greece's Aganaktismenoi movement. At the height of the 2011 protests the "sky-blue and white" national flags were very prominent in Syntagma Square in Athens, and in demonstrations all over the country. The meaning of the flag's use was however highly conten-

Image 4.3: National symbols in the Zuccotti Park protest encampment, New York, November 2011 (Courtesy Lara Pelaez Madrid)

tious. During the occupation of Syntagma, the use of national flags denoted a cleavage between two parts of the square, divided by their political leanings. While in the "lower square"—the part facing west where assemblies were held, tents were pitched, and more progressive protesters stationed—few flags were to be seen, the national emblem was ubiquitous in the "upper square", above the marble steps leading towards the parliament, which became the gathering point for right-wing groups and individuals, including the Free Greeks (*Eleutheroi Ellenes*) who called for an exit from the euro, and even occasionally members of the newly formed neo-fascist group Golden Dawn. Yet, national flags were also adopted by a diversified swath of protesters with no clear political allegiance, who saw it as a symbol of national pride and independence, made relevant again by perceived foreign interference and economic colonisation by Germany and the European Union. As Christos, a 31-year-old Greek participant in Syntagma, notices, "the flag was also used by many non-politicised people, and for older people it might have reminded them of the resistance against the Germans [in the Second World War]." By the same token the European Union flag was often

121

Image 4.4: European flag overlaid with the squatters' symbol in the Syntagma Square encampment, Athens, June 2011 (Paolo Gerbaudo)

used as a symbol of scorn, due to the imposition of austerity measures as conditions for offering bail-out packages (Image 4.4).

Conversely, the Spanish national flag, known as the *Rojigualda* and introduced in 1978 at the end of the dictatorship, was never seen at protest camps and Indignados demonstrations. This had to do with the fact that the flag, an adaptation of monarchist flags already in use in the nineteenth century, carried connotations of Franco's dictatorship, and offended the sensibilities of Catalans, Basques, other minorities, and leftist activists alike regarding emblems of the Spanish nation-state. Yet, even in a country with such a staunchly anti-nationalist Left, national symbols eventually emerged in the protests. During the civic tides ("*mareas ciudadanas*") of 2012 and 2013 which followed the occupations of 2011, many protesters came to adopt the flag of the Second Spanish Republic—which existed from 1931 to 1939 before its defeat by Franco— so that its colours of red, yellow and murrey became symbols of patriotic pride rooted in the nation's history and its struggle against fascism, while also serving as an expression of republican sentiment toward the existing monarchy. In fact, the latter issue became particularly heated during the summer of 2014, when the monarchy's crisis of legitimacy eventually led to the abdication of King Juan Carlos and the coronation of his son as Felipe VI. In general, the Indignados protests were a powerful demonstration of both national indignation at the present state of the country and national pride in a glorious past, and particularly of the heroic struggle against fascism during the civil war, thematised in the music, theatre, and street art of protest camps. This patriotic vein of the 15-M movement would later be reflected in the discourse of Podemos, whose leader Pablo Iglesias made frequent references to the homeland (*patria*) in a left-wing re-imagining of patriotism.[10]

In the US, the use of national symbology was also striking when compared with the earlier anti-globalisation movement. During my visit to the Zuccotti Park protest camp in New York, I was surprised by the abundance of American flags planted by protesters around the area. They were there to express Occupy's ambitions to be a movement of national regeneration and renewal, as discussed by Todd Gitlin in the aptly titled *Occupy Nation*,[11] aimed at salvaging the true spirit of American democracy from its current state of corruption, and addressing the legitimate grievances of the overwhelming majority of its people. However, whether the flag's presence was welcome was also a matter for dispute. During one of my visits, I witnessed a flag deliberately hung the wrong way around (the traditional method for signalling distress on ships) and a group of scruffy protesters stomping on a flag before dramatically setting it on fire for the benefit of passers-by. Besides national flags many other symbols contributed to this narrative of Occupy as a movement of American renewal, as seen for example in a protester dressed as the patriotic cartoon hero Captain America and another dressed as a Unionist soldier from the American Civil War.

Equally significant was the use of national symbology in the 2013 protests in Turkey and Brazil. In the case of Turkey, the protests, sparked by the violent eviction of Gezi Park in late May 2013, saw copious usage of the national white star and crescent flag, introduced in 1844, and other national symbols. The flag flew prominently above the crowds gathered in the adjoining Taksim Square during the days of protest in May and June 2013, with its visual impact re-doubled by the presence of an enormous flag towering above a flagpole at the centre of the square, and big flags hung by protesters on the Atatürk Cultural Centre, named after Mustafa Kemal Atatürk, founder of the Republic of Turkey and its first president. The use of the flag signified the sense of national unity against the governing elite and the expression of a new national pride in seeing one's people reclaim their dignity through rebellion. But it also stemmed from the view of Erdoğan's government, and particularly his Justice and Development Party (AKP), as fundamentally anti-national, given the president's nostalgia for the days of the Ottoman empire and AKP hostility towards the figure of Atatürk, accused by Islamists of having introduced alien Western customs and demonstrated scarce respect for religious morals, due to rumours of his passion for women and alcohol. While again the flag had a far broader meaning than a simple expression of nationalism, the protests also saw the participation of nationalist groups such as the Cumhuriyet Halk Partisi [Republican People's Party], founded by Atatürk and the far-right Milliyetçi Hareket Partisi [Nationalist Movement Party], whose presence led to verbal and sometimes physical clashes with Kurdish and other minority activists.

In Brazil, the June movement witnessed the use of a variety of national symbols. While national flags were absent during the first days of protest, when the streets were dominated by anti-authoritarian protesters mobilised by the autonomist Movimento Passe Livre (MPL), they made a boisterous appearance towards the middle of June when large sections of the Brazilian middle class joined the protests, bringing to them a more conservative agenda and worldview. Flags, often worn by participants as hoods, and the national colours of green and yellow painted on people's faces became a common sight in the protests. This use of the national flag, which also given the impending World Cup was reminiscent of football *torcidas* [Brazilian "Ultras"] choreography, bothered many leftist participants among the protesters who, like 42-year old artist Leandro, saw in these practices the manifestation of the "conservative and nationalist sector of the Brazilian population." This became particularly visible in the anti-government protests that swept Brazil in the aftermath of the 2014 elections, denouncing corruption in the governing PT, and eventually led to the impeachment of President Dilma Rousseff in 2016. Yet also in this case the use of national symbology was more ambiguous than an outright expression of nationalism. As Pablo Ortellado, a 40-year-old activist and academic in São Paulo and one of the founders of the Movimento Passe Livre [Free Fare Movement] in Brazil, argues, the presence of the flag could also be seen as "an affirmation of the public, of the collective. It reminded me of what happened in 2001 and 2002 in Argentina, where people from the autonomist movement were using the national anthem and the national flag in the assemblies."

The adoption of a national symbology did not mean that these movements were deprived of a supranational dimension. Rather they built mutual solidarity connections across borders, which often used the very same language of the nation, seen most strikingly in the use of other countries' flags during the protests. Egyptian activists displayed the Libyan, Tunisian and Syrian flags in their protests, while in turn other countries invigorated by the Arab Spring flew the Egyptian flag. Similarly, Spanish protesters often used Icelandic flags to express their admiration for the so-called Icelandic Revolution of 2009, in which citizen protests forced the finance industry-friendly government to resign. In turn, Greek activists used Spanish flags in the protests in Syntagma Square to express their solidarity towards the Indignados, from whom they drew so much inspiration. Finally, Turkish and Brazilian protesters, due to the simultaneity of their movements, often used each other's flag in solidarity. Activists certainly expressed solidarity with each other across borders, and often made appeals to the prospect of a global revolution. However, they mostly did so starting from the assumption that they were largely independent national movements, each with its own idiosyncratic national characteristics and specific goals.

The homeland as political battleground

The national turn of the movement of the squares is not just a matter of symbology; it also reflects a change in strategy and operations. The 2011–13 movements tried to root protest action in the political structures of their respective countries, through targeting either national enemies, such as prominent politicians and bankers, or global foes framed as "enemies of the nation," and by trying to exploit the political opportunities that presented themselves in their national space, much like many prior movements in history that organised nationally coordinated campaigns. In so doing, they claimed the nation, rather than global space, as the central battleground.

This rescaling of the struggle to a national space was informed by an awareness that the global framework the anti-globalisation movement had proposed made it difficult to connect with large sections of the population, due to the sense of abstraction elicited by global issues, with their perceived distance from the everyday life of ordinary people, and that it was therefore necessary to also develop the protest inside a national framework. Marina, an Occupy activist, argues that, "campaigning on climate change was very difficult, because its something very abstract and it is difficult for people to understand and see it," while the economic crisis hit far closer to home, and was therefore an easier issue to mobilise people on. Paique Duques, a 28-year-old activist involved in the Movimento Passe Livre in Brasilia, takes a similar view: "The anti-globalisation movement did not speak the language of the people, [and because of that] it did not attract people from poor areas. Because it had themes that were very international, and people were not interested in struggling against the WTO, if struggling against the WTO did not bring them water." He goes on to explain that the birth of the MPL and its establishment as a national, rather than global, network drew inspiration from the wave of national struggles which developed in Latin America in the mid-2000s, including the water revolt in Bolivia, as well as the successful slew of populist-socialist governments from Hugo Chávez to Evo Morales. Javier Toret, a Spanish activist from ¡Democracia Real Ya!, argues that the "antiglobalisation movement was a bit like Manu Chao [the famous political singer]: very global, idealistic and hope-driven. This movement is more concrete. It starts from demands that are far more connected to people's everyday life. And it is more national, more connected with the population of different countries."

Protest movements from Egypt to France tried to exploit national political opportunities, attuning the rhythm of mobilisation to the national agenda and its most resounding events. Unlike the anti-globalisation movement which, in opposing the global order, adopted a "summit-hopping" strategy,[12] following the schedule of the global meetings of the powerful from the G8 through to the WTO, the movements of the squares focused their attention on topical national events—elections, phases of high political tension, negotiations around rescue packages, or the hosting of large sporting events—as moments at which to target mobilising efforts. The Egyptian Revolution was scheduled to start on 25 January—the national "Police Day"—and also only a few days after the victorious conclusion of the Tunisian uprising. The beginning of the 15-M movement in Spain was timed to coincide with an important round of local elections in May 2011 that, as a consequence of the protests, resulted in a debacle for the governing Socialist Party (PSOE), hastening the resignation of Prime Minister Zapatero. The Greek Aganaktismenoi's rapid rise was in no small part a consequence of their contemporaneity with the climax of the negotiations between the Troika (IMF, ECB, and EC) and the governing Socialist Party (PASOK) of George Papandreou, who was soon forced to resign. Finally, in the case of Brazil the protests exploded in the days immediately before the Confederations Cup of 2013, in preparation for the World Cup the following year: a time at which activists knew they could inflict the greatest disruption and reputational damage.

The targets chosen by these movements also reflected their predominantly national rather than global framing, as seen in the way they preferred to target local representatives of the oligarchy like politicians and bankers. When targeting global actors they mainly did so through framing them as foreign forces interfering with national democracy. Among the most prominent foes picked by these movements were national political elites: Mubarak in Egypt, Zapatero and then Rajoy in Spain, Papandreou and then Papademos in Greece, Obama in the US, Dilma Rousseff in Brazil, and Erdoğan in Turkey. Similarly, national economic elites featured prominently in protest discourse and action, as seen in the attacks against local crony capitalists in Egypt; Bankia's chief Rodrigo Rato in Spain; Alpha Bank and Eurobank, who were involved in a questionable merger deal in Greece; Bank of America, Chase, Wells Fargo, JP Morgan, and Goldman Sachs in the US; Halkbank in Turkey, involved in a major corruption scandal that also implicated then Prime Minister Erdoğan; the media monopolist Rede Globo and national transport entrepreneurs in Brazil. Global economic forces—a traditional foe of the anti-globalisation movement—were also targeted, but not so much as agents of a global empire confronted by a global multitude. Rather these enemies were mostly framed as foreign forces interfering with national society, as seen most clearly in the Spanish and Greek criticisms of the Troika (made up of the International Monetary Fund, the European Commission, and the European Central Bank) which oversaw the "rescue" operations of several debt-laden European countries, as well as the enmity against the German government, accused of "economic colonisation."

From the metropolis to the province

A map of the mobilisations of the anti-globalisation movement would show a truly global protest wave, as the protesters gathered in far-flung localities, many of which became synonymous with counter-summit demonstrations and large gatherings, from Seattle, Prague, and Genoa through to Porto Alegre and Florence. In keeping with its refocusing on the nation as the central protest battleground, the movement of the squares instead took the form of an array of nationally coordinated campaigns, reflecting the "modular" character of many modern popular movements, whereby a certain form of action was repeated in similar ways and at coordinated times all over the national territory.[13] Practically all the major movements of 2011—with the exception of the Tunisian Revolution which emerged from the backwaters of the Gafsa mining district—started in metropolitan areas, as seen in the prominent role of the protests in Madrid, Athens, New York, Istanbul, and São Paulo, and their status as unofficial "capitals" of their respective national movements. However, none of them limited themselves to these dense urban cores, well known as traditional heartlands for anti-authoritarian protest movements, due to the concentration of the highly educated and progressive "new middle class", the main social base of new social movements.[14] On the contrary, one of the most impressive and innovative feats of this protest wave was the degree to which it managed to reach deep into the nations' hinterlands, and into the periphery and rural areas, in a way that was instrumental to targeting "anybody and everybody," including the less affluent, less progressive, and less educated demographics, traditionally at the margins of progressive protest movements.

In the case of the Spanish Indignados the local diffusion of the movement started from the first day of protest on 15 May that saw parallel demonstrations in fifty-eight cities, and gathered pace in the course of the mobilisation. After the first occupations at Puerta del Sol in Madrid and Plaça de Catalunya in Barcelona, a series of copycat protests emerged in over 100 centres all across Spain, and abroad solidarity actions and camps were pitched by Spanish expats. Protest camps popped up even in faraway towns in Castile and Extremadura, rural areas known for their conservative political orientations. The localisation of the movement intensified after the main occupations in big metropolitan centres were dismantled, with the movement focusing on the creation of neighbourhood assemblies, in order to bring the new politics ever closer to the local population, as well as on a series of *"marchas indignadas"* [marches of the outraged] that, starting from eight different corners of the country, converged towards the capital city, in a powerful demonstration of the imaginary of national unity and regeneration that underpinned these movements. These marches were an emotionally charged immersion in the nation's geography and history, contributing to the narrative of national redemption proposed by the 15-M movement. Thus, for example, Gregorio Herrero, a 72-year-old participant in the "southern march" who was once a militant in the Communist Party, describes in his diary that when crossing the region of La Mancha he was reminded of Don Quixote de La Mancha, that Indignado of old.[15]

Much like the Indignados, the Greek Aganaktismenoi reached well beyond the main metropolitan areas, namely those in and around Athens, which hosts around half of the national population. The movement rapidly sprang up in other large cities such as Thessaloniki, Sparti, Larissa, Patras, and Heraklion, and there was virtually no part of the country—island or sizeable village—where assemblies and actions connected with the mobilisation were not present.

No less locally distributed was the Occupy Wall Street movement. If the overall number of participants did not reach the levels of the Indignados and the Aganaktismenoi in proportion to the local population, the level of movement diffusion was impressive, demonstrating its appeal even in areas that might have been otherwise dismissed as Tea Party heartlands. As noted by Los Angeles-based, 41-year-old activist and researcher Joan Donovan, one of the features of Occupy Wall Street was that "people did not need to carpool to the protest", as was the case for large anti-war or anti-globalisation protests. Rather, "Occupy was a distributed protest," which allowed people to demonstrate in their own areas, thus allowing the movement to mobilise people who would never have considered travelling hundreds of miles just to partake in a protest action. Occupy counted at its peak over 1,000 occupations in the US alone, while hundreds of other protest camps, small or large, were set up abroad either in solidarity with the American protests or as part of separate national campaigns. Among the areas covered in the protest map of Occupy were staunchly conservative states such as Mississippi, Missouri, Alabama and North Carolina. *Le Monde Diplomatique* reported on a camp set up in the town of Jackson in Mississippi, which counted among its participants a woman who was registered as a Republican voter, and was so fond of her gun that she even jogged with it.[16] It was in these remote localities that the constituency of Occupy Wall Street criss-crossed with the base of the Tea Party demonstrating its ability to appeal to people beyond those self-identified as leftists.

The protest movements in Brazil and Turkey also experienced an impressive level of local diffusion, testament to their truly broad-based nature. In the case of Turkey, the police raid against the protest encampment in Gezi Park in late May 2015 quickly instigated a series of protests all over the country, including in the capital Ankara and several other cities such as İzmir, Antalya, Adana, Bursa and Hatay among others, with solidarity demonstrations worldwide among the Turkish diaspora. A similar degree of local penetration was achieved by the Movimento de Junho, which after beginning in the big metropolitan areas of the so-called "axis" [*eixo*] of Rio de Janeiro and São Paulo, where a large part of the population and the country's wealth is concentrated, soon reached into the various regions of the country, including remote towns like Cuiabá, São Luís, and Maceió, usually left on the side-lines of national politics. Finally, Nuit Debout in France had quite a high level of local penetration, with protests held in many other cities beyond Paris, including Nantes, Rennes, and Toulouse, though there were debates about the difficulty of reaching poorer areas with high unemployment, where the opposition against the el-Khomri labour law did not resonate as much.

The highly diffuse character of these movements surprised analysts, who sometimes read it simply as a result of the proliferation of digital communication technology, and their proverbial "virality," rapidly disseminating news of protests across informal networks and allowing people in remote areas to easily replicate the protest format they saw applied in the large urban centres, the traditional trend-setters for protest as in other domains. While this factor was undoubtedly important, equally so was the way in which the movements represented themselves as occasions of national regeneration; events that were not the preserve of the metropolitan youth, but were also of direct concern for ordinary people living in smaller centres and rural areas, who if anything were even more severely affected by the issues that motivated the protests, including the effects of the economic crisis and of political disenfranchisement and corruption. Thus, the national framing of the movement of the squares made it possible to penetrate into conservative and rural areas which had remained remote from the anti-globalisation struggle against the global governance structures of the IMF and the WTO, strongly contributing to the impact of the new protest wave on public opinion.

A national entrenchment?

This return to the nation was the result of reflection upon a hard truth that anti-globalisation activists had preferred to ignore: that at the global level there remained little chance of gaining any substantial concessions despite significant campaigning effort, due to the lack of a clear institutional interlocutor for protest movements, and the in-built unresponsiveness of global institutions to popular demands, all being non-elected bodies and therefore unconcerned about public opinion regarding them, as has been argued by Nancy Fraser.[17] Given this situation of a global democratic deficit, it should come as no surprise that protesters felt compelled to focus their mobilising efforts at the national level, where it appeared easier to leverage political energy when opportunities were presented, and construct more focused and sustained mobilisations. The return to the national also constituted the obvious result of these movements' reaffirmation of popular sovereignty, since the only space where such a principle can be satisfied at the present time is the nation-state. This shift reflects the widespread conviction that, where on the global scale social movements have no clear interlocutor, "at the national level there is an actor that can respond to people's demands", to use the words of Brazilian activist Pablo Ortellado. "That actor is the state, and the demands are public policies". The new wave of movements brought about "a realisation that there is little leverage at the global scale, and that there is also a need to use the national level".

The return to the nation also needs to be read as a reflection of the crisis of the project of globalisation, itself hastened by the economic crisis of 2008, which is highlighted by the current discussion on "deglobalisation," such as that proposed by economist Walden Bello[18] or "flowback of globalisation," as proposed by Paul Smith,[19] in which the apparently inexorable path of yet more integration seems to be in question. Already the failures of the 2001 WTO negotiations in Doha, Qatar, and the stalling of similar initiatives, stood to demonstrate the falling political support for the liberalisation of global markets. The crisis of legitimacy for globalisation was clearly exacerbated by the 2008 crash, which demonstrated the fragility of economic interconnectedness through financialisation, and in popular consciousness cast the global economy as a predatory force upsetting the economic and political stability of countries the world over. In this context, globalisation—which during the Roaring Nineties appeared to be delivering on its promise of endless wealth—increasingly appeared to be a synonym for the uncontrollable forces that endanger people's economic security and undermine the effectiveness of national politics.[20]

This trend of global disarticulation has been particularly evident in the European Union, which since the explosion of the crisis has come under increasing criticism for the austerity politics it has imposed, coordinated by the European Commission and the European Central Bank. In the case of the bail-out programmes forced on a number of countries, mostly in southern Europe, the EU has come across as an explicitly anti-democratic force, at the service of global capital, and this has led to a major rise in euro-scepticism. A further example of the crisis of globalisation is the strong opposition that the new Transatlantic Trade and Investment Partnership (TTIP) between the European Union and the United States has encountered, and the fact that during the 2016 US presidential primaries both Bernie Sanders and Donald Trump declared themselves to be for a revision of free trade treaties. In recent years we have seen how the reality of a multipolar world has been accompanied by the return of strong state politics, as manifested in the bellicose realpolitik of countries like Russia, China, and the US, and their frictions in areas such as Syria and the South China Sea, showing the increasing risk of global conflict between world superpowers. The Brexit referendum in June 2016, leading to the prospect of a dangerous disintegration of the European Union, is the latest evidence of this worrying trend.

In this context of global economic and geopolitical instability the return of the nation runs the risk of being a retrenchment; a defensive retreat to an apparently more secure environ, where the nation is seen as a dam against the tempest of the world. By focusing on the national scale, activists risk losing sight of the ways in which many policies, and in particular economic agendas, are coordinated at the supranational level, as became very evident during the European sovereign debt crisis of 2011–12. Economic decisions—which have negatively impacted upon southern European nations—have largely being overseen by technocrats in Brussels, the European Central Bank and the European Commission, without any popular movement being able, despite the effort of the protest days of Blockupy against the European Central Bank, to mount a convincing resistance to such anti-democratic economic autocracy. The more sinister underside of this return of the nation is that by using national symbology and identities, protest movements risk playing in to the hands of right-wing groups. This was seen in infiltration attempts by fascist movements like Golden Dawn in Greece, anti-Semitic groups in the US, and far-right groups in Spain that would wander near these movements, trying to influence their agendas and proselytise to their participants.

The crisis of globalisation has forced protest movements to get to grips with the national question, which to its discredit the radical Left has traditionally preferred to ignore. Nations are not just "imagined com-munities" as Benedict Anderson supposed,[21] but a fact of history; a real-ity hard-wired in our linguistic differences, our schooling systems, traditions, and customs. Furthermore, they deeply shape the way our politics is organised, since political authority continues to primarily reside in national government. This does not mean to say that nations are inherently good or bad; as Isaiah Berlin opined of nationalism, one can only say that "it is responsible for [both] magnificent achievements and appalling crimes."[22] Ignoring this reality, or prophesising its ultimate withering-away, is akin to the same infantile attitude of those who think capitalism will collapse simply because of its internal contradictions. What matters ultimately is which understanding of the nation activists adopt. In this respect the populist appeal to the nation that informed the 2010s upheavals is not the ethnic *Volksgeist* nation of Johann Gottfried von Herder,[23] the frame of reference for xenophobic populists from the FPÖ in Austria to the Front National in France, but rather the "civic nation" proposed by the Abbé Sieyès, the French cleric and theorist of the Third Estate, for whom the nation was "a body of associates, living under a common law, and represented by the same legislature."[24] They proposed not an exclusive nationalism, but a democratic patriotism that saw national pride as a necessary scale of a more universal emancipatory project that could progressively embrace the entire humanity. This democratic patriotism is arguably the best antidote against the right-wing mobilisation of national identity that is at the heart of xenophobic popu-list movements. It is a revealing fact that wherever left-wing populist formations have arisen they have acted as a bulwark against the rise of the extreme Right. This stands to demonstrate how left-wing populism and its progressive patriotism is the best antidote against right-wing populism and its xenophobic nationalism. .

In conclusion, the movement of the squares' success was to a great extent premised on their ability to reclaim national space and to use national identity as a resource for mobilisation. However, this should not mean that we take the nation to be the only real political space and consider all other political scales, such as the local, the regional, the transnational and the global, insignificant. A successful political strategy for coming movements in the post-neoliberal era will involve an articulation of these different levels, and possibly also a reclamation of that global political vision which constituted such an important advancement on the part of the anti-globalisation movement. Despite the crisis of neoliberal globalisation, such a global perspective is still fundamental to help us to understand issues like climate change and the globally interconnected economy, and to construct an alliance between movements across borders. Significant parts of this strategy will need to be revived and built upon.

5

SOCIAL MEDIA AND CITIZENS' MOBILISATION

Organise online—Occupy offline.

Occupy Wall Street meme

Don't worry, we're from the internet.

Anonymous slogan

Our revolution is like Wikipedia.

Wael Ghonim, Egyptian Revolutionary

You are messing with the youth who grew up fighting police in GTA [Grand Theft Auto].

Gezi Park protest slogan

With the explosion of the Arab Spring in the early months of 2011, pundits, journalists, and academics competed in coining expressions such as "Twitter revolution", "Wiki-revolution" and "Revolution 2.0"[1] to emphasise the nexus between digital media and protest—a signature of contemporary movements. If one removes the hype from the discussion, a result of contemporary culture's inordinate fascination with technology, these assertions retain a kernel of truth, in that nobody with any direct knowledge of these movements could deny the importance of digital media. From Egypt to Brazil and Turkey, social network sites like Facebook and Twitter, along with many other online tools, featured prominently in the protester experience. They became key channels for information diffusion, public discussions, and calls for mobilisation both in preparation for, and during, major protest events. As argued by

Spanish activist Javier Toret, those movements of 2011–13 "were the first in history whose mass mobilisation relied primarily on the internet", far more than was the case with the anti-globalisation movement, which emerged at a time when the internet was still a peripheral phenomenon and smartphones did not exist. 48-year-old Asun Villar, who was involved in various activist committees in the Puerta del Sol occupation in 2011, states that, "if such revolutions happen now it is due to the freedom the internet gives". Similarly, 27-year-old Brazilian activist and student Mariana Marchesi argues that, "it would be impossible to conceive of these movements without the internet".

The movement of the squares emerged at a time in which the internet had become part and parcel of everyday life, and at which economic stagnation was paralleled by one of the heaviest waves of technological innovation in human history. It is significant that 2007 was not just the start date of the economic crisis, but also the release date of the first iPhone, a product that epitomised the ubiquitous connectivity experience brought about by the worldwide diffusion of smartphones. Furthermore, many activists were heavily influenced by "internet freedom" movements, and the open-source software movement, and they collaborated with hacker groups (such as Anonymous) that supported the protest wave with a number of connected "ops", from OpTunisia and OpEgypt to direct declarations of support for Occupy. By now the debate on whether digital media did have an impact on these movements should hopefully be settled, despite some techno-pessimists and nostalgic Leftists still clinging to the idea that digital organising is all just hype manufactured by Silicon Valley. What is far more contentious and interesting is the debate about *how* exactly the use of the internet, and social media in particular, affected the way protesters communicate, organise and mobilise, and what kind of organisational forms accompanied this wave of technological innovation.

Much of the debate about the consequences of social media for organisation has followed a typical techno-libertarian line. Social media use has ushered in a totally personalised politics whereby autonomous individuals involved in "connective action" no longer require the unity and leadership typical of traditional forms of collective action, or so runs the argument of Lance Bennett and Alexandra Segerberg.[2] This line of analysis emphasises the neo-anarchist and individualist element of contemporary forms of protest communication, but it seems to overlook the persistence of collectivity in digital protest[3] and the fact that the use of social network sites has been accompanied by the rise of new forms of leadership, rather than leaderlessness.

As we will see in this chapter, reflecting a populist change of mentality, and the majoritarian ambition that underpinned the movements of the squares, they pursued what I describe as a "cyber-populist" strategy of "occupation of the digital mainstream", making use of the power of Facebook and Twitter as means of mass mobilisation. This approach overturned the spirit of tech activism during the anti-globalisation movement, which sought to construct an autonomous communication infrastructure, as seen in the establishment of alternative Internet Service Providers, activist mailing lists, and the information website Indymedia; instead it pragmatically focused on tapping into the huge outreach afforded by corporate social network platforms used by millions, notwithstanding the notable risks involved, namely surveillance and censorship.

Table 5.1: Digital communication in comparison

	Anti-globalisation movement	*Movement of the squares*
Media practices	• Mailing lists • Indymedia • Activist websites	• Facebook • Twitter • Tumblr, YouTube
Orientations	• Cyber-libertarianism • Separatism • Virtualisation of small group politics	• Cyber-populism • Pragmatism • Interactive mass mobilisation

Using the mass outreach possibilities of corporate social media, 2011 activists scaled up of the practices of participatory communication that lay at the heart of the anti-globalisation movement's digital communications. They did not use digital media mainly for the purpose of internal organising, as was the case with prior movements, but as an external means of mobilisation of the citizenry, a public megaphone to address the "netizen", or what I describe as the "generic internet user,"[4] an updated version of the "common man" of earlier populist imaginaries. This change in strategy was accompanied by a change in the style of communication. Eschewing the militant style of the ultra-Left, activists opted for a simplified and emotionally charged form of political communication, geared at eliciting internet users to post, comment and share activist messages. Internet memes, hashtags, emoticons, and the interactive and participatory features of social media were all used within this new repertoire of protest communication. Political Facebook pages and Twitter conversations were transformed into rallying points for the online mass aggregation[5] of a highly dispersed and diversified constituency of internet users, and as a training ground to prepare protesters for their ultimate jump "from the screens to the streets"; from the physical isolation of web interactions to the bodily immersiveness of protest action in the occupied squares.

Counter to the discourse of leaderless ness and horizontality that had often accompanied digital protest communications, activist social media were far from being leaderless spaces; the reliance on user participation did not equate with an absence of organisation and leadership. The communications of the movement of the squares in fact saw strong leadership dynamics at play.[6] They witnessed the rise of "digital vanguards"—collective and informal leadership structures—who steered the process of online mobilisation, as seen in the emergence of social media teams and communication collectives that managed key accounts with hundreds of thousands of followers and likes. As we shall see, the mismatch between the discourse of leaderlessness and the reality of emergent and informal leadership led to a number of major clashes within activist circles around the control of internet assets, raising difficult ethical and political questions about the nature of power and organisation in a digital era, which have continued to preoccupy protest movements ever since.

Occupying the digital mainstream

"To be honest, at the beginning we were having a bit of a laugh about this Facebook and Twitter thing," admits Petros, a 34-year-old veteran of anti-globalisation and Left campaigns, and a participant in the Aganaktismenoi movement in Athens. This speaks to the suspicion and sneering reactions of more experienced activists towards the use of social networks. The seemingly enthusiastic adoption of corporate platforms such as Facebook and Twitter for communications purposes generated disapproval from many activists, and in particular seasoned tech activists and veterans of the anti-globalisation movement, who often took it as a sign of political naivety and ignorance of past struggles, which had strived to construct alternative and self-managed communication infrastructures.

This divergence in practice was not just due to technological evolution. It reflected a more general difference between the anti-globalisation movement and the movement of the squares in philosophy; in how the internet was conceived of as a space for communication and mobilisation. The anti-globalisation movement largely adopted a cyber-libertarian and separatist approach, geared at constructing an "alternative internet": an autonomous communication infrastructure beyond the control of capital and the state. The 2011 activists opted for a more pragmatic cyber-populist strategy of occupation of the digital mainstream, making use of the powerful capabilities of social network sites like Facebook and Twitter as the best suited means to fulfilling their aspiration of constructing a "politics of the indignant citizen". This change of approach stemmed from the belief of many younger activists that previous forms of internet communication, while securing some control over the infrastructure, had ultimately led to self-ghettoisation in activist-only spaces; "virtual communes" of the alternative internet. This conviction led them to attempt to "occupy the 'digital mainstream'": the set of popular platforms and services utilised on a daily basis by the majority of the digitally-connected population.

The spirit that underpinned the anti-globalisation movement's internet operations is condensed in American punk rock musician and activist Jello Biafra's statement, "Don't hate the media, become the media", which was adopted as a motto by the alternative news website Indymedia,[7] the internet journalism voice of the anti-globalisation movement. In order to have their voice heard, activists believed they first needed to create their own communicative infrastructure since there was no way to develop genuine and free forms of communication within a capitalist system always bound to prioritise profit and censor radical content, with the state's complicity. This approach was inspired by the long struggle for alternative media in the 1960s, 1970s, and 1980s that led to the underground press and pirate radio stations, by which social movements circulated content that would otherwise have found no space in the mainstream media. Drawing on this tradition, activists engaged in the development of various internet services for the activist community, such as the provision of server space for websites, email accounts and mailing lists, as well as grassroots education efforts through various hacking spaces and events.

The most important digital channel developed by the global justice movement was Indymedia, short for Independent Media Center, "a collective of independent media organisations and hundreds of journalists offering grassroots, non-corporate coverage". Formed during the 1999 Seattle protests, Indymedia reported on various local struggles and campaigns to provide an alternative view to that of mainstream news media. At the core of Indymedia lay the philosophy of "open publishing",[8] a system without editorial control and filtering and in which users could freely publish what they wanted, in a way that anticipated the "user-generated" logic of Web 2.0.

Besides using the internet as a means of "counter-representation", to balance what was perceived as the distorted account of mainstream news media, activists also used the web for internal discussion and as an organisational platform through which to exchange information in preparation for various protest events. Tech activists set up a number of alternative ISPs (internet service providers), including Riseup[9] and Aktivix[10] in the UK, Inventati[11] and Autistici[12] in Italy, and Nadir[13] in Germany. Their remit was to furnish a variety of activist communication services, encrypting individual email accounts and managing listservs on different topics of interest, from practical information about counter-summit protests to discussions about squatting, cycling, permaculture and similar radical political issues. Public mailing lists such as g8-int, Radical Europe, Dissent, Gipfelsoli, and Peoples' Global Action (PGA) were a key means of coordination for local and transnational mobilisations, through which information about upcoming protest events, such as anti-G8 protests or anti-nuclear power protest camps, was circulated.

The internet operations of the anti-globalisation movement reflected its imaginary of autonomy and self-management that opposed the dominance of both the state and the market and sought to construct, in autonomist jargon, "the commons", a space that is neither private, nor public, and is constantly reproduced by its users. This strategy reflected what Hakim Bey called the Temporary Autonomous Zone or TAZ, a fleeting anarchist "pirate utopia" emerging in the interstices of the system.[14] One of the most important alternative internet service providers in Italy was Isole nella Rete [Islands in the Net], conjuring up an image of small pockets of resistance in the sea of the enemy, under the control of the twin mortal enemies of State and Capital. Internet activism constituted a prolonging and virtualisation of the small group politics of collectives, affinity groups and squats that, as we saw in Chapter 4, made up the texture of neo-anarchism's countercultural politics of resistance.

Contemporary digital activists have moved on from this cyber-autonomist imaginary. The adoption of corporate social networks constitutes a sort of digital update of the eternal populist desire of "going to the people". If activists decided to use these corporate platforms, "it was because the people are on Facebook and Twitter, and it was there that we could reach them," as Marta Franco, a 32-year-old Indignados activist, explains. Joan Donovan, an Occupy activist heavily involved in digital communications work during the mobilisation, explains: "We were not staunchly anti-capitalist in the sense that we were not going to use Facebook or Twitter, or other things, just because they were a tool of capital. Our idea was to communicate everywhere, use this plurality of means of communication, let it run wild and see what happens in different places." Asun Villar, an Indignados activist, has a similar attitude, saying, "If it can be used, it must be used. Are we not in the system anyway?" She goes on to say that while there are evident risks in using social media, such as "the ability to be monitored", there are also benefits to them in that "people in power are not able to control information in the same manner as in the past," and "what is important is the capacity of these media to transport mass amounts of information that the authorities don't want us to have". These testimonies illustrate the pragmatic attitude that informed internet communications in the movements of 2011, and the way in which, while activists were cognisant of the corporate nature of these channels of communication, they strategically saw the potential benefits as outstripping the drawbacks.

The cyber-populist turn in digital communications was a reflection of the popularisation of the internet during the last fifteen years and the new opportunities it unlocked for activists. While in 2001, at the peak of the anti-globalisation movement, only 8 per cent of the world's population, and 30 per cent in developed countries, had access to the internet, total internet users in 2012 stood at 2.7 billion globally, 40 per cent of the global population.[15] Furthermore, all the countries swept up in the movement of the squares experienced an impressive growth of internet and social media use in the years preceding these insurgencies, with possession of an internet connection no longer an elite indicator but fairly commonplace. What we face in this context is not just the "social web", as it is often described, but also a mass web; social media have integrated

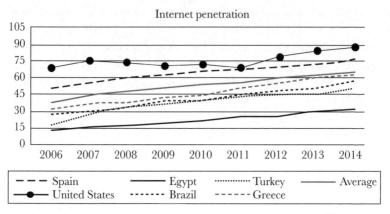

Figure 5.1: Internet access (% of adult population)[16]

one-to-one and one-to-many communicative logics, leading to unprecedented outreach possibilities as suggested by Manuel Castells with his concept of "mass self-communication."[17] It is within this communication eco-system that "a new global generation has arisen" for which digital connectivity, used to keep in touch with friends and family, is part and parcel of everyday experience, as argued by Javier Toret, and as such "the movement arises directly from the internet, from a very transversal section of the population that shares the use of digital technology." Through daily engagement with the internet many young people have had an opportunity to cut their teeth in politics, because as Paique Duques, a Brazilian activist in the Movimento Passe Livre, observes: "People are less afraid to intervene on an internet forum than in an assembly". For many millenials, participating in political discussions on the internet has constituted a sort of "political baptism", as argued by Mustafa Shamaa, a young Egyptian protester.

Using corporate social networking platforms such as Facebook and Twitter, activists reclaim for the people platforms that are "people's platforms" in two respects.[18] Firstly, these corporate services owe their success to the active participation of millions, who freely contribute their invisible "net labour" and personal data, from which these companies extract huge profits. Secondly, these corporations have directly profited from the creativity of social movements, and in particular from the experimentations with new forms of digital communication conducted by hackers and digital activists during the anti-globalisation movement. As observed by Brazilian activist Pablo Ortellado, "the tools of Web 2.0 were created by us", that is, by protest movements (in fact a number of the key developers of Twitter, Flickr and Craigslist had formerly been tech activists with Indymedia). Corporations such as Facebook and Twitter "brought to the market the participatory logic introduced by Indymedia" and its philosophy of open-publishing, and successfully converted this into a mass-scale commercial logic that enables billions of people the world over to communicate with one another. But, in turn, "activists lost control over the platforms", Ortellado goes on to explain. In using corporate social networks for purposes that have possibly little commercial value to their hosts, activists are in a way "expropriating the expropriators", reclaiming for popular use what legitimately belongs to the people.

This occupation of the digital mainstream did, however, force digital activists to play on enemy territory, and therefore exposed them to serious risks. These dangers, already suspected by activists at the time of the 2011–13 protest wave, became well documented after the revelations of the NSA Prism scandal.[19] Systems analyst Edward Snowden revealed the extent to which the US National Security Agency (NSA), its British counterpart Government Communication Headquarters (GCHQ), and many other intelligence organisations utilised social networking sites as mass surveillance tools. These revelations raised reasonable concerns about the risks involved in using corporate platforms for protest purposes, when the back-end of these tools could be so easily accessed by security services. Activists also faced censorship on social networks, as seen in the repeated closing down of Facebook pages such as Anarchist Memes[20] and the Turkish page Ötekilerin Postası [the Other Post], with similar episodes taking place on Twitter.[21] More generally the commercial nature—with the dominance of celebrity news and entertainment content—of social network sites may lead to the banalisation of political communication.[22]

All in all, we can understand the reasons for this strategy of occupation of the digital mainstream, in spite of the evident disadvantages, as a pragmatic move to exploit the unique window of opportunity that emerged at the beginning of the 2010s, when these platforms were experiencing a peak in adoption rates but had not yet reached a point of saturation, and their news feeds algorithms were more favourable to the underdogs. As ever, protest movements are adept at locating historical opportunities and this was no exception, leading to mass outreach possibilities that were beyond the wildest dreams of the previous generation of activists, thus allowing an escape from the virtual activist ghetto in which tech activists had been corralled during the anti-globalisation movement. However, this window of opportunity now seems to be rapidly closing, as social network sites turn ever more towards their commercial imperatives, pushing paid promoted content, and changing their algorithms in ways that are unfavourable for non-profit groups. This was the case with the modification to Facebook's news feed algorithm that significantly limited the visibility of content coming from organisations' Facebook pages, which were some of the most important channels used by activists. Twitter has been discussing similar modifications. It is clear that in the mid to long term activists will also need to go back to the question of control over infrastructures and services, which was the focus of concern for anti-globalisation "techies". The ultimate aim is creating services that can be truly described as "people's platforms", not because they are used by ordinary people, but also because they are under their management and control, as prefigured by current debates about federated social networks and "platform co-operatives."[23]

Mobilising the netizen

For each of the movements of the squares from Egypt to Turkey, social media were "the way information was disseminated for the masses", argues Turkish activist Sarphan Uzunoğlu, and the technologies through which "masses can be mobilised", as put by Spanish activist Asun Villar. This "mass" element is well described by Manuel Castells and is key to understanding the shift in the logic of protest communication introduced by 2011 activists. Reflecting its commitment to the politics of autonomy, the anti-globalisation movement used the internet as an extension of its small group politics, always in connection with more traditional structures of activist mobilisation, including the thick personal networks of social movement scenes, and still relying on mainstream media reporting of upcoming actions to mobilise more people. The movement of the squares instead moved to an expansive populist model of online communication that, rather than simply "networking" individuals and groups, signalled a process of mass aggregation of atomised and dispersed participants into one single online "crowd", to use a term that has become current in the Web 2.0 lexicon.[24]

This shift in protest communication revolves around the foregrounding of the public and external functions of digital media over their use as internal means of organisation. Of course, these two functions—the internal and external—have both been represented within contemporary agit-prop's toolkit, which uses different apps and services for various purposes. As described by Spanish activist Marta Franco: "Facebook and Twitter [were] used as a space for networking, information diffusion and public discussion; video services such as YouTube and livestream apps such as Bambuser as means to distribute movement propaganda, represent protest events and document police violence; and chat services like Skype and Mumble to have internal organisational meetings." However, the public and outreach components were what made the difference to the new model of online communication.

"The key shift was when we passed from using Facebook mainly as a platform for internal discussions to a platform for public communication with people outside of our group," says Ahmed Maher, the 31-year-old co-founder of the 6 April Youth Movement, a key protest organisation in the Egyptian revolution. While the internet had previously been utilised chiefly as an internal coordination platform, providing geographically dispersed activist groups with the opportunity to organise from a distance, the 2011 upheavals utilised social media as soap-boxes aimed at maximising mass outreach among the general populace. In doing so, Arab digital activists demonstrated to the world "the power of social networks, their capacity for diffusion and for contagion", argues 24-year-old Segundo Gonzalez of Juventud Sin Futuro [Youth Without a Future]. It led activists in Spain and other countries to develop an expansive strategy that, according to Fabio Gandara of ¡Democracia Real Ya!, revolved around the intention "to use the power of the internet, the network structures to organise ourselves state-wide and to carry out a citizen's call for mass protests throughout Spain from a citizen point of view".

The clearest sign of the public reframing and scaling up of digital media activism was the emergence of so-called "power" social media accounts (channels with several tens of thousands of followers), official movement Facebook pages and Twitter accounts, with audiences of hundreds of thousands, if not millions, of people, which constituted the most important channels for mobilising participants. In the case of the Egyptian revolutionary movement, the most prominent ones were the "Kullena Khaled Said" Facebook page (with 3.7 million likes)[25] and the

"6 April Youth Movement" Facebook page (with 1.3 million likes as of July 2016).[26] In the 15-M/Indignados movement, central social media accounts included the ¡Democracia Real Ya! Facebook page, with around 546,000 likes,[27] and its Twitter account, with 233,000 followers, alongside other prominent channels such as Acampadasol with 73,000 followers on Twitter, and Juventud Sin Futuro on Facebook, with 123,000 likes.[28] In the case of Occupy Wall Street in the US, the main social media channels were the Twitter accounts @OccupyWallStreetNYC, with 205,000 followers,[29] and @OccupyWallStreet with 214,000 followers,[30] and the Facebook pages Occupy Wall St. with 815,000 likes[31] and Occupy Together with 310,000 likes.[32] These numbers were two orders of magnitude above the typical online audience of the anti-globalisation movement.

This unprecedented reach allowed the movements of the squares to reach well beyond the usual activist circles. Activists attempted to sidestep traditional media and directly substitute themselves into the intermediary role of representation the mainstream had typically played, seen almost without exception by activists as a force in thrall to the establishment. Thus for example Jorge Izquierdo, a 38-year-old Spanish activist, explains that through social media, "I can now bypass all the media including the supposedly progressive ones. I can bypass *Publico*, *El Pais*, or La Sexta. This is a very new thing." In this context the addressee was no longer the activist or the already politicised internet user of the elitist Web 1.0, but the generalised audience of the news media that activists wanted to substitute: it was the "anybody and everybody", the "netizen", or the "generic internet user"[33] as a surrogate (within the space of the internet) for the People and the citizens to whom the movements of the squares appealed.

The cyber-populist strategy of the 2011 wave was accompanied by a modification to the style of protest communication, with activists from Egypt to Brazil tailoring content to the specificity of social media and their publics.[34] As Isham Christie, an activist with Occupy Wall Street, expresses, a constant concern for activists responsible for maintaining Twitter and Facebook accounts was to develop a discourse "that was both radical and popular"; that could express the urgent need for social change, but in such a way that addressed those many "people who do not already identify as activists", in the words of UK-based activist Kirsten Forkert, who has been active in student protests and anti-austerity campaigns. According to 23-year-old Pablo Gallego, who has a degree in business management and is an organiser in ¡Democracia Real Ya!, it is precisely this change of approach to content that led to "normal people, people like me and you who had no political commitment [answering] the call to go out".

To this end they made use of the tropes of what could be called digital-popular culture, in reference to Antonio Gramsci's idea of "national-popular,"[35] as a cultural space at the intersection of popular and digital culture which had been emerging on mass social networks such as Facebook, YouTube, Instagram, Twitter, and many others. Specifically, they applied three stylistic solutions that best allowed them to tap into the customs of social media users: crisp text for posts, avoiding the verbosity and obscurity of the militant Left; emotionally charged expression to motivate prospective participants; abundant visual content in the form of internet memes, pictures and videos; and the harnessing of the logic of interactivity and crowd-sourcing, as seen in collective activist blogs.

Digital activists forsook the wordy and often overly intellectualised content of radical Left communication. Instead, they perfected the concise writing style of Facebook and Twitter, channelling their content into short, incisive and sometimes sloganeering texts or even simply hashtags, such as the 100,000 Occupy-themed hashtags that were created at the height of the movement. According to Segundo Gonzalez, an Indignados activist and later an MP for Podemos, "the internet demands you develop your discourse in a very simplified way, because if there are too many words, people do not read. Nobody reads a six-paragraph-long text, nobody shares it". Furthermore, to avoid scaring away non-politicised internet users, activists from Egypt to France almost entirely eschewed terms that might sound too political, difficult, or ideological, opting instead for what Pablo Gallego refers to as "euphemisms", such as "rich" instead of "capitalists" and "poor" instead of "the working class".

As well as brevity, activists tried to emphasise emotional over informational content. This can be seen in the deeply emotional tone of many status messages and tweets sent by activists, rife with emoticons, exclamation marks, and capitalised letters to elicit attention and engagement from the audience. Activists also tried to use positive language, expressing the emancipatory possibilities of grassroots action, sometimes also acquiring a prophetic tone, asserting with certainty the ultimate victory of popular mobilisation. Consider, for example, the status message posted on the Facebook page, Kullena Khaled Said, on 25 January 2011, at the beginning of the revolution:

> I never saw this on Facebook before… The Jan25 invitation reached 500,000 Facebook users. 27,000 have RSVPed. People in the villages must know there is a solution. That we will take action and say "No". That we demand our rights. Let's do this Egyptians. Let's show the world that we are not cowards and that we are ready to sacrifice anything for our rights.[36]

Similarly, the ¡Democracia Real Ya! Facebook page wrote on April 10 that, "We already have 20,000 indignant followers on Facebook!" and on April 26 announced, "We are already 30,000 indignants confirming their participation in the state event!! Invite your contact and let's continue growing!!!" These messages highlight how social media communications were geared towards motivating participants and infusing them with a sense of collective enthusiasm, or what I have described elsewhere as "digital enthusiasm,"[37] all the more important due to the physical dispersion and individualisation of their online interactions.

Social media is well-known for having an eminently visual character and digital activists put a lot of emphasis on visual material including internet memes, propaganda videos published on YouTube, and livestreams of protest events. Examples of this trend were various popular internet memes, or more precisely "image macros", such as the Turkish "Lady in Red" meme, or the "Pepper Spray Cop" meme.[38] The "Lady in Red" meme stemmed from a photo taken during the attack on the Gezi Park occupation at the end of May 2013, where a woman in a red dress was attacked by the police. The "Pepper Spray Cop" meme was ignited by a photo of a policeman casually pepper-spraying a group of protesters sitting on the ground at the University of California, Davis on 18 November 2011. The two photos set in motion an avalanche of photo-shopped variants, with the silhouette of the UC Davis policeman pasted onto John Trumbull's *Declaration of Independence* painting and Michelangelo's *Creation of Adam* in the Sistine Chapel. They conveyed, in an immediate and ludic format, the stupidity and brutality of police repression and its vile targeting of defenceless individuals, proof of police service to the oligarchy rather than of ordinary citizens.

A final element of the digital-popular rhetoric used by 2011 activists was the adoption of the Web 2.0 logic of crowd-sourcing. Wael Ghonim in fact described the Egyptian revolution as like Wikipedia, in which every user contributed by collectively suggesting slogans, preparing visual materials, and the like.[39] Digital activists systematically appealed to the imaginary of the "wisdom of the crowd,"[40] and the discourse of co-operation and peer-to-peer sharing of Web 2.0, trying to tap into the creative and co-operative potential of internet users. Like anti-globalisation tech activists they were informed by "the idea of participation and creating a dialogue," as put by 40-year-old Brazilian activist and academic Pablo Ortellado, an activist with Indymedia, though they operated at a much larger scale than their predecessors.

An example of this participatory mass communication which informed the movement of the squares' digital activism are the many social justice crowd-sourced blogs that have become a symbol of the participatory spirit of the 2011–13 movements. The most famous is the "We Are the 99 Percent" Tumblr blog, created by Occupy Wall Street activists, which hosted hundreds of short stories of distress from US citizens, and in particular from the "squeezed middle", in the wake of the financial crisis. Protesters were asked to take a selfie while holding a message explaining their situation, thus turning the selfie, the symbol of the vacuity of digital culture, into a means of political expression. Gathering hundreds of contributions—which stood to confirm as if in an experimental trial the seriousness of various social issues such as poverty, homelessness, racism or precarious working conditions—these crowd-sourced blogs work as a means of aggregation of otherwise isolated individuals, making them feel part of the same "crowd", sharing a similar experience and similar grievances. Thus, these blogs were not just crowd-sourced, but also "crowd-building".

Counter to the idea of "slacktivism" proposed by techno-pessimists like Evgeny Morozov,[41] these online communications were never meant to be substitutive of offline protest action. Their philosophy was summed up in Occupy Wall Street's motto, "Organise online—Occupy offline"; the idea was that activists had to be brought together in online discussions as a preliminary stage before the ultimate "jump to the streets" [*salto a la calle*]. Activists explicitly and insistently emphasised the urgency of transforming online dissent into offline protests, as seen in exhortations like the Spanish slogan "*toma la calle*" [take the streets], the synonymous Brazilian "*vem pra rua*", appropriated from a Fiat car advertisement, and the connected call "let's exit Facebook". As Egyptian activist Ahmed Sabry argues, "Facebook is good, everything is good, but unless you have real people really wanting and willing to protest, you go nowhere."

Similarly, Mark, a 25-year-old Occupy Wall Street activist explains, "The internet should be looked at as something to get the ball rolling, to get the word out there. People still have to get out on the streets." As Asun Villar summarises, "Through the internet and through Facebook and Twitter people have seen there are people like them, who think like them. They are just as outraged. And I think that this is what has made them dare to participate."

Social media were conceived of as a sort of "training ground" that could enable largely non-politicised prospective participants to gain the necessary self-confidence, mutual trust, and enthusiasm to take part in actual protest on the streets. To translate this potential into actual partici- pation activists made use of those features of social media that allow the organisation of specific events, such as Facebook's popular event feature, as funnelling channels providing an otherwise highly dispersed social base with a focal point for mobilisation in space and time. This was seen in the Egyptian 25 January protests that were launched through a dedicated Facebook event, and led activists in Egypt to talk of their revolution as the first to be "pre-programmed". This practice would later be adopted by activists the world over, facilitating the transformations of the online crowds gathered around Facebook pages and Twitter hashtags, into the offline crowds occupying public squares from Tahrir to Syntagma.

The emergence of digital vanguards

One of the dominant narratives about the movement of the squares is that they were completely spontaneous and leaderless, and that their commu- nications reflected this non-hierarchical nature, as argued by authors like Paul Mason and Manuel Castells among others, who often depicted these movements as networks fighting against hierarchies.[42] Many of my inter- viewees indeed believed that the key contribution of social media was that they could make social movements more horizontal.

This discourse of leaderlessness and horizontality hints at the way in which digital communication disrupted previously rigid and formalised modes of organisation, and left organisations more flexible and porous. However, it is wrong in assuming that the flexibility and greater degree of openness of digital organising equates to the disappearance of leader- ship and hierarchy. As I have argued in *Tweets and the Streets*, far from disappearing from the online world of Facebook pages, Twitter conversations, and Instagram threads, new forms of leadership emerged which made use of the interactive affordances of these platforms such as liking, sharing, commenting, re-tweeting, and favouriting, as well as of the massive scale of their reach, which far surpassed anything available during the era of the so-called Web 1.0 to construct new forms of direction of collective action.[43] This persistence and transformation of leadership was in fact part of a broader trend: many digital phenomena that people consider leaderless—from Linux to Wikipedia—have in fact their own forms of leadership and hierarchy. Even hacker group Anonymous, supposedly the most horizontal of contemporary protest groupings, has its own leaders and factions.[44] It should not come as a surprise that—despite its appeal to leaderlessness—the movement of the squares also had its own leaders (and, more noticeably, leading groups) who utilised digital media as a means of directing collective action.[45]

One of the reasons for the widespread suspicion of hierarchy among activists is its identification with individual leadership and its authoritarian manifestations. This element of individual leadership was, however, mostly absent in the movement of the squares, due to ist collectivism and a suspicion of personality politics. It is true that these movements saw the rise to prominence of certain individuals, some of them thanks to their social media presence, including Wael Ghonim, the administrator of the "Kullena Khaled Said" Facebook page, as well as bloggers Gigi Ibrahim, Wael Abbas, and Alaa Abdel el-Fattah in Egypt; activists like David Graeber, David Ross, Justin Wedes, and Micah White in the US; Elisa Quadros or "Sininho," an activist who was thrust into the limelight during a trial after the protests in Brazil; or Kurdish film director and MP Sırrı Süreyya Önder, who stood in front of the bulldozers in the first day of the protests in Gezi park. Furthermore, there were also showbiz celebrities who lent their support to the movement, such as Javier Bardem in Spain, and Michael Moore, Tim Robbins, and rap producer Lupe Fiasco in the US. However, as Asun Villar says, "there was no Gandhi in these movements", that is, no single recognisable leader. In fact individual leaders repeatedly proved to be great disappointments, no less so when protesters initially had some hope in them. This was seen most glaringly in Egypt, where Nobel Peace Prize laureate and former presidential candidate Mohammed el-Baradei repeatedly blew the opportunity to take the lead of the movement due to his indecisiveness.

The impact of individual leaders paled in comparison with the collective leadership structures built by these movements. Protest organisations such as the 6 April Youth Movement in Egypt, ¡Democracia Real Ya! in Spain, the Movimento Passe Livre in Brazil, and Convergence des Luttes in France played important roles in launching the mobilisations. However, they did not possess the typical mass base and extensive structure of popular and revolutionary organisations of the past. As Brazilian activist Rodrigo Nunes argues, the movement of the squares "was the first to experience a mass mobilisation without mass organisations". As a consequence these protest organisations had a limited degree of control over the evolution of the protests: once the movement gathered in the square they could no longer direct the force they had unleashed. While the 6 April Youth Movement was pivotal in launching the Tahrir protests, it did not manage to establish itself as a leading force in the aftermath of the revolution and its membership did not grow substantially. In Spain, when the protest camps began ¡Democracia Real Ya! decided to stand on the side and allow the process to develop autonomously. The Movimento Passe Livre decided to withdraw itself from the mobilisation at the height of the protests in mid-June 2013, because it realised it had lost all control of its evolution and was concerned about an incipient right-wing turn. Finally Convergence des Luttes, which had called the first day of protest in France, repeatedly expressed suspicion about the assemblies in Place de la République which it saw as too naïve and lacking in a clear strategy. These groups were bullhorns for the movement, instigating mass mobilisation but mostly incapable of directing them. Also important for "on the ground" organising was the role played by experienced activist groups who helped with the setting up of the camps, as well as by subcultural groups such as football ultras, who acted as a sort of revolutionary militia in countries like Egypt, Brazil, and Turkey.

Besides these protest organisations and social groupings, the movement of the squares saw the presence of more invisible but no less important leadership structures that I describe as "digital vanguards", to indicate their similarity to historical political vanguards and their use of digital media as means of direction of collective action.[46] The clearest example was the prevalence of social media teams: groups ranging from two to twenty people with responsibility for managing movements' social network accounts. These groups emerged both within specific protest organisations such as those previously discussed, and within protest camps, in the form of committees or working groups accountable to the general assembly. For example, to manage its social media communications ¡Democracia Real Ya! had two separate groups: four to six people were responsible for the Twitter feed and six to eight people worked on the Facebook page, as reported by Javier Toret, one of its participants. The Puerta del Sol protest encampment set up a specific committee with ten to fifteen people responsible for maintaining two Twitter accounts (@tomalaplaza and @acampadasol), member Marta Franco recounted. In the case of Occupy Wall Street around fifteen people were involved in managing the main Facebook account and around twenty managed the Twitter account @OccupyWallStNYC, though the size of these groups significantly varied at different stages in the evolution of the movement, with new people brought in to cope with the increasing workload as the movement continued to grow.

As Marta Franco describes, social media teams followed principles of "openness" and "consensus", with internal coordination both through face-to-face meetings and various online chats and forums: Skype conference calls and voice or text chats via services such as Mumble and Telegram. As reported by Andrew, a 26-year-old Occupy activist involved in various communication teams, the everyday life of these groups was characterised by "invisible conversation work" where people "spen[t] hours and hours talking with one another". However, the application of the philosophy of horizontality was repeatedly contradicted by the presence of power differentials and a clear division of political labour. While in these collectives there was supposedly never a leader, from time to time some individuals took a prominent role, argues Klaudia Alvarez, a 37-year-old communication team organiser with ¡Democracia Real Ya!

The presence of an internal hierarchy was exacerbated by the fact that to streamline collective work most activist groups utilised social media management systems, such as Hootsuite, CoTweet and Buffer, with their hierarchical structure of user permissions.[47] In this context, participants were assigned different "rights", with some only able to produce new content, such as new tweets or Facebook status messages, while others were also entitled to edit and approve previously submitted content. At the top of the structure stood the "admins", those who controlled access to the social media management system and the passwords of the accounts. As 30-year-old Tim Fitzgerald, an Occupy Wall Street activist known for his Twitter handle @diceytrooper, explains, due to the registration policies of social media companies which only allow for individuals (or registered companies and organisations) to apply for an account, "whoever made the account on day one [could] reclaim the account, ultimately there [was] an owner". As a consequence some "people ended up acquiring all these assets [which] made them centres of gravity in ways that really distorted the network". Additionally, some of these teams were dominated by close-knit groups of friends and activists, with only limited possibility for outsiders to become fully included, also due to fears about the infiltration of police agents or people with different political agendas. 33-year-old Steve Reid, an organiser in UK Uncut, an anti-austerity campaign that was a recent predecessor of the movements of the squares, admits, "saying that we were horizontal was a bit dishonest because there was a central group".

The presence of this hierarchical structure and reasonably clear core groups, coupled with the lack of alertness about risks or viable policies on how to deal with internal controversies, prepared the terrain for misunderstandings and recriminations that sometimes escalated into excruciating power struggles around the control of social media accounts, with dire effects for the reputation of the connected social movements and their official communication channels.

In Spain, a split opened up in ¡Democracia Real Ya! in early 2012 and exploded around the time of the first anniversary of the 15-M protests. One group, named "Refundación" [Refounding], comprised those who wanted to turn ¡Democracia Real Ya! into a legally registered association. The other, named "Reinicia" [Restart], instead wanted the group to remain a network. The fight between the two groups escalated into a vociferous spat over the control of social media platforms, and the Refundación group managed to get hold of the main Facebook page of ¡Democracia Real Ya! The Reinicia group retaliated by securing control over the main Twitter channel. Alternative Facebook and Twitter channels were set up by each of the two factions to discredit each other, each claiming to be the "real" ¡Democracia Real Ya!

In the case of Occupy Wall Street, low-level conflicts around the management of key accounts accompanied the entire lifecycle of the movement, but only exploded publicly after the movement had begun to decline. The most famous incident took place in February 2014. Justine Tunney, a Google engineer and an early organiser in the movement, who had set up various internet accounts, including occupywallst.org (known among activists as STORG) and the main Facebook page, claimed control of the main Twitter account, @OccupyWallSt. Disappointed by a perceived lack of recognition for her contribution to the movement, and disillusioned by the direction it had taken, she voiced her frustration in a cascade of messages, some of them rather bizarre, in what one of her friends described as a "very public breakdown."[48] Later the same year Justin Wedes, another high profile Occupy Wall Street activist based in Detroit, after a longstanding argument with people on the "Tweet boat" social media team asserted control over another key social media asset of the movement, the @OccupyWallStreetNYC handle, before suspending the account. Similar stories of activist spats over the control of social media accounts emerged from many other movements operating at the same time and sharing a similar horizontalist philosophy, such as the Israeli Indignados movement and the Canadian indigenous people's movement Idle No More.

It would be too easy to read these episodes simply as the result of personal weaknesses, or the egomania and opportunistic tendencies that are so prevalent in contemporary neoliberal societies. We need to understand them also as reflections of the unrealistic puritanism unleashed when horizontality is adopted not as part of a utopian vision of the world the movement wants to achieve, but as a strict prescription for actual practice. Horizontality is not a solution to the question of leadership; it only sweeps the issue under the carpet. Appeals to horizontality often provided a convenient smokescreen for *de facto* leaders to prevent any collective discussion about leadership, and to avoid relinquishing their privileged position or being questioned about their behaviour. It is not by chance that, as Stephanie, a 27-year-old Occupy Wall Street participant, describes, "Often within the communication teams created by these movements, the most fanatic defenders of horizontality and leaderlessness were precisely the *de facto* leaders!" These problems call for a serious rethinking about the viability of the principle of horizontality, and the plausibility of other collective principles and organisational protocols that could make emergent forms of leadership more transparent and accountable.

6

THE CAMP AND THE AGORA

Toma la plaza [Take the square].

Indignados slogan

Lost a job, found an occupation.

Occupy Wall Street sign

Everywhere is Taksim, Everywhere is Resistance.

Turkish protest slogan

Tens of thousands of people are assembled in Tahrir Square. Six months have gone by since the revolution of 25 January 2011 that forced Mubarak to step down, and three since the last occupation of the square in April. The atmosphere is something between a popular festival and an insurrection, the beginning of a new mobilisation and a social reunion of veterans. At the entrances to the square unmarked stewards check people's IDs and search them swiftly to make sure nobody is carrying weapons. Past the controls, inside the square it feels safe and welcoming, a convivial space, full of families, old people, and workers, beside the masses of the Egyptian youth, the *shabab el-thawra* [youth of the Revolution]: students, football hooligans, young workers, and street children. The centre of the square is occupied by a protest camp, similar to that set up during the days of the revolution. A complex of white marquees hangs in the breeze, held by twenty ten-metre-high wooden poles, to protect people from the scorching Egyptian

157

summer sun. Below them is a series of tents, big and small, housing activists and families, political groups, and various protester necessities—medics, food, and electronics.

The small topiary trees that have miraculously survived the many battles waged in the square have been turned into popular billboards on which to stick revolutionary messages: "Bread, freedom, and end to military rule", "Freedom for the prisoners", "Work, health, education". On the concrete perimeter of the roundabout sit groups of people and individuals, holding home-made propaganda: caricatures of Mubarak, Assad, and Qaddafi as infants, a maquette of Field Marshal Tantawi (the military president), and various posters celebrating the revolution. Small groups of friends are chatting, or listening to the people speaking and the music coming from the different stages set up around the square. People stream out of the adjoining underground station, many dressed in national colours. Street sellers push their carts selling popcorn, roasted potatoes and *koshari* (an Egyptian favourite consisting of rice, pasta, and lentils with a tomato sauce). Others sell revolutionary souvenirs, Egyptian flags, 25-January–themed T-shirts, Arabic copies of *The Prince*, and other political books. From a loudspeaker comes a song by the revolutionary singer Ramy Essam. Ahmed, a 24-year-old 6 April Youth Movement activist who has come back to the square for the first time since 25 January, reads out the leaflet with all the demands raised by the occupation, which ends by saying, "We will stay until our demands are met."

Since the occupation of Tahrir Square in January 2011, the tactic of "all out" or "no end date" protest camps—also called "protest encampments" or "*acampadas*" in Spanish, to avoid the military connotations of the term "camp"—located in central public squares became the signature practice of the new protest wave, hence the name "movement of the squares". From the Kasbah camp organised by Tunisian activists a few weeks after the fall of President Ben Ali, to the occupation of Puerta del Sol by the Spanish Indignados and the tents set up by Israeli activists in Rothschild Boulevard in Tel Aviv, as well as those in Zuccotti Park in New York, Gezi Park in Istanbul, and Place de la République in Paris, this "take the square" tactic was variously adopted and readapted. As Micah White, an instigator of Occupy Wall Street, explains, it became a "viral social ritual" that served as a means of dramatisation of the conflict between the citizenry and the oligarchy, and their vision of a politics of citizenship, re-democratising society from the bottom-up.

Table 6.1: Protest repertoires in comparison

	Anti-globalisation movement	*Movement of the squares*
Protest tactics	Counter-summit protests Creative direct action Black bloc tactics	Protest camps in highly visible public squares
Protest rationale	Countercultural and militant protest	Peaceful gathering of the citizenry Ritual of popular communion

The protest camp has a long history within protest movements, and has been used in the environmental, anti-war, and anti-globalisation movements.[1] Before the movement of the squares however, it had mainly been an "accessory tactic", a means to sustain and defend participants who were taking part in direct action and large demonstrations. Starting with the protests of 2011 this tactic underwent a fundamental change in meaning and purpose. It acquired an unprecedented centrality in the action system of the movement of the squares, going from being a logistical support structure for other tactics to the main form of protest action waged by these movements.

Where the anti-globalisation movement and direct action campaigns erected ephemeral protest camps in suburban or rural areas, often inaccessible to movement outsiders, the movements of the squares had their camps in central city areas easily accessible to sympathisers and the simply curious. Where protest camps were previously communal spaces, replete with countercultural mores, for the movement of the squares they were marked as public spaces open to anyone. Finally, where anti-globalisation camps had rather militant connotations likely to scare away many prospective participants, the 2011 camps were marked by a friendly and reassuring look and feel that was instrumental in attracting many participants to their first experience of protest action.

The 2010s occupations aimed at constructing a new "agora", which, like the ancient assembly place of Athenian democracy, would be designed to gather the citizenry and involve it in public discussions, the most elementary of political acts. Furthermore, the camps served as a outdoor psychotherapeutic and pedagogical space in which thousands of individuals, all carrying their own personal story of failure and frustration amidst the economic crisis, could demolish the many barriers set up by neoliberal society, freeing themselves from loneliness and cultivating a sense of unity and mutual empathy that became one of the driving forces of the protest wave.

This protest tactic incorporated aspects from both anarchist and populist politics, including the former's participatory spirit and the latter's focus on popular mobilisation. However, they also displayed the deep-seated contradictions between these different inspirations. Anarchists often saw the camp as a commune or autonomous community, a sort of biotope amidst the urban jungle in which to construct an alternative society in the here and now. Populists instead understood the camp as an agora, a people's stage on which to articulate common narratives and a springboard from which to commence a process of systemic change that would generalise the spirit of the occupied squares. These two narratives clashed with one another in the everyday life of the camp, leading to different interpretations of the meaning of the occupations and of the movements they incubated.

The protest party and the Black Bloc

Protest camps, like protest tactics more generally, are not just practical means to achieve specific ends. It is reductive to understand them simply as "instruments" of protest, whose efficiency can be objectively assessed by measuring their capacity for disruption and the pressure they put on power-holders. Rather, protest tactics are always to be understood also as a form of communication, a symbolic practice that conveys a certain understanding of the present society—its problems and possible solutions—to both their participants and to various publics; supporters, sympathisers, and opponents. Charles Tilly speaks of protest tactics as part of a "repertoire of contention,"[2] a theatrical metaphor to indicate how protests are "symbolically coherent phenomena,"[3] utilising different tactics to dramatise people's claims.[4]

An expert on eighteenth and nineteenth century social movements and revolutions, Tilly identifies two main repertoires of contention corresponding to pre-modern and modern social movements, with the French Revolution the watershed moment. Pre-modern protest was highly localised and focused on an immediate redress of grievances, often through the use of violent direct action.[5] It encompassed such practices as break-ins, assaults, "*charivari*,"[6] pulling down culprits' houses, and seizing grain. It was only in the late eighteenth and early nineteenth century, during the epoch of the great bourgeois revolutions and the rise of the labour movement, that a "modern" protest repertoire was formed.[7] Cognisant of the political opportunities introduced by the consolidation of the modern nation-state, protests progressively became more coordinated at the national level, concentrating all forces on the centralised apparatus of the state as a means to exact various concessions: civil rights, representation in political institutions, labour legislation, control of food prices, and elementary public services. It was at this time that a number of familiar protest practices—such as the protest march and the strike—crystallised.

The modern repertoire of contention, strongly associated with the history of the labour movement and the industrial era-Left, is a blueprint against which many post-'68 new social movements, such as feminism, environmentalism, the squatter movement, and the anti-globalisation movement, have constructed their political praxis. Activists within neo-anarchist movements have often ridiculed protest parades as "marches from A to B" (while also highlighting their disturbing militaristic connotations) and strikes as ritualistic events with no real disruptive effect on a system that has found many workarounds for them. As an alternative to what they saw as the tired rituals of the Old Left, activists developed a new series of creative protest tactics that could be characterised as being part of a "postmodern repertoire of contention", to distinguish it from the modern repertoire, given the way in which it reflects some typical features of postmodern culture such as reflexivity, irony, and fondness for pastiche.

The new way of doing protest pursued by anti-globalisation activists at the time of the millennium comprised two main streams: "spiky" and "fluffy". On the one hand, it saw a pursuit of militant means, and in particular the black bloc tactic, with targeted property destruction and confrontations with police. On the other hand, it saw the development of a stream of creative and non-violent protest tactics, taking the form of a "protest party" which framed protest as an act of joy and vivacity.[8] These two streams, while differing in their level of militancy, both stemmed from a view of protest as a countercultural activity, involving small groups sharing a common culture and participation in a common movement scene.[9]

The black bloc tactic was widely utilised between the late 1990s and 2000s in both local and global protests. This practice originated from the German Autonomen in the 1970s and then rapidly spread to other countries in Europe and the US, more recently acquiring a truly global reach. The tactic involves a simple script: everybody dresses completely in black from head to toe, covering their faces by using sunglasses, hoodies, caps, and the like, so as to minimise the risk of being identified and prosecuted. Militant sections of the anti-globalisation sections have used this format of protest to engage in attacks against symbols of global capitalism—McDonald's restaurants, banks, etc.—and fought intense battles with the police. The relationship of the rest of the movement with the Black Bloc, which—as the name suggests—often appeared as a specific bloc within demonstrations, has been problematic. It is true that in certain anti-globalisation demonstrations the presence of the Black Bloc was welcome, and some people saw them as a sort of steward corps for the entire movement, protecting it from police attacks. However, more often they have been seen as adventurists opting for militant tactics not shared by the majority of participants, and ultimately playing into the hands of the police and the mainstream news media, only too eager to publish pictures of broken windows as a pretext to unleash repression against protesters and depict them as criminals.

Very different in spirit is the format of the "protest party" that informed many anti-globalisation movement activities.[10] Examples include the anti-roads movement Reclaim the Streets blocking roads and intersections to protest against "car culture"; the collective bike rides dubbed "Critical Mass", which disrupt vehicle traffic by "being the traffic"; the political theatre of the Insurgent Clown Army; the colourful parades against labour precarity coordinated by EuroMayDay; the padded bloc of the White Overalls, with protesters dressed in ungainly defensive gear to confront the police forces during counter-summit protests; and the pink blocs of queer protesters seen in various demonstrations. Instead of marching like armies, as the labour movement would, protest participants were invited to act creatively like performers or dancers, as first proposed by German writer Magnus Enzsensberger and prefigured by Emma Goldman's famous (though possibly misquoted) proclamation, "if I can't dance, it is not my revolution!"[11] This refusal of the linearity of the traditional and political union marches, sometimes derided as "march from A to B", was epitomised by the "star march" format utilised in many anti-globalisation protests, in which different blocs would try to confuse police forces by staging separate converging marches, with columns splitting into sub-columns and smaller groups when approaching the target area.

Within this postmodern protest repertoire protest camps have featured frequently, appearing in the context of counter-summit protests hosting thousands of protesters, but also in smaller direct actions, such as in anti-border demonstrations, protests against military installations, or in environmentalist actions. Their role has however been for the most part a logistical one. They served to provide a global and nomadic activist community converging on a given location with all that was necessary to participate in protest action: shelter, running water, sanitation, and popular kitchens (*Volkskuche* in German) that would offer protesters a menu of vegan food—with great quantities of hummus, beans, organic bread, and soy milk—as well as protest training sessions. Besides such practical considerations, the camp also constituted an important community space, allowing participants to partake in a moving though fleeting experience of "holiday communism," as ironically phrased by German activist Matthias.

Anti-globalisation protest camps reflected the multiple nuances of neo-anarchist and radical left cultures, and of the various political clans that made up the larger tribe. They were usually organised into politically themed neighbourhoods (such as Zapatista, Trotskyist, queer, green, and so forth), or *barrios* in Spanish, where like-minded people sharing the same politics could get to know each other and construct bonds of mutual solidarity. Despite their practical and psychological importance, protest camps were in fact a sidepiece. The climax in the dramaturgy of protest coincided with the large demonstrations and the direct action days, a customary component of counter-summit protests during which activists would attempt to break into a securitised "red zone" in which power-holders were gathering. Thus the protest camps retained some of the function of the military camps from which they genealogically derived. They were a kind of guerrilla bivouac providing logistical and psychological support for the battles ahead, places in which to find nourishment and shelter, and to embolden the rebel army before its assault on the enemy lines. Their location bespoke this function being at "striking distance" from the target, be it the site of a global summit, the HQ of a global institution, a military installation, a migrant detention centre, a coal-powered station, an airport, or other sources of greenhouse gases.

From the outside anti-globalisation camps appeared as militant spaces, marked out from the surrounding ground. They were often defended by heavy barricades because of the fear of overnight police raids, and displayed aggressive visual messaging. Consider for example the protest camps erected during the Rostock anti-G8 protests of 2007. Around the perimeter of the protest camps of Reddelich and North Rostock stood an array of defensive structures, including wooden observation towers resembling those of an American fort in the Old West. At the main gate of the Reddelich camp stood a sign with the words "You are now leaving the EU", the same words found at the entrance of the anarchist commune of Christiania in Copenhagen, in a caustic claim to extra-territoriality. Within both camps "No Photographs" signs abounded, reflecting a fear of police infiltrators and of the identification and prosecution of protesters. Yet even more militant was the setting of the anti-NATO protest camp in Strasbourg I attended in April 2009. To get to the camp, participants had to pass three massive barricades made of destroyed cars and salvaged street furniture, on a tarmac punctuated by large burn-marks and small piles of broken glass left behind by Molotov bombs hurled at police forces. An appealing adrenaline experience for those of an activist mind-set, perhaps, but a sight certain to scare off pretty much anybody else.

The new citizenist protest repertoire developed by the movement of the squares incorporated many elements of the anti-globalisation movement's postmodern techniques, including the emphasis on creativity, improvisation, and the search for authentic relationships. However, as part of the movement's attempt to appeal to the majority, it shed the countercultural and inward looking attitude, as well as the antagonism and militancy displayed in many anti-globalisation actions. Firstly, the protest camp shifted from a communal and countercultural space to a public space, a redefinition aided by its central location and reassuring external appearance. Secondly, the protest camp became a site for a ritual of popular communion; for the display of various acts of solidarity aimed at breaking down the barriers between different sections of society and between individuals.

"Yes we camp!"

If toponyms such as Tahrir, Puerta del Sol, Syntagma, and Taksim have become synonymous with the movement of the squares it is because these iconic public squares became the centre of its political dramaturgy, the nodal point around which the protest narrative—centring on the invocation of the agora as the classical scene of democracy—was woven. Obviously the 2011 protests were not just limited to protest camps; they encompassed demonstrations and various forms of "mass direct action". However, except for a handful of major protest events, for example Occupy Wall Street's 15 October 2011 occupation of Times Square in New York or the largest 15-M marches, more traditional demonstrations paled in importance and public visibility in comparison with the myriad activities (assemblies, meetings, debates, community services, and so on) conducted within protest camps, which became the ingredients of a public spectacle represented in the news media and in activist media. In the new repertoire of contention the protest camp was no longer just a support tactic, a logistical infrastructure, or an intermediate stage towards large actions and demonstrations. It was not a prologue to protest; it was the manifestation of protest itself.

Protesters used the tactic of the protest camp in a way that reflected the citizenist spirit of inclusivity and unity. On the one hand using this tactic often stood to denounce the situation of social emergency in which many people were on the brink of homelessness, of having to "sleep rough" as people did in protest camps. As Patrick Gill of Occupy puts it, the camps came to resemble Hoovervilles, the shanty towns that appeared around the US during the Great Depression and took their name from President Hoover. It was a "burning building" that announced to the public "how bad things really were," in the aftermath of the 2008 crisis. On the other hand, this tactic also had a larger ambition: the reclamation of public space as a necessary pre-condition for a popular re-composition of a fragmented and atomised society. The meaning of protest camps was informed by the diagnosis of a society suffering from a lack of public space, thanks to the neoliberal trend towards privatisation and individualism, leading to a generalised crisis of civic life, as depicted in the US by authors such as Michael Sorkin, Don Mitchell, and Robert Putnam.[12] Many protesters felt that "there is no public space for people to gather", and that "the public spaces that we have are not public"; that is, what we today call public spaces are in fact better described as spaces of transit and consumption, rather than as spaces of assembly and genuine interaction.

Public squares were chosen as sites of occupation because in the social imaginary these squares have always been "the people's place"; the sites in which the People is visible in its extreme heterogeneity, and the sites in which the People has repeatedly manifested itself through history as a political force, against tyranny and for democracy. As 25-year-old Mahmoud al-Banna, an Egyptian socialist activist argues, "Revolutions in past centuries all took place in squares, because there is this idea of all the people going there for political reasons in moments of crisis." In this context, the protest camp shed its erstwhile function as a militant outpost in conflict space and became something more akin to the Athenian agorā: a public space in which ordinary citizens, the 99 per cent, could meet, discuss and find common ground against the oligarchic power oppressing them all. Shawn Carrié, a 24-year-old Occupy activist in New York, argues that the aim of the protests was to "reactivate a public space" where there could "be real interaction in person, and in conversation, with actual people, reaching out to people." Similarly Vicente Martin, a 30-year-old squatter and a participant in the Indignados camp in Barcelona, asserts that the camp's main function was to be a place in which "people can meet, can discuss and can share." Brazilian student and protester Mariana Marchesi argues that while the movement in São Paulo did not use protest camps, it was animated by the same desire for reclamation of public space, whereby "the Avenida Paulista [the most important thoroughfare] became the symbol of that space that we wanted. We did not have squares, but we had the Avenida Paulista."

The narrative of the protest camp as an agora was borne out by the central location of protest camps in the 2011 protest wave. While anti-globalisation protest camps were often set up in remote areas, the encampments of the movement of the squares "picked the most central sites of major urban centres", according to John Jordan, a veteran of Reclaim the Streets and the Climate Camp movement; places like Tahrir Square in Cairo, Puerta del Sol in Madrid, Syntagma Square in Athens, and Taksim Square in Istanbul: areas of high visibility, under the constant watch of the media, but also sites of heavy traffic at the intersection of mass transit systems. On the one hand the central location of the encampments stemmed from considerations of convenience. The aim was to make the camp as open and accessible as possible to supporters and sympathisers without asking them to travel hundreds of miles to participate in a protest event. One could say that if the logic of the Narodniks was "let's go to the people", the logic of the protest camps was more along the lines of "let the people come to us". On the other hand,

Image 5.1: Protester reading a leaflet carrying protest demands in Tahrir Square, Cairo, November 2011 (Courtesy Lara Pelaez Madrid)

it served to express these movements' claim to the imaginary Centre of the People and of the Nation—its pulsing heart—as suggested in the description of Tahrir by Mohammed Mido, an Egyptian activist, as "the centre of the country and of the revolution."

The centrality of protest camps in the protest dramaturgy has been reinforced by their all-out character; their conveying of an ultimatum against the establishment. All the 2011 camps were explicitly or implicitly underpinned by the idea that the occupation would continue until "all our demands are met", as we saw in this chapter's epigraph. In this they sought to emulate the Egyptian Revolution, whose protracted fight against Mubarak's dictatorship ultimately resulted in his resignation on 11 February 2011. As Anastasia, a 28-year-old participant in the Aganaktismenoi movement explains, the fascination with the example of Tahrir led to the fact that, "people wanted to stay as long as they could [in Syntagma Square]. That was not something we did in previous movements." The "long haul" character of these protest gatherings, and the way it evoked a spirit of heroic collective determination, earned them the attention of the news media for protracted periods. While anti-globalisation protests only attracted news coverage for a few days at a time, coin-

Image 5.2: A moment of relaxation in the protest encampment in Puerta del Sol, Madrid, May 2011 (Courtesy Lara Pelaez Madrid)

ciding with counter-summit protests, and often in connection with episodes of violence, the 2010s occupations managed to harness attention for much longer, with, most surprisingly, the coverage predominantly focusing on the positive and constructive aspects of these movements: their grievances, their spirit, and their democratic practices.

The framing of protest encampments as new agoras was accompanied by an emphasis on openness, publicness, and inclusivity towards prospective participants. This was clearly visible in their external appearance, and their abandonment of the militant and aggressive look and feel of neo-anarchist camps in the anti-globalisation movement. All camps from Tahrir to Syntagma had, by necessity, a rather haphazard layout, reflecting their having been erected at break-neck speed and often under the watch of the police. Despite their chaotic impromptu and amateur character, activists were careful to avoid the camps looking dangerous, decadent, dirty, or scruffy. On the contrary they wanted them to feel as safe and accessible as possible so that they could attract citizens of different backgrounds and make them feel that it was "their" movement. Reflecting this emphasis on inclusivity, protest camps were for the most part free of the intimidating markers of militancy and recognisable political symbols that were omnipresent in anti-globalisation camps. Furthermore, they did not usually feature defensive structures separating them from the surrounding world. The exceptions were those erected by police, for example the barriers erected around Zuccotti Park by the New York Police Department, and when there was a justifiable demand for security, as in Tahrir Square, where activists set up check-points at the entrances so as to prevent provocateurs from carrying weapons into the square.

The internal layout of protest camps was deliberately arranged to fulfil this aim of inclusivity. Activists wanted the camp to attract passers-by; they wanted them to gain a direct experience of the camp, visiting it, talking with people and, for those so inclined, participating in assemblies and meetings. The protest camp was something to be experienced directly argues Nora, an Egyptian activist, who at the height of the uprising exhorted a sceptical friend: "Just go to Tahrir Square, just go to the square and watch for yourself. Just don't stay at home and watch [it on] television." Anna Turull, a 27-year-old architect who participated in the Indignados movement in Barcelona, recounts how while initially participants wanted to clump all the tents at the centre of the square, they eventually decided that that layout would have appeared too defensive and opted to line them along the square's circular edges, with wide gaps in-between to allow people to enter easily "because we did not need to defend ourselves from anyone." The fact that the camp was a space to be visited and explored was made explicit by the paths cutting across these small tent cities, sometimes named, as in the case of the Zuccotti Park occupation, after inspiring political figures of the past, from Gandhi to Kropotkin, as well as by the display of maps of the camp, so as to allow for an easy circulation of visitors.

Counter to what happened in the anti-globalisation camps, the 2011 encampments also had a very positive attitude towards photographing and filming. Far from displaying "No Photographs" signs, as was customary in anti-globalisation camps, they strongly encouraged photography and filming for the benefit of those at home, sometimes termed "internet occupiers". For example, one could often see protesters deliberately holding cardboard signs to allow passers-by to take a snap. Consequently protest camps looked like a political attraction; a family-friendly revolutionary theme park or a fair from a possible utopian future, beyond the present neoliberal predicament. Indeed, some militant activists complained that camps had turned into an "activist zoo" where ordinary people would go to see if protesters were really as scruffy as they looked on TV. Yet this "spectacular" element of protest camps was also instrumental to their mission of representing the people to itself, or to act as a "people's stage", as suggested by a message I encountered in the Zuccotti Park occupation.

A moment of popular communion

Enthusiasm, amazement, happiness, compassion, brotherhood, magic, and camaraderie: all terms that frequently recur in participant testimonies when asked to report their experience in protest camps. This lexicon bespeaks the intensely emotional atmosphere that hung over the tents, plastic tables and chairs, and sleeping mats and sleeping bags of the 2011 occupations. Spanish activists famously claimed that the 15-M was an "emotional state" and they celebrated the way the taking of the square had led them to a collective awakening. Imbued with such strong emotional content—a powerful mixture of indignation, anger and hope— protest camps became the venue for a collective experience of community, togetherness and solidarity, which made them appear like something between a popular festival and a political boot camp, or as 34-year-old Turkish activist Harun Burak puts it, "It was as if the Soviets had gone to Woodstock."

Protest camps can be understood as the sites of a particular kind of political ritual: a popular communion geared at bringing together the divided people. This political liturgy is reminiscent of the moments of collective effervescence described by Emile Durkheim, examining the events in which tribal communities gather to reassert their common culture and whose participants experience intense feelings of common bonding.[13] In addition, it echoes the project of a "civic religion", proposed by Jean-Jacques Rousseau,[14] as a set of symbolic practices aimed at constructing solidarity and mutual responsibility among all free citizens, such as the ritual of the planting of the revolutionary tree during the French revolution. One could see the unifying function of the encampments in the way they attempted to break the many cultural and social barriers dividing the body politic, how they endeavoured to overcome the condition of loneliness and isolation condemning citizens to apathy and depression, and their attempt to construct concrete forms of popular solidarity, starting from the satisfaction of the basic needs of those living in and visiting the camp.

Due to the diverse cross-section of society they attracted, protest camps allowed participants the possibility of questioning the manifold divisions cutting through the body of contemporary complex societies, divisions suspected by activists of facilitating the oligarchy's strategy of "divide and rule". Ahmed Sabry, a 41-year-old Egyptian activist, said in reference to Tahrir Square, "We created a space, where all our differences were gone and we had just one goal, we wanted the downfall of the regime and it would stop only when Mubarak was gone". Similarly Richard, a 42-year-old priest and Occupy Wall Street participant, described Zuccotti Park as "a space where we tear down the walls and the barriers that have divided us, where we question the prejudices we have about one another". Indeed, one of the most moving spectacles of the occupations was seeing previous antagonists eventually coming to terms with one another, in the name of a common goal and in opposition to a common enemy: Christians and Muslims fighting together and protecting each other's prayer times during the Egyptian Revolution; feminists and more traditional women finding ways to discuss their differing views of femininity; people of progressive and conservative beliefs, leftists and nationalists gathering in the same square, though sometimes at opposite ends, as in Athens; and poor people discussing their condition with well-off activists. Harun Burak relates his amazement at seeing "Kurdish nationalists, and Fascist Kemalists who would have normally strangled each other" co-existing in Taksim Square.[15]

Protest encampments became a space wherein different demographics mobilised by this movement—such as the lost generation, the squeezed middle, and the new poor discussed in Chapter 1—encountered their social and political "Other" only to almost invariably discover them as an unexpected ally, someone also affected by systemic social and political problems, and therefore sharing an enmity towards the real "Other": the political and economic oligarchies responsible for their common suffering. These encounters provided participants with concrete proof of the possibility of acting together despite significant differences in background, worldview and values. Ayşegül, a 29-year-old Turkish participant, describes her experience in the square and the enthusiasm experienced in witnessing very different people finding a way to work together:

> The Gezi protests were the happiest moments in my life. Because I saw a lot of different people and different ideas, because we can meet each other. We did not push each other. We are all holding our hands. We just told each other

we can be different, but we can work together fruitfully. We are different and we have a lot of problems, but we can be together.

Shawn Carrié describes the "thousand realisations" such encounters elicited among protesters in Zuccotti Park and hundreds of protest camps all over the world:

> You meet people who are homeless and they are dirty and smelly, but they are some of the smartest people you have ever met. Also all your ideas of ordinary people as racists or homophobic fall down. Meeting people changes your ideas, you start to question what we do in the world. You start thinking about if it has to be that way.

This experience of encountering the social "Other" had a profound impact on many participants, concretely demonstrating the possibility of constructing a popular alliance against the oligarchy.

Equally important was the function of protest camps as a remedy against social atomisation: the painful experience of extreme individualisation and loneliness that constitutes the hallmark of neoliberal societies. As José Ordóñez, an Indignados participant, reports, within the movement the saying went that "where there is the 15-M [movement] solitude disappears." Constructing a convivial space comprising various occasions for socialising, from debates, assemblies, and popular dinners to casual conversations among strangers, camps acted as spaces where individuals could overcome their isolation, construct new personal relationships, and realise that those which had first appeared to them as individual problems were in fact the reflection of systemic issues, only to be resolved through the pursuit of collective action. Nora Shalaby, an Egyptian activist, recounts the strange feeling of conviviality experienced in Tahrir Square during the eighteen-day revolution of 2011, explaining that while—in the gargantuan masses gathered in the squares—one might have felt a stranger among strangers, "You felt as if you knew everybody in the square, and everybody in the square knew you. Every man and every woman were more like your brothers and sisters. You were not afraid. You felt that this is how the world should be." Casually meeting other people in the camp sharing the same problems and the same preoccupations relieved many from the feeling of isolation that had long paralysed and disempowered them. As Caiti, a 22-year-old student and Occupy participant in New York, said, it was "important as a space to meet between different people to share their grievances. Because there are many people like you who have lost a job, or cannot find one and don't know what to do." This sharing of experiences engendered for many a feeling of relief, as recounted by Jorge Izquierdo, an Indignado in Barcelona: "There are many people who are saying, 'Finally! I was tired of thinking I was the only one saying that it was enough and telling the other people, don't you realise what is going on?'"

Nowhere was this experience of collectivity and mutual empathy more vivid than in those moments of collective affection that interspersed the everyday life of protest camps, giving those present goose bumps and reinforcing their commitment to the movement. Vicente Martin recounts an assembly in which people ended up hugging each other: "It seemed to me a necessary gesture. It might be hippie, it might be romantic, but I think that we needed that. Because we lack love, we lack physical contact, we lack honesty." Georgios, a 46-year-old participant in the protest in Syntagma, recounts how on the first night of the protest the crowd was taken by a moment of collective weeping, understandable considering the dire economic situation faced by many Greeks in the aftermath of 2008: "We all wept, because there are all these problems that you live individually, but then you come to realise that there are many people who are living the same problems, and you feel that you are not alone." Thus, the camps also acted as psycho-therapeutic spaces, which relieved people from a sense of guilt about their own misfortunes, and provided participants the sense of being cared for and looked after by others, something especially important in countries like Greece where economic disarray had led to an increase in suicides and people suffering from depression.

The push for collective solidarity had its most concrete results in the self-organised services offered by protest camps[16]—sanitation, security, education, libraries, crèches, kitchens, clinics, media, and so on. These services, like similar services in anti-globalisation protest camps, were set up first and foremost to satisfy the immediate needs of the occupiers: those actually living in the camp, and those supporting it day by day. To deliver these services the movement relied on the generosity of individual participants, who brought food, medicines, and electric equipment, or ordered pizza deliveries for the occupiers. Ayşegül, a participant in the Gezi protests, recounts how participants shared everything at their disposal:

> We did not buy anything. We did not use any money. There were some people who made breakfast, other people who brought medicines. We felt that we are a people, we are a community, and everybody should bring something there and just use that. People shared with other people what they had. People

learned to share stuff. I have tea and you have biscuits, I give you tea, and you give some biscuits. People were so happy because everybody offered things to one another.

As Shimri Zameret, a 33-year-old Occupy London protester noted, the fact that camps provided people with free accommodation and free or inexpensive food allowed them "time to concentrate on political campaigning and protest organising". However, they also had a more general and public purpose, catering for the needs of all visitors to camp and of the many poor and homeless people who gathered there, and embodying the movement's affirmation of mutual help and solidarity. Stephanie, an Occupy participant, explains the understanding behind these services: "We are upset about the fact that there is no universal healthcare, OK, there is a health tent here. Or we are angry that there is no housing… OK, there is housing here. People are without food, OK, there is some food here." Protest encampments proposed a reversal of the everyday experience of neoliberal societies at times of economic crisis and austerity, in which state services were on the decline. In so doing they incarnated the aspiration of constructing a society based on solidarity and reciprocity, rather than greed and competition.

The camp under siege

Square encampments were a largely successful tactic. They afforded activists a resonant and flexible format of protest, easily reproducible in different countries, that allowed them to effectively dramatise the connection between the movement and the people it stood to represent: the 99 per cent, the majority, the People; the grievances raised (poverty, homelessness, disenfranchisement); and the movement's values (empathy, community, solidarity). However, they could also be a liability, sucking enormous energy out of participants and making the movement a sitting duck for the inevitable arrival of police repression. This tactic frequently became an object of fixation and an obstacle, preventing the movements from developing into new forms. While the protest camp was the venue where all the enthusiasm that allowed these movements to emerge was accumulated and concentrated, it was often also the point where much of that enthusiasm was eventually expended.

Protest encampments raised serious questions of sustainability for the movement. They tested the determination and strength of their participants and especially of the "full time occupiers" who dedicated all of their time to the movement, sleeping in the protest camps, dealing with their everyday maintenance, participating in various working groups and committees and organising most of the camps' activities. The everyday life of the occupations involved a considerable amount of labour and stress, which in the long run became particularly taxing for the most committed participants, with some camps lasting many weeks or even months, leading many to exhaustion and "activist burnout".

Referring to his experience in Tahrir Square during the revolution, Ahmed Sharqawi, a 22-year-old university student and activist in the 6 April Youth Movement, reported how the many enjoyable aspects of the life in the camp, such as those discussed in the previous section, were balanced out by considerable downsides: "Life in the camp is difficult. You get little sleep, you are in constant danger, and there are some crazy people and thieves going around, and you need to constantly look after your own stuff." Certainly the experience of protesters in Tahrir, who were under the constant threat of the police, pro-government thugs and even snipers, is an extreme case in point. But it hints at a more general trend: the wear produced by constantly being in a space with no separation between the private and the public, except for the thin surface of one's tent, in which meetings and activities are held. All sorts of conflicts can arise and, worse still, the threat of a police attack is a constant. It is telling that the Nuit Debout protesters decided not to have a protest camp. As argued by Baki Youssofou, a 37-year-old organiser, "Nuit Debout is not an occupation because we believe the movements of 2011 have been defeated precisely because they were occupations. The problem is that when you occupy, the army or the police can always come and evict you from the square."

The inevitable fatigue from a long occupation also contributed towards driving a wedge between various categories of participants. For example, during my visit to Zuccotti Park in early November 2011, I met a protester who sat on a step leading to the exit of the small square and held a hand-written sign that said that he was striking. He complained about what he called "hipster protesters", middle class participants, who never slept in the camp and joined it only in the afternoon to take part in its public activities, such as assemblies and working groups. This episode was illustrative of a wider tendency towards class division inside the park, with the East Side of the camp occupied by middle class professionals, students and graduates and the West Side of the camp by the poor and homeless. Thus, far from being an ideal and utopian space, an enthusiastic community where the evil of the world could be suspended, as it seemed during moments of collective emotional effervescence, the camp contained within itself all the contradictions of an unequal society. It was not a green land set apart from the "desert of the real" but rather, as some protesters described it, a "microcosm of society", a random and uncontrolled sample of society in which one could see on a smaller scale both its contradictions and potential.

An additional problem raised by protest camps was the relationship with the local community. Despite all the attempts to make them as peaceful and orderly as possible, in line with the movement's desire to appear reasonable, the occupations inevitably generated considerable disruption for people living and working in the area. Among the issues that most bothered local communities were the continuous crowding; the presence of riot police in the area; the tendency of camps to attract the downtrodden of society, including people with mental health, drug and homelessness issues; restrictions to traffic and public transportation; and drops in revenues from tourism-related business for shopkeepers, hotels and the like. A good example of these frictions was the controversy surrounding a group of drummers gathered on the West Side of Zuccotti Park who created serious frictions with the local community playing at all hours of the day, including during general assemblies. The local community board repeatedly asked protesters to stop the continuous noise, also mentioning the disruption caused to children at a nearby school. However it took the occupation several days to come to some compromise agreement with the drummers, who justified themselves by arguing that drumming for them amounted to a religious practice.

It is significant that despite all these problems, when the possibility of disbanding the camp was raised in the occupations that lasted longer, strong internal opposition made the move impossible. Only in Egypt and Spain did protesters lift the occupations of their own accord. Tahrir was dismantled after Mubarak's departure, because the majority of the movement considered that to be a clear victory (a reading that would later prove over-optimistic). The Puerta del Sol occupation folded up on the basis that it had become unsustainable—it was starting to alienate the local community, and the bulk of protest participants were well beyond the point of exhaustion—but more importantly, the occupiers recognised that it was time to evolve "beyond the squares". In all the other cases the occupations erected by the 2011 and 2013 movements ended as a consequence of state repression. The occupation in Syntagma Square was violently evicted by the police after sixty days of occupation, and the same fate was meted upon protest camps in the US, which fell victim to a coordinated wave of evictions in November 2011 that hit Oakland, Denver, Albany, Salt Lake City, and many other sites. The Taksim protest camp was evicted on 15 June 2013 after eleven days of occupation, by a vast and violent police operation.

The strong attachment to the tactic of the protest camp, despite all the problems, reflected its great organisational importance as an "anchoring point" for a movement otherwise deprived of solid organisational structures, and therefore always at risk of drifting where the stream took it. Occupy activist Andrew Conner argues that, in New York, the importance of the protest camp was that, "it was a place that people knew they could go to and where to find us." Since the eviction of the park, the movement lost that sense of orientation afforded by its physical presence, with a disruptive effect upon the movement: "People [were] not able to get involved. They [were] not able to find information about the movement [and be active within it]." The aftermath of the raid confirmed that activists had been right in their initial diagnosis of the lack of a public space, since the net result was that once again "nobody ha[d] a place, there [was] no place to have civic discussions with other citizens," as argued by Shawn Carrié.

While movements such as the Spanish Indignados partly managed to evolve beyond the camp, adopting new tactics, such as the popular marches of the "citizens' tides" [*mareas ciudadanas*], most others, including Occupy Wall Street and the protests in Turkey, did not manage to extricate themselves from the occupied square and its communal experience. Once deprived of the material and symbolic support of the protest camp, protesters seemed to be back at square one, without a public space and therefore also without a movement.

The camp as commune and people's stage

Two competing narratives shaped the life of protest camps, proposing different explanations of what they meant and stood for. For the more anarchist-inclined activists, protest camps were a commune; self-standing rebel islands on which to erect an activist utopia here and now, in which to realise an "ideal democratic and participatory system"—as described by Patrick Gill, a 32-year-old activist in the Public Relations Working Group in New York—and hope that somehow it would survive to grow and be joined by other communes the world over. For those subscribing more to a democratic populist view—whom anarchist writers like David Graeber and Mark Bray disdainfully call "liberals"—it was something altogether different: not so much a space, but an event; not an autonomous commune, but a people's stage; a public ritual that could rally an otherwise dispersed citizenry and thematise the numerous challenges facing society, as the first stage in a total reclamation of society and political institutions away from the grip of oligarchic power.

The anarchist view of the protest camp as a commune, autonomous space, or rebel island amidst the tempestuous waves of state and capital, was (as we have discussed) influential for the anti-globalisation movement and its understanding of occupied spaces. The camp was thereby conceived as a self-governed space, autonomous from the surrounding territory that constantly tried to encroach it once again. In the 2012 award-winning documentary *The Square*, Ahmed, a participant in the protests in Cairo, says in a moment of illumination that, "This is our space. This might just be an acre of space, but it is an acre we control."[17] Protesters in Egypt often referred to Tahrir Square as *Dawla el-Tahrir* [the Nation, or State, of Tahrir], a country smaller than the Vatican whose borders were marked by the checkpoints erected at the square's entrances. Yet, as related by many of my Egyptian interviewees, this fetishisation of Tahrir—this idea that "Tahrir is the Revolution"—contributed to activists losing touch with the sentiment of the Egyptian street and the priorities of the majority of the population, increasingly remote from the activists in their acre-sized free republic.

A similar situation developed around the protest camp in Taksim Square, which some protesters referred as the "Taksim Commune" in reference to the Paris Commune of 1871, as some anarchist activists were concerned that it was not really an autonomous and self-sufficient space. Firstly, many of the people who participated in the camp did not interrupt their everyday routines; they continued to go to work and joined the occupiers only in the afternoon. Secondly, all the material resources expended in the camp—food, tents, kitchen equipment, and so on—were brought from the outside world (though one wonders what possible alternative to this there could have been), which bothered those who went as far as entertaining the bizarre notion of the camp as a biotope—an independent habitat—in which people could produce everything they needed.

This conception of the camp as an autonomous commune—informed by the anarchist imaginary of occupied spaces, squats, and social centres—thus reflected the most counterproductive elements of neo-anarchist culture and its influence on the movement. Unable to imagine more broadly beyond that which could be immediately touched or experienced, it also was marked by primitivism: the tendency to look for models of a utopian alternative in historical, or indigenous, societies and villages. It was an obstacle to the ability of the movement to connect with the wider population, leading to a juxtaposition in Turkish popular discourse between Gezi and Gazi, a poor neighbourhood in Istanbul and a base of support for Erdoğan, where the protests were overwhelmingly viewed with hostility. In fact, this narrative of autonomy was contradicted by slogans that emphasised being untethered to any specific place, as in the Turkish, "Everywhere is Taksim, everywhere is resistance."

The populist view of the camp took a radically different route. Instead of seeing the camp as a sort of extra-territorial domain, a discrete area under the control of the movement, it approached it as a people's stage—a space of representation rather than just of participation; not so much a place but an event. In this view the essence of the protest camp did not revolve around its autonomy, or its capacity to sketch an approximate outline of a social order without coercion and without government. Rather, it saw the camp as a symbolic ritual, whose value was found not in the direct experience of those living in the camp, but rather in the relationship occupations constructed with society at large, and the way they acted as a point of identification; a moment of re-composition of the Citizenry, otherwise divided by innumerable barriers. According to this view the camp itself was not the embryonic embodiment of a utopian society, but simply a stage from which the present dystopia could be denounced and a future utopia articulated; the camp was merely a means to an end, not an end in itself as anarchists may have desired. Thus rather than a prefigurative politics—seeking to construct an alternative society here and now in the concrete experience of communal life in the protest camp—the populist view of the camp was more akin to a prophecy about the coming of a "new politics", starting with the moral resolve of the occupations and progressively permeating the entire texture of society.

7

THE PEOPLE'S PARLIAMENT

The General Assembly is a gathering of people committed to making decisions based upon a collective agreement or "consensus." There is no single leader or governing body of the General Assembly—everyone's voice is equal. Anyone is free to propose an idea or express an opinion as part of the General Assembly.

New York City General Assembly (NYCGA) description[1]

"Yo tambien soy una indignada" [I am also an indignant]. So said a woman in her mid-forties talking about the difficulties in juggling work and family life because of cuts to childcare, enacted by the government as part of its austerity programme. Person after person took to the microphone in Puerta del Sol, Central Madrid, in a Sunday afternoon assembly during the first days of the occupation. The second to speak was a man in his late thirties talking about the problems he was experiencing with his job at an IT company nearing bankruptcy. The third was a man in his fifties; his son had duly completed his university studies but could not find a job amidst the pitiful economic situation. All these speeches—lasting for just two minutes each in accordance with the assembly's rules, designed to ensure as many different people as possible could participate in the discussion—varied greatly in their actual content, as diverse as the people expressing them. Regardless of the heterogeneity of backgrounds and grievances, all interventions ended with the same ritual formula, asserting the adherence of the speakers to a common movement: *"Yo tambien soy un(a) indignado/a"*: "Me too—I am an indignant".

181

This scene in central Madrid on 21 May 2011, similar to others I observed in protest camps in Barcelona, Athens, New York, and Paris, provides a snapshot of the practice that best embodies the spirit of popular democracy of the movements of the squares: large meetings, described as "popular assemblies" or "general assemblies," which had become a signature tactic of the protest wave. Criticising an unresponsive political system and the politicians who had betrayed them, protesters set to work by formulating a grassroots democratic system that could embody their demand for a real and better democracy. From Spain to the US and later France, most of these movements adopted a fairly standard model which inherited much from the culture of horizontal decision-making in the anti-globalisation movement and the long tradition of participatory direct democracy that began with the New Left in the 1960s. This encompassed popular assemblies, large plenary meetings open to all citizens, as well as a panoply of smaller committees and working groups: a self-organised movement bureaucracy responsible for more specific and practical issues. These meetings abided by the principle of "consensus"—aiming at achieving a collective agreement among all those involved, instead of using hierarchical structures and majority vote—and adopted a number of other typical procedures of neo-anarchist movements, including the presence of a facilitator moderating the discussion and the use of a number of hand signs, such as wiggling hands pointing up to express approval, pointing down to express disapproval, and crossed arms to block a decision one disagrees with.

At the peak of the mobilisation these meetings—described by Azzellini and Sitrin as "mass horizontal assemblies"[2] to reflect both their mass scale in terms of participation, and their principles of horizontality and consensus-based decision-making—achieved remarkable success. They attracted great numbers and enthusiasm with the larger ones, in big occupations in metropolitan centres, sometimes hosting several hundred or even thousands of people, including many outsiders with no prior experience of protest participation. Furthermore, these movements also created hundreds of smaller assemblies in urban neighbourhoods or towns, many of which survived after the evictions of the main protest camps, thus making the gatherings accessible to people who could not visit the larger occupations.

Popular assemblies were spectacular demonstrations of the power of direct democracy, and of the enthusiasm it can generate among many ordinary citizens, against the background of a post-democratic society in which opportunities to voice one's opinion and participate in collective decision-making are scarce. They stood to demonstrate the open, work-in-progress character of these movements; the fact that they, in contrast to many previous movements, did not start with the assumption that they had a solution, but proposed to create arenas of public discussion where common solutions could be identified. The popular assemblies thus became, possibly even more than the protest camps, the movement's signature practice, that which most strikingly embodied their idea of a radical politics of citizenship, aiming at re-democratising society from the bottom up, starting with a return to face-to-face discussion in public space, which constitutes the most basic custom of democratic life.

Table 7.1: Democratic practices in comparison

	Anti-globalisation movement	*Movement of the squares*
Democratic practices	• Social forums • Spokescouncils • Movement assemblies	• General assemblies • Working groups • Committees
Orientations	• Autonomy • Diversity • De-centralisation • Horizontality	• Horizontality • Inclusiveness • Popular sovereignty • Unity of general will

In analysing popular assemblies in this chapter, I aim to explore elements of both continuity and difference vis-à-vis previous cycles of struggle, and in particular the anti-globalisation movement, from which the 2011 gatherings drew much in terms of procedure and ethos. I focus on three aspects: the new centrality of the popular assembly as a "people's parliament"; the radical openness of the assembly, with its aim of including the entire citizenry; and the tensions between the mass scale of participation in assemblies and the use of consensus procedures originally devised for small group meetings.

First, counter to previous movements' push for de-centralisation, the popular assembly format of the movement of the squares reflected a renewed desire to construct centres of decision-making, which might unify the movement around collective decisions binding for all participants. Popular assemblies convened in the occupied squares, and in particular those held in these movements' "capital cities" (Madrid,

Barcelona, New York, Athens, Istanbul), became in the movement's imagination a "people's parliament", an organ that could (if slightly hyperbolically) claim itself to be a legislature of popular sovereignty, the latter hitherto betrayed by elected delegates inside parliament.

Second, a further novelty of these assemblies was their radical openness and ability to attract a diversified cohort of participants. While in the anti-globalisation movement assemblies were an internal process, involving those already part of the activist community, the assemblies of the move-ment of the squares were framed from the start as "popular assemblies", and therefore open to people from very different walks of life. This inclu-sivity was facilitated by the adoption of the procedure and ethos of con-sensus with its emphasis on the importance of listening to other people's opinions. Furthermore, it derived from the assemblies' locations: highly visible public spaces, often at the centre of large urban areas, rather than social centres and similar activist spaces as in previous mobilisations.

Third, I show how this mass character of assemblies, and the diverse background of participants, raised problems of efficiency and sustaina-bility, with meetings regularly disrupted and running overtime, ultimately contributing to their rapid decline. These organisational quandaries were the result of a "crisis of growth"; the fact that the swell in popular par-ticipation had ultimately overwhelmed the capacity of decision-making structures. Some of these movements shifted to more simplified proce-dures like majority vote to cope with the mass scale of participation, but this only partly solved the problem. However, the dysfunctionality of popular assemblies ultimately contributed to the movements alienating many of the ordinary people they had initially managed to attract, and ultimately depriving these movements of a clear strategic direction beyond the squares. Thus, while popular assemblies became the most recognisable signature of these movements, widely covered in main-stream news and activist media alike, they were also synonymous with the movements' shortcomings.

The path of grassroots democracy

Meetings, assemblies, caucuses and similar forms of discussion and deci-sion-making constitute a familiar feature of virtually all social movements, as spaces where individuals need to come to collective agreements about the issues affecting them, investigate possible political solutions, and deal with the nitty-gritty of organisation.[3] The labour movement of the nineteenth and twentieth centuries eventually opted for a bureaucratic and hierarchical model of decision-making, as embodied in its most important organisations: trade unions and parties, which came to resemble a sort of "state within the state,"[4] from which the labour movement could progressively prepare for a peaceful conquest of state power, as indeed began with the advent of social democracy in the twentieth century.

This model, often criticised for its oligarchic tendency, as already denounced in 1911 by Robert Michels,[5] became a spectre—the ghost of the Old Left—which continues to elicit suspicion or outright hostility to this day. Against the centralism and bureaucratism of this tradition a number of democratic experiments developed that put an emphasis on de-centralisation, to assert autonomy from oppressive large-scale institutions, such as the state, parties, or trade unions. Anarchist movements had already, since the nineteenth and early twentieth century, developed an alternative blueprint, based on the idea of council democracy, and federations of communes in which workers would organise from the bottom up. This project of an alternative grassroots democracy was revived during the upheavals of the 1960s in which the New Left, criticising bureaucratic organisations, developed an alternative organisational model based on notions of autonomy and de-centralisation, and on the principle of consensus.

While 1968 will forever be associated with large assemblies in the occupied universities, as in the Sorbonne or the University of Frankfurt, its aftermath saw the move towards de-centralisation, with large formal organisations such as Students for a Democratic Society in the US, and Lotta Continua in Italy, deciding to dissolve themselves to be replaced by thousands of different collective initiatives and campaigns, united by their immersion in a common countercultural and activist scene. The autonomist movements in Italy and Germany became a rhizome of collectives, campaigns, occupied buildings, festivals, co-operatives, and militant groups, immersed in their local territory: the inverse of the centralism of Left parties and trade unions. Similarly in the US, the movements of the 1970s and 1980s acquired a molecular and diffuse structure, whose basic organisational unit was the affinity group: small groups of between five and fifteen people who shared a common vision or collective campaign, and participated together in demonstrations and direct actions.[6]

This trend towards de-centralisation and diffuseness was compounded by the adoption of consensus-based decision-making in assemblies, in place of majority rule. Consensus decision-making can be described as an ethics and praxis that involves the reaching of a common agreement, through taking into account the positions of all participants. Instead of trying to impose a majority decision on everybody, consensus decision-making is concerned with reaching arrangements that everybody in the assembly can live with. As Graeber explains, "the essence of consensus is just that everyone should be able to weigh in equally on a decision, and no one should be bound by a decision they detest."[7] When adopting a "pure" consensus methodology, it is sufficient even for one person to "veto" or "block" the decision and thus for a proposal to be struck down. In order to overcome the objections that are always likely to emerge around certain decisions, assemblies thus typically involve complex negotiations, refinements, adjustments, and a lot of "nudging", until decisions can be made. While in Europe most post-'68 movements did not fully adopt the technicalities of the decision-making procedures developed in the US, they utilised a similar spirit, with assemblies proceeding instead by unanimity.

De-centralisation and consensus informed the emergence of spokescouncils as a central organisational structure for these movements. A spokescouncil is a meeting of "spokes" (short for spokesperson), representing the various groups involved in a campaign or movement. As described by Barbara Epstein, one of the major experts on direct action movements:

> [W]henever a decision had to be made (often several times a day) the clusters would meet to work out their views and arrive at consensus. Anyone who disagreed strongly with a collective decision had the right to block it, although it was understood that this power should not be used unless a fundamental moral issue was at stake. Each cluster sent a "spokes" to a "spokescouncil" that met with the clusters; runners were sent between clusters and spokescouncils, bringing questions to be addressed to the clusters and conveying the decisions to the spokescouncils. Spokes were rotated daily, so as to discourage the emergence of a leading group.[8]

This structure that came to be used in a number of protest movements, from environmental and anti-nuclear protests to the feminist and squatters' movements, is the clearest manifestation of the post-'68 anti-authoritarian movements' move away from the large assembly format and towards smaller groups, coordinated over a greater scale through a networked system, with local units acting as autonomous micro-sovereign bodies organised upward in increasingly large federations.

The anti-globalisation movement inherited much from this tradition and busied itself with creating forms of alternative democracy, to the point that, as argued by David Graeber, its internal organisational forms were its own ideology.[9] As explained by Marianne Maeckelbergh, the movement was a "networked democracy" that aimed at "a decentralisation of various forms of power so that there may be many loci of power."[10] Spokescouncils "were organised on the basis of small group discussions that feed into the larger discussion", so that "everyone has to have the opportunity to speak."[11] The movement mostly eschewed large meetings, considered too unwieldy to moderate using consensus, and not conducive to the sufficient participation of all individuals.

The most important democratic innovation introduced by the global justice movement was without a doubt the Social Forum, a meeting of civil society organisations and activist groups opposed to neoliberalism. The social forum movement, as it was sometimes described, began with the World Social Forum (WSF) in Porto Alegre in Brazil in January 2001, timed to coincide with the World Economic Forum in Davos, Switzerland, where each year businessmen and policymakers meet to discuss how to manage the world economy. The movement then developed into a number of continental social forum events, starting with the Florence European Social Forum of 2002 and various local social forums, which in countries like Italy, Spain and Greece played a very important role in coordinating social movements.

The social forum reflected in its structure the project of a participatory direct democracy, valuing of autonomy and diversity, and suspicious towards all forms of centralisation and strong coordination. These democratic arenas were defined as "open spaces" in which social actors could come together and "inter-link", but without the need to come to a common decision binding for all participants. Thus, the World Social Forum's original charter of principles notably affirmed:

> The meetings of the World Social Forum do not deliberate on behalf of the World Social Forum as a body. No one, therefore, will be authorised, on behalf of any of the editions of the Forum, to express positions claiming to be those of all its participants. The participants in the Forum shall not be called on to take decisions as a body, whether by vote or acclamation, on declarations or

proposals for action that would commit all, or the majority, of them and that propose to be taken as establishing positions of the Forum as a body.[12]

Emphasising its "plural", "diversified" and "de-centralised" nature, the WSF proposed to function—as the name itself suggested—just as "a forum for debate"; a network of different movements, NGOs, and political groups. It rejected the notion that it could be seen as a unified decision-making platform for the global movement, and mostly utilised a format of small thematic meetings running in parallel, with few plenary sessions that could be seen as an assembly of sorts.

In truth, the World Social Forum, among other fringe events such as autonomous activist camps, usually hosted a "movements' assembly" where various decisions—mostly revolving around the global coordination of various single-issue campaigns—could be taken. However, the organisers were always careful to insist that the assembly did not represent the collective will of the Forum. The dominant organisational logic of social forums firmly remained one of "networking", of loose coalition building among pre-existing collective actors, jealously guarding their own autonomy and diversity, and with no desire or hope to unite all the movements around a common strategy.

This de-centralised and molecular organisational model undoubtedly had its merits. It emphasised diversity and authenticity against a traditional Left incapable of catering to the demand for participation, which has instead been the hallmark of practically all new social movements. Furthermore, it revolved around an assertion of autonomy at the smallest possible level, incidentally similar to the Catholic notion of "subsidiarity,"[13] thus providing activists with an effective way to embed their action in local contexts. However, this loose organisational logic led to the inability to make common front in critical situations. This problem was most glaringly seen in the disastrous results of the controversial principle of "diversity of tactics,"[14] widely accepted by anti-globalisation protesters.

The diversity of tactics, often invoked in the context of counter-summit protests, meant that different groups were allowed to decide, independently from one another, their preferred "level of confrontation" with police forces, regardless of the majority opinion of movement participants. Thus, while in global mobilisations most groups and participants would abide by principles of non-violent civil disobedience, other groups such as the anarchist Black Bloc felt legitimised to engage in property destruction and intense fighting with police forces, often with the net result of indiscriminate police reprisal against the entire movement as was most clearly felt during the anti-G8 protests in Genoa of the summer of 2001. The Italian police exploited the public outrage at a number of Black Bloc actions as an excuse to conduct vicious beatings and psychological torture against harmless protesters, in what Amnesty International described as the greatest suspension of human rights in Western Europe since the end of the Second World War.

These painful episodes, which left lasting scars in the collective psyche of social movements, as well as outlining more generally the limits of the de-centralised model of decision-making used by spokescouncils and activist gatherings like the World Social Forum, were something the new generation of activists of 2011, as well as the veterans of the anti-globalisation movement that took part in the movement of the squares, remained cognisant of as they constructed their own organisational structures.

"All power to the assemblies"

While borrowing several procedures and techniques from the anti-globalisation movement, and abiding by the general ethos of neo-anarchist direct democracy, the 2011 activists internalised important lessons about the need for stronger unity and solidarity within social movements, even at the expense of the autonomy of constituent groups. Whereas in the anti-globalisation movement grassroots democracy, especially in the form of spokescouncils and networks, was geared at de-centralisation, at creating "multiple loci of power,"[15] in the 2011 movements the decision-making structures came to revolve around the attempt of creating a unified space of decision-making for the entire movement. The movement of the squares displayed a centralising drive, most clearly in the imaginary of the popular assembly as the centre of the movement. Protesters in the occupied squares wanted the movement to speak with one voice; a voice that comprised all individual voices and fused them into a collective will, which was ultimately considered binding for all those involved in the movement. Thus, participatory decision-making practices initially developed as a means of *de-centralisation* were transformed into a new model of *centrality*.

What will be proposed here is an admittedly idealised "organogram" of the decision-making structure of the movement of the squares that necessarily abstracts from local variations (Figure 7.1). The model most closely reflects the practices of the movements of 2011 in Spain, the US, and Greece, and the 2016 Nuit Debout movement in France. Some of its aspects are also applicable to the movement in Turkey, where different assemblies of various political hues co-existed, but less so in Brazil, where assemblies became a prominent feature of the movement only in Belo Horizonte and a few other cities, and in Egypt, where rallies or more informal discussions predominated.[16]

The organogram shows three basic units: general assemblies, committees, and working groups. At the centre lies the general assembly: the deliberative and, one might say, "legislative" body. It was the organ responsible for making decisions, establishing principles, and representing the collective voice of the movement on important matters. Only

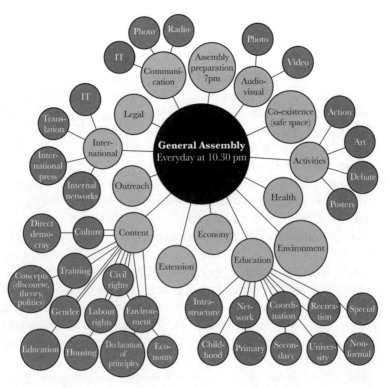

Figure 7.1: The organisational structure of the Barcelona encampment

resolutions and declarations approved by the general assembly could be considered "official" positions of the movement. The assembly branched out into a number of secondary structures located in a subordinate position: committees and working groups. These executive sub-organs acted as delegates of the assembly; as Graeber explains they "[were] created by the General Assembly or larger group, in order to fulfil a specific task or carry out some work."[17] They constituted an executive body that dealt with various specific tasks for the protest camp and the movement as a whole, such as kitchen labour, sanitation, outreach, assembly facilitation, direct action, and so forth. The difference between committees and working groups was fundamentally a temporal one, with working groups tasked with "more specific necessities, often with a fixed term," with the possibility of reforming groups into committees to give them permanence if it appeared that their tasks would require a more durable structure. Thematic committees were akin to parliamentary task forces with a mandate to draft law proposals that would then be discussed in the people's parliament. More practical committees and working groups resembled people's ministries, organising various aspects of the micro-republics erected in the occupied squares.

This organisational structure was at loggerheads with the decision-making practices of the anti-globalisation movement, and in particular spokescouncils and social forums, which followed a de-centralised and networked dynamic whereby small groups fed into larger group discussions. In contrast, the general assembly acted as a means of re-centralisation, locating all the most important decisions at the higher hierarchical levels, while small groups were simply tasked with executive roles. Within this structure popular assemblies—reminiscent of the assemblies described by Rousseau in *The Social Contract*, in turn styled after the *comitia centuriata* and the *comitia tributa*, the local assemblies of the Roman Republic—acquired a clear symbolic and functional centrality. Only decisions taken by the general assembly were considered official and binding for the whole movement, as expressed in the Statement of Autonomy of Occupy Wall Street thus: "Any statement or declaration not released through the General Assembly and made public online at www.nycga.net should be considered independent of Occupy Wall Street."[18]

Perhaps we could see in this structure a paradoxical, inverted form of the Leninist—and prior to this, Jacobin—principle of "democratic centralism". As testified to by slogans such as the Spanish, "All power to the

Image 7.1: Nuit Debout Assembly, Place de la République, Paris, April 2016 (Paolo Gerbaudo)

assemblies", echoing the Russian revolutionary slogan, "All power to the Soviets", popular assemblies reflected a revived craving for a centre of democratic authority that might establish a general will out of thousands of different individual wills, contra the postmodern cult of diversity and autonomy before unity and solidarity. While for Leninists the centre of decision-making was the central committee of the party, away from the turmoil of the crowd, in the movement of the squares thecentre was the masses participating in the popular assembly, that by their presence became delegates of the Citizenry. The assembly was the place in which, to use another Leninist maxim that paradoxically acquired new reso-nance in this context, the movement could unify all the different indi-vidual wills into a collective will, and guarantee that "diversity in debate" would lead to "unity in action", as a fulfilment of its claim to collective solidarity expressed in slogans such as "We Are the 99 Percent".

Vicente Martin, an activist involved with the Indignados in Barcelona, described the general assembly as "the small people's parliament, where people go to speak and give their opinion." It presented itself as the legitimate voice of the People, the seat of a more authentic democracy than that peddled by corrupt politicians; a revolutionary assembly tasked with the objective of founding a new republic, or the re-founding of the existing polity. This imaginary of the people's parliament was reinforced by the fact that, despite the existence of various general assemblies in all the camps, inevitably the assemblies in the capital or largest cities of the movement (such as New York, Madrid, Athens, and Istanbul), came to be seen by the news media and by many participants alike as the power loci whose decisions were taken to represent the will of the entire movement, thus giving these assemblies the semblance of alternative national parliaments, purporting to represent the people's will.

This aspiration to embody popular sovereignty is visible in the language of the popular assembly declarations, whose tone was different from the often technical manner of anti-globalisation assemblies, and more closely resembled the language of the National Constituent Assembly of the French Revolution, wresting sovereignty from King Louis XVI, or of the US Constitutional Convention of 1787. Emblematic of this was the content of various documents approved by general assemblies, such as the 27 May 2011 declaration from the general assembly at Syntagma Square, pointedly located in front of the Greek parliament, in which participants affirmed that: "When we, the people, start discussions without fear, fear grips them inside the parliament building."[19] Similarly, the Declaration of the Occupation of New York City struck a solemn tone when it repeated the excerpt from the US Declaration of Independence reading: "That whenever any Form of Government becomes destructive of these ends [Life, Liberty, and the Pursuit of Happiness], it is the Right of the People to alter or abolish it...."

This return to an emphasis on unity and solidarity—so at variance with the postmodern cult of networks and rhizomes which informed the millennial politics of the anti-globalisation movement—reflected a larger change in attitude and ethos of the movement of the squares, which was also visible in other practices connected, but not limited, to popular assemblies. An example is the "people's mic", one of the most famous tactical innovations of Occupy Wall Street, introduced to allow individuals to have their voice heard during assemblies and demonstrations despite the NYPD prohibiting demonstrators from using megaphones in the park. People who wanted to speak would first call for a "mic check", and then express short sentences that were repeated by the crowd. As explained by Matt, a 24-year-old Occupy participant, the "people's mic":

Is a representation of walking in someone else's shoes, it is the literal representation of that, because you are actually repeating their words, you are repeating their words in the first person. And if they said "I am a victim of racism," you repeat that back, and you say, "I am a victim of racism," you don't say, "You are a victim of racism"… You are actually taking a part of that yourself. And it is a beautiful thing that way. It is really like empathy in action.

Through unifying practices such as popular assemblies and the people's mic, the multitude of participants became temporarily fused and synchronised in one voice, ideally the voice of the People the movement stood to represent, rather than simply the voice of the individual that was first expressing the sentence.

The turn towards centralisation in the decision-making structure of the movement of the squares was, however, tempered by some manifestations of an opposite trend towards functional diversification and autonomy, which on the one hand bespoke how organisational unity can never be total, needing to find forms of articulation with multiplicity and singularity, and on the other reflected the resistance of some sections of the movement to the drive for unity. As we saw in Chapter 5 these movements also encompassed a number of separate political collectives and organisations—such as ¡Democracia Real Ya! in Spain, the 6 April Youth Movement in Egypt, the Movimento Passe Livre in Brazil and Convergence des Luttes in France—which often pursued their own individual strategies with limited coordination with the general assemblies. A further sign of this trend was the proliferation of sub-organs, such as working groups and committees that mushroomed during the occupations.

In Spain, a total of 562 committees and working groups were counted all over the country, with around thirty in Madrid alone.[20] In the Puerta del Sol occupation committees included the legal team, providing legal advice to protesters; the assembly "dynamisation" committee, responsible for organising the facilitation of assemblies; the infrastructure committee, charged with maintaining camp infrastructure; and the sanitation committee, upon whom rested the task of keeping the camp clean and tidy. Working groups dealt with issues like the environment, feminism, migration, and even included a bohemian-sounding taskforce for "love and spirituality". Similarly abundant were the committees and working groups in Occupy Wall Street. In New York—where almost ninety separate structures had emerged towards the later phase of the movement—groups dealt with food, facilitation, sanitation, direct action, infrastructure, security, medication, alongside more policy-oriented committees such as the "Demands" working group, and one dealing with alternative banking. Also in Athens and various other Greek occupations, as well as in the Nuit Debout protests in France, this structure was followed, with various groups responsible for media work, assembly organisation, security and sanitation.

While many of these structures played important and productive roles, their uncontrolled growth also reflected a certain narcissistic and self-centred tendency of the movement, its excessive focus on internal organisation often taking energy away from discussions about political strategy. This tendency was often ridiculed by the news media as a demonstration of the Left's tendency, whether socialist or anarchist-inspired, to keep creating superfluous levels of governance. Pablo Gallego, a member of ¡Democracia Real Ya!, chastised this "excessive bureaucracy", constantly producing yet another committee and working group, as if they were the solution to the problems that arose. Indeed this binge of committees is a paradox for the culture of informal organising, namely that while such arrangements operate against the negative background of the state and bureaucratic organisations, they are nevertheless bound to create their own incipient informal bureaucracy; a sort of libertarian proto-state.

Working groups and committees, usually composed of more committed and experienced activists, often entered into collision courses with the general assembly and sometimes tried to claim autonomy for themselves, in the manner of the networked democracy of the anti-globalisation movement. This tendency was particularly apparent in the US, where it became the subject of open discussion within general assemblies. During the last days of the occupation a resolution was approved moving a lot of day-to-day decision-making to a spokescouncil that represented committees and working groups. This decision came too late to have any significant impact on the direction of the movement. But it reflected a process that had already been *de facto* maturing in the actual practice of the movement, whereby working groups and committees moved from being secondary sub-organs emanating from the general assembly, into primary units with representation in a coordinating spokescouncil. Often, as explained by anarchist activist and scholar Mark Bray, the assembly came to be viewed more as an external outreach branch of the movement, merely political theatre,[21] while the real decision-making was done in committees and working groups, or worse, in closed meetings outside the camp.

The use of secondary structures was premised on practical considerations, due to the way in which large assemblies became more and more unmanageable as the movement grew, as we shall see in this chapter.

Isham Christie, an Occupy activist in New York, explained that in working groups and committees, "you could get things done that you could not get done through the assembly". But it also reflected the unease of some activists, especially those of an anarchist bent, towards the strong collective unity implied by the centrality of the popular assembly. Thus, the controversies around the decision-making structure of the movement illustrated the contradictions between populist and anarchist models of direct democracy: the more unity-oriented model represented by the general assembly, together with the idea of a more plebiscitary and centralised democracy; and the more molecular model of affinity groups and spokescouncils, working groups and committees. While the populist model revolved around the assembly as a space where many otherwise atomised individual wills could be fused into a common general will,[22] the neo-anarchist model clung to a faith in small groups, seen as best suited to allow the greatest degree of individual participation in decision-making. These two models found only a partial and conflictual amalgamation in the practice of decision-making in the occupations, with the populist vision of direct democracy eventually prevailing over the anarchist idea.

A sea of twinkling hands

A further distinguishing element of the democratic practices of the movement of the squares was their radical openness and inclusivity, well beyond anything that had been achieved in the gatherings and meetings of the anti-globalisation movement, or previous anti-authoritarian movements. Combining the ethos and procedures of consensus decision-making derived from their predecessors with their own mass scale and diversity, these assemblies became potent experiments in self-organised "people power", best visualised in the sea of twinkling hands sometimes seen during mass assemblies, with hundreds or even thousands of people physically expressing their emerging consensus.

The most remarkable feature of the 2011 popular assemblies was their ability to attract outsiders: ordinary citizens angered with the economy and disaffected with mainstream politics, who were often at their first protest experience; people who, while having initially scant understanding of the culture of protest movements and their decision-making practices, were nonetheless willing to give direct democracy a try. The curiosity of

Image 7.2: Popular assembly in Puerta Del Sol, Madrid, 21 May 2011 (Courtesy Lara Pelaez Madrid)

Image 7.3: Popular assembly in Plaça de Catalunya, Barcelona, May 2011 (Courtesy Lara Pelaez Madrid)

ordinary people about direct democracy, and their willingness to experiment with it, astonished many activists. Harun Burak, a participant in the Gezi protests, remarks, "I was amazed in Gezi by how much people were so anxious to implement these horizontal principles, as far as decision-making was concerned. Not just young people, also middle aged people and people from the working class. And they had no idea of how to do it, by the way. It was exhilarating to see that contradiction." He recounts the demeanour of attentiveness and respect during an assembly in the last days of the Gezi Park occupation: "over 100 people were standing in a circle, trying to decide on whether to evacuate the park or not. It was just the way people were listening so attentively. I don't think that those people ever listened to something so seriously and earnestly."

Popular assemblies offered ordinary citizens an unprecedented opportunity to have their say on the various issues affecting them, and more importantly to have their views heard. As Anastasia, an architect involved in the Syntagma occupation, remarks, the movement emerged at a time when, "people had seen that there was nothing else to lose, and wanted to try something different than they had done previously". Assemblies were important "because most of the people who participated, even older people, did not have any chance to talk about their problems, and about what was happening in Greece". As argued by Stephanie, an Occupy Wall Street participant, in these participatory, open and "non-vanguardist" assemblies, "many people felt the opportunity to take their own individual ownership, and exercise their own agency". Key for the assemblies was "the reappropriation of political speech, the fact that everybody and not just politicians, could talk about politics", as proposed by Selyne, a 32-year-old unemployed woman and a participant in Nuit Debout. Thus, popular assemblies became a vehicle for the re-politicisation of society pursued by the movement of the squares; a space in which ordinary citizens could re-engage themselves with politics, starting from the most basic of political acts: discussing politics in public.

The radical openness of assemblies was facilitated by two connected elements: on the one hand the movement's adoption of consensus both as a procedure and an ethos, emphasising the importance of listening to other people; on the other the location of these assemblies in highly visible public spaces, facilitating the participation of ordinary citizens.

Since their inception, most of the movements of the 2011 wave expressed clear adherence to the principles and procedures of "consensus-based decision-making," striving to achieve a collective agreement among all participants by integrating various points of view and finding compromise decisions, instead of seeking majority votes. Consensus was adopted both as a general ethos of decision-making and as a series of specific procedures on how decisions should be made; with the customary sequence of proposals, requests for clarifications, declarations of agreement and disagreement, and then various rounds to try and establish a resolution everybody or almost everybody would be happy with, sometimes at the cost of watering down the initial proposal. As explained in a document produced by the facilitation team of the occupation of Puerta del Sol, widely circulated in the activist community and translated into English, it was stated that:

> The consensus process is diametrically opposed to the kind of thinking propounded by the present system. The normal response of two people with differing opinions tends to be confrontational. They each defend their opinions with the aim of convincing their opponent, until their opinion has won. The aim of consensus, on the other hand, is to construct. Two people with differing ideas work together to build something new. The [goal] is not my idea or yours; rather it is the notion that two ideas together will produce something new, something that neither of us had envisaged beforehand. This focus requires that we actively listen, rather than merely be preoccupied with preparing our response. Consensus is born when we understand that all opinions—be these opinions of our own, or opinions of others—need to be considered and that a collectively created idea can transform us and our own opinions.[23]

The application of this philosophy in the movement of the squares was "a gamble", in David Graeber's words, given that these procedures had, until that point, only been used for small meetings, like those nooks and crannies of the organisational structure of the anti-globalisation movement.[24] Indeed, as Mark Bray notes, "Occupy had an organising model designed for smaller groups of relatively like-minded people cemented by personal relationships."[25] Techniques stemming from small group politics had to be hastily scaled up to unprecedented levels of mass politics, and as we shall see this adaptation had only a limited degree of success. Despite the problems created by this mismatch between consensus procedures and mass participation, to be discussed in the next section, it can hardly be denied that adherence to the ethos of consensus was instrumental in creating a spirit of community and empathy which made popular assemblies so inspiring and attractive to outsiders.

Besides the adoption of consensus, another important feature of assemblies was their radical openness, inherent in their very designation as "popular" or "general" assemblies—e.g. assemblies open to every-one—rather than movement assemblies, the preserve of a tribal activist counterculture. This redefinition of the meaning of assemblies was aided by their outdoor location in occupied central squares and similar public spaces rather than in activist enclosures. Aitor, an activist based in Barcelona, thus contrasted the assemblies of the movement of the squares with those of the anti-globalisation movement:

> The assemblies we were doing during the anti-globalisation movement were in the base of a specific movement, in one social centre or another. Now it is different. Because they are assemblies that [come to] pass through a re-appro-priation of public space, of the streets and of the squares, that are opened to the entire citizenry. This is something very important. If you do it [an assem-bly] in a community centre, in an activist place, an assembly will never be as inclusive. The idea was to re-appropriate that space, as [with] the original meaning of the agora.

The location of assemblies in highly visible public spaces signified that they were events that concerned the entirety of the citizenry and not just those from a politicised section of society. It reflected their intention to be the voice of the Citizenry, rather than the voice of activists alone. "Nobody could accuse us of discriminating [against] anybody," argues Selyne, a participant of Nuit Debout, "because the assemblies were in a central public square where everyone could come and join".

This public reframing of the assembly, which goes hand in hand with the public re-definition of protest camps described in the foregoing chap-ter, also impacted the definition of who could participate and how. Social forums and spokescouncils made prior organisational affiliation (in a movement, collective or organisation) almost a pre-condition for partici-pation. It was implicitly assumed that people participating in these meet-ings were there as representatives, or "spokes," of a certain group. Because of this framework, such events ended up de facto excluding, or at least marginalising from the process, all those individuals who were not involved in any group or were new to the movement.

Counter to this federative group-of-groups logic, the 2011 general assembly instead embraced participants as individuals—as citizens—without any further qualification in terms of membership, or of political belief, and without any intermediary layer. As Krinis, a Greek activist involved in the Aganaktismenoi, confirms, "in the anti-globalisation movement people were participating in the movement as groups, now they are participating as individuals". In fact, in certain circumstances affiliation to organisations, such as political parties, could almost act as a criteria for exclusion, because as Petros, a Greek activist, puts it, "political people were not allowed to speak", in the sense that interventions of people belonging to parties or organisations in the assemblies were looked at with suspicion by the majority of participants, in line with a typical populist "anti-groups" spirit which predates Rousseau's enmity towards intermediary groupings. A number of practices were developed in order to avoid assemblies being dominated by organised groups. For example, in Greece an organiser chose the "stack" (that is, the list of speakers) by lot, reinstating a famous practice of ancient Athenian democracy. As recounted by Babis Christopoulos, organised groups did however often find workarounds, with participants belonging to a certain group giving all their numbers to one person who had been fielded to speak on behalf of the group.

The radical openness of popular assemblies was arguably one of the most refreshing features of the grassroots democracy system created by these movements, and it aptly embodied their ambition of constructing a "politics of citizens," rather than a politics of activists. However, the radical inclusivity of the popular assemblies also ended up raising significant problems, due to the incapacity of consensus procedures developed for small activist meetings to cope with the huge influx of participants. The movement of the squares was the moment in which participatory direct democracy, and its ethos of consensus, had reached its highest popularity among the populace at large; but it was also the event that most glaringly laid bare its weaknesses and contradictions.

Boredom is an endless meeting

While at the height of these movements these unprecedented "mass horizontal assemblies" functioned relatively well, in the long term these large meetings showed themselves for the haphazard stopgap that they were. Assemblies soon became clogged and frustratingly sluggish, and sometimes ran for several hours or even days before coming to a decision. They transitioned from a symbol of these movements' power and resonance among the general populace into an emblem of one of their most significant shortcomings: their incapacity to find a workable compromise between idealism and pragmatism. Thus, Juan Carlos Monedero, one of the founders of Podemos, could argue that the assemblies were both "radically democratic and radically inoperative."[26]

The "horror stories" about assemblies are as frequent as celebrations of their transformative power. In Spain many people came to refer to assemblies as "iron-ass democracy" (*democracia del culo de hierro*), due to the fact that only those with a metal posterior could sit for so many hours in discussion. For example, the *acampada* assembly in Puerta del Sol took three days to make a decision on whether to dismantle the encampment. In the US, an equally long discussion deliberated over what to do with a group of resident drummers who had infuriated the local community, and exhausted the mental energies of all the other campers, until finally the assembly managed to approve a community agreement. The high tide of participation also carried its own problems, in particular the arrival of the odd mentally unstable or egomaniacal individuals, who became known for disrupting meetings, thus adding to the sluggishness of consensus and infuriating all the other participants who were taking the process very seriously. Isham Christie, a participant in Occupy Wall Street, recounts how the general assembly process soon became "very dysfunctional". He complains about, "having to spend all the time listening to crazy people, fighting for five hours and nothing getting done; my ability to stand people soapboxing and people saying completely tangential things was really put to the test." Similar problems were experienced in the Occupy London Stock Exchange occupation. As recounted by Shimri Zameret, an Occupy London participant, while many people wanted to ban alcohol consumption in the camp, the proposal was blocked on several occasions by some camp residents—incidentally those who were indulging in drinking the most. Finally, the assembly was cunningly convened at 7am one morning, when it was rightly assumed that the vetoers would still be in deep slumber, and the decision was passed.

One could interpret the decline of the assemblies as resulting from a "crisis of growth". The failure of assemblies stemmed from the inadequate consensus-making procedures: devised for small group meetings, they were unsuitable due to the size of the popular assemblies. Assemblies became flooded with thousands of people, many of them politically inexperienced, and not necessarily in line with the worldviews and social norms of the activist community, thus making it difficult for the movement to integrate them using their fragile protocols that assumed adherence to some common political ideas and standards of behaviour. This situation was exacerbated by the lack of any formal structure or coordinating council that could compensate the tendency toward organisational entropy. Decision-making became painstaking, with meetings regularly running over time and often ending without reaching a consensus solely due to the opposition of a few individuals, either out of a cynical attitude or a deliberate attempt at political sabotage. In a way, one could say that assemblies fell victim to their own success, stretching themselves far greater than could be sustained.

The experience of long and dysfunctional assemblies submerged by discussion about trivial details, soapboxing, and petty confrontations eventually led many of these newcomers to abandon a movement they had only recently joined. If, to quote social movement researcher Francesca Polletta's book title, for many core activists in this movement "freedom is an endless meeting,"[27] for many new participants the endless meetings were more of a nightmare of insufferable boredom.

The collapse of popular assemblies reflects the limits of the "proceduralism" that has informed both neo-anarchism and citizenism. Proceduralism can be described as a view that emphasises the importance of process over content—of the means rather than the ends—and thus argues that if the right procedures are utilised the outcome is necessarily going to be correct (or at least the process will be correct, and this is all that matters). Pablo Ortellado recounts, for example, an anti-globalisation assembly in which the facilitator concluded the meeting by saying that the end-result had not been good, but the process had been excellent. This dogmatic adherence of some activists to often painstaking procedures of "full consensus", allowing one or few individuals to block decisions otherwise supported by the great majority, made assemblies unmanageable. This resulted from the fact that consensus-based procedures were applied to a constituency that was far more heterogeneous in social background and political views than the activist communities that had initially developed these procedures, and often lacked a basic initial consensus about the nature of their grievances and aims. This situation was compounded by the cultural tendency Mark Bray has called a "liberal libertarianism"[28]— a knee-jerk rejection of everything that smacks of coercion—which led to a tolerance of disruptions in the collective process coming from a few egomaniacs or psychologically troubled participants.

Protesters often countered such criticisms by asserting that the sluggishness of decision-making was a necessary downside of their radically democratic practices, far superior in any case to the pseudo-democratic pageantry adopted by politicians. Thus, Spanish activists proclaimed: "we go slow, because we go far" [*vamos lentos, porque vamos lejos*], or referring to Spanish poet Antonio Machado, they quoted: "Walker: there is no walk, the walk is made walking" [*Caminante no hay camino, el camino se hace al andar*],[29] itself redolent of the Zapatista maxim "*caminando preguntamos*"— "as we walk we ask questions"—explaining that these movements had no pre-established doctrine, but developed one as they went along. Yet these justifications did not seem to convince many assembly participants, who ultimately came to the conclusion that consensus-based decision-making seemed very good in theory, but proved a nightmare in practice, especially when applied to such a large and diverse movement.

It is significant that to cope with the swelling of participants and in order to make assemblies more efficient some of the movements, as in Spain and the United States, soon veered towards a more majoritarian procedure of "modified consensus", where there were some fall-back mechanisms, in case it were not possible to reach a collective decision without anybody in the crowd vetoing it. The more practical Greeks avoided consensus decision-making procedures from the beginning and adopted the alternate procedure of "supermajority" rule—usually 80 or 90 per cent of all participants—and tried to simplify some of the often tortuous procedures of participatory direct democracy.

We can interpret this shift from consensus to supermajority not just as a technical change, geared at making direct democracy work in face of the high level of popular participation, but also as a political shift, which, running parallel to the re-centralisation of decision-making around the popular assembly, as discussed at the beginning of the chapter, reflects how a more populist and plebiscitary model of direct democracy ulti- mately prevailed over the anarchist version. Or, more precisely, while the form of assemblies remained mostly anarchist, as seen in their procedur- alism and principles of horizontality and consensus, their content became increasingly populist, as seen in the language of many declara- tions and resolutions, and their appeal to the notion of popular sover- eignty, and the view of the popular assembly as a people's parliament.

The movement of the squares thus reintroduced a number of demo- cratic and republican principles that are at loggerheads with neo-anar- chist grassroots democracy: the idea that decisions need to be taken by everyone together, rather than in small groups; the idea that one person equals one vote, rather than a person equalling one bloc; and the idea that the will of the majority has priority over the desire of the minority. As we shall see in the next chapter this populist and majoritarian approach, and its emphasis on values of unity and solidarity over the principles of autonomy and diversity, has gone on to inform the establishment of new organisations, parties and candidatures which emerged in the aftermath of the occupations, many of these attempting to fulfil their aims and address some of their organisational failures.

8

THE ASSAULT ON THE INSTITUTIONS

Tenim més poder del que ens han fet creure [We have more power than what they made us believe]

Ada Colau

El miedo va a cambiar de bando [Fear is changing side]

Pablo Iglesias

Straight Talking, Honest Politics
Jeremy Corbyn's Labour Party leadership campaign slogan

A Political Revolution Is Coming
Bernie Sanders' 2016 presidential campaign slogan

"We want to be citizens. We want to take back our institutions." The words, spoken by Leonidas Martin, a 38-year-old Spanish activist and artist based in Barcelona, and a 15-M participant, sent a wave of disbelief across a meeting hall packed with militants and researchers, mostly stemming from northern Europe's autonomist and anarchist movements. Many in the audience did not seem at all comfortable with that lead. When had anybody last heard terms like "citizens" and "institutions" utilised in such a context, not as pejorative terms more commonly associated with the enemy—mainstream society's—discourse, but as words relevant for the construction of a radical politics? Such a sentence would certainly have been met with hostility had it been expressed in an anti-globalisation assembly on the eve of a major action against the WTO, the IMF or the G8. Yet in 2013, in the aftermath of the movements of the squares, those words seemed not only "expressable", but also able to capture something important about the political horizon newly opened up, and the way the focus had shifted away from the occupations and towards the reclaiming of political institutions for the citizens, including through the foundation of new parties and the re-foundation of old ones.

Looking at the new progressive politics that emerged out of the mobilisations of 2011 and 2013 it becomes apparent how, while the movement of the squares ultimately suffered multiple defeats in its attempt at democratic regime change, it also acted as the propellant for a phase of political renewal, marking its entrance as a sort of "year zero" from which to re-found democratic politics. Animated by the collective spirit of solidarity introduced by the movement of the squares, but also wary of the limits that informal organising structures place on collective action, protesters have started to develop more structured campaigns, organisations, and even new political parties, a turn completely out of character with radical politics before 2011.

The strategy embraced by activists in Spain, Greece, Turkey, and other countries has sometimes been described as an "assault on the institutions"[1]—an active and radical, but strictly peaceful, engagement with the institutions of the state, in order to place them under the auspices of popular sovereignty and restore and expand the rights of the citizen. This vision, which can be seen as the contemporary equivalent of the post-'68 "march through the institutions", which led to the foundation of various European Green parties and civil society organisations, asserts the need for the liberation of political institutions from the existing political caste—the self-serving politicians who are occupying them—and their subsequent takeover by ordinary citizens as a necessary step to regain political power, and ultimately be in a position to address the various social and economic ills that blemish contemporary society.

This strategy of the assault on the institutions has developed along two parallel tracks. Some activists from the movement of the squares have gone on to populate an array of civic campaigns to directly engage the state on questions of housing, unemployment and public services, set up alternative media projects aimed at representing "the people's voice," and launch constituent assembly initiatives aiming at rewriting the fundamental laws of the country. But also, many 2011 "veterans" have participated in the foundation of new democratic-populist political parties and municipal initiatives, as in the case of Podemos and Barcelona en Comù in Spain, or the re-foundation of existing parties, as with the case of Syriza in Greece and the pro-Kurdish People's Democratic Party (HDP) in Turkey. Furthermore, the effect of the movement of the squares has made itself felt in other recent victories for the Left, such as the election of Jeremy Corbyn as leader of the Labour Party in Britain, and the impressive, though ultimately unsuccessful, Bernie Sanders campaign for the presidential nomination in the 2016 primaries for the US Democratic Party. The remarkable growth of support for these Left groupings is strongly related to the movement of the squares; much of the activist support has come from networks established during the occupations and a strong correlation exists between the base of support for the 2011 movement and these later initiatives. These phenomena point to the development of a new twenty-first century party-politics, informed by the discourse of the movement of the squares.

Table 8.1: Relationship between protest movements and political institutions

	Anti-globalisation movement	Movement of the squares
Political logic	Anti-statist politics of autonomy	Politics of citizenship reasserting control over public space and state institutions
Relationship with political parties	Uneasy collaboration	Genesis/regeneration

This new strategy contrasts markedly with the dominant approach in the era of the anti-globalisation movement, which harboured a far more pessimistic view of institutions and political parties. Where anti-globalisation activists mostly shied away from a direct engagement with state institutions, and considered them increasingly irrelevant in a global era, many participants in the 2011–16 upheavals saw political institutions as one of several structures in society to "occupy" and put under the control of "ordinary citizens". Where anti-globalisation activists sneered at political parties, seeing them as relics of a bygone era, and appealed instead to civil society as a space autonomous from institutional politics, the new organisers and leaders bred in the occupation of the squares participated in the foundation and re-foundation of political parties, seen as necessary cogs in the process of a popular reconquest of power. Thus, whereas anti-globalisation mobilisations aimed at creating forms of "counter-power" and a politics of resistance, the movement of the squares aspired to construct what could be described as forms of "under-power": a power surging from the grassroots and from the self-organisation of the citizenry, but ultimately aiming at a complete re-foundation of the political system. The movement of the squares was thus not just a "destituent" moment, undermining the legitimacy of the neoliberal order, but also a "constituent" moment: an event of foundation of a "new politics" matching the requirements of the post-neoliberal era.

Change the world while taking power

To appreciate the latitude of the change introduced by the movement of the squares in the relationship between state and institutions, one only needs to delve briefly into the discourse on state power that dominated the anti-globalisation movement, particularly among neo-anarchist activists. For the global justice movement, and in particular its autonomist section, political parties were viewed as servants of the State, often liable to betray popular demands, while the nation-state was a scourge, the entity responsible for deploying riot police against demonstrators and jailing activists, as well as the relic of a bygone era, retaining less and less power in a time of global interconnectedness.

This anti-statist vision was most programmatically expounded in Marxist theorist John Holloway's *Change the World Without Taking Power*,[2] a reference text for anti-globalisation activists. Holloway argued that the defeat of communism discredited the Leninist idea of seizing the state. He cautioned that such an option was not only politically impractical but ethically wrong, because by taking power one ultimately accepts the principle of the state's right to coerce, and its logic of "power-over", rather than the more positive and grassroots notion Holloway calls "power-to":

> You cannot build a society of non-power relations by conquering power. Once the logic of power is adopted, the struggle against power is already lost. The idea of changing society through the conquest of power thus ends up achieving the opposite of what it sets out to achieve. Instead of the conquest of power being a step towards the abolition of power relations, the attempt to conquer power involves the extension of the field of power relations into the struggle for power... For what is at issue in the revolutionary transformation of the world is not whose power but the very existence of power. What is at

issue is not who exercises power, but how to create a world based on the mutual recognition of human dignity, on the formation of social relations which are not power relations.[3]

Holloway, whose work was inspired by the example of the Zapatista uprising in south-eastern Mexico, called for a utopian society in which power and money would eventually be abolished; a stateless polity, based on voluntary organisation, reminiscent of Kropotkin's self-governed federated communities.

The anti-statist position expressed by Holloway and his comrades reflects a longstanding suspicion of state power on the radical Left. Its origins can be traced back to early Marxism and anarchism. Thinkers as diverse as Karl Marx, Pierre-Joseph Proudhon, and Mikhail Bakunin each fantasised about the day when the state would eventually breathe its last, only differing in their prognosis of how that would happen. While the anarchists called for an immediate elimination of the state, Marx forecast an intermediate phase in which the state would have become the instrument of a "dictatorship of the proletariat."[4] Lenin followed in Marx's steps, building a theory of a vanguard party who could take state power, and far from hastening the dissolution of the state into civil society—as proposed by Marx—Russian Soviet socialism used the state as a means of authoritarian power, reminiscent of Tsarist absolutism, in which the party bureaucracy left no space for diversity in debate, let alone in action. Instead of democracy, state socialism delivered a ruthless dictatorship responsible for the bloodbath of the Stalinist Great Purge of the 1930s, among many other heinous crimes.

For anarchists the authoritarianism of Bolsheviks in power was just a confirmation of their deeply ingrained suspicion of the state, seen as the root of all forms of coercion; the state being the armed guardian of a system based on the domination of one class over the other, and on the ruthless oppression of individuals and local communities. Instead of the state, the anarchist movement imagined a world based on voluntary organisation: on co-operatives and communes, organised in federations, at the local, national and international level; a blueprint that continues to inform many protest movements to the present day.

The anti-globalisation movement reflected this anti-statist attitude and extra-parliamentary orientation of the radical and anarchist Left, which sometimes seemed to serve as a rationalisation (in addition to a consolation) for the impossibility of taking state power at times of rampant neoliberal hegemony. The novelty, introduced by activists campaigning against corporate power and international financial institutions, was the conviction that the geopolitical arrangement of globalisation, with its increasing interconnectedness and supranational governance, had severely weakened state sovereignty, thus making the classic socialist blueprint of taking state power less relevant. As we have seen, this prophecy was the thesis underpinning *Empire*[5] and *Multitude*,[6] both authored by autonomist thinkers Antonio Negri and Michael Hardt at the turn of the millennium, and which had a tremendous influence upon anti-globalisation activists. The nation-state was not just evil, as affirmed by Marxist and anarchist thinkers alike, but also destined to become politically irrelevant. Eventually it seemed that Marx's prophecy and the anarchists' wishes were coming to fruition, not due to popular insurrection, but because of the transformative effects of global capitalism.

Stemming from this vision of a weakened and irrelevant state, anti-globalisation activists saw themselves as part of a "global civil society", or "international civil society"; a global networked movement to whom the appeals of the Zapatistas were addressed. But this antipathy towards the state also left the movement without a clear interlocutor from which to exact concessions, given the impossibility of obtaining any concrete gains from global institutions.[7]

Besides considering the state irrelevant in a time of global interconnectedness, global justice activists were also highly sceptical of political parties and the possibility of them delivering solutions for the many issues raised by the movement, precisely because the only power political parties could win was at the state level. Activists, in particular those stemming from the neo-anarchist scene, were particularly critical of social-democratic parties they saw as sell-outs, who had converted to the neoliberal gospel. But they were also suspicious of the parties of the far Left, chastising them for their hierarchical organisational structure and their incapability of adapting their political discourse to a post-industrial and globalised society. This anti-party attitude reached far further than the radical sections of the movement alone. Significantly, within the World Social Forum, though all participants were politically left and some were party members, the parties themselves were not allowed inside the forum.

Despite this suspicion anti-globalisation activists maintained levels of an uneasy collaboration with left parties. This was seen in various forms:

left parties participating in anti-globalisation demonstrations; activists working within parties and sometimes running for office at local or state level; support for left parties from activists during electoral campaigns; and parties integrating some demands of social movements in their policy platform. The partnership between radical Left parties and protest movements was particularly strong in Italy. Rifondazione Comunista, the party born of a split in the Italian Communist Party when it shed the word "communist" in the aftermath of 1989, played an important role in the anti-globalisation movement, and counted many anti-globalisation activists among its members. Synaspismós/Syriza in Greece played a similar role to Rifondazione, describing itself as a "movement party" because it gathered various movements, represented by the purple flag in the logo, along with communist and Green parties.

The relationship between movement and parties was particularly strong in Latin America, with the left-wing "pink tide" of Chávez in Venezuela, Morales in Bolivia, and Correa in Ecuador, and left-wing parties in power in Argentina, Brazil, and Nicaragua enjoying strong links to popular movements, a crucial factor in their electoral success. Many of these parties drew inspiration from the Partido dos Trabalhadores [Workers' Party or PT] in Brazil that had, since its foundation in the 1980s, developed a strong relationship with the workers' movement and various popular mobilisations, and like Syriza and Rifondazione defined itself as a "movement party". However, neo-anarchist and autonomist activists understandably looked with much suspicion at these parties and their attempts to co-opt social movements.

The movement of the squares advanced a different relationship of social movements with the state and with political parties that repudiated some of the tenets of the anti-globalisation era. Within the emerging vision of the assault on the institutions, the state is not seen merely as an enemy's castle to be destroyed, but also a piece of the solution: an institutional apparatus to be restored under the auspices of popular sovereignty and opened to the participation of the citizenry. It is only by taking the state, activists once again reason, that it is possible to address that hollowing out of institutional political power and its subservience to financial interests that has led to the present conundrum. Thus, rather than seeing themselves acting on behalf of civil society against the state—as neo-anarchists did in their construction of counter-power from below—activists have instead resolved toward "taking it all" [*ir a por todo*], an expression often heard during the Spanish mobilisations, with the intention of exploiting the current wave of popular discontent to regain state power and radically transform state institutions. Furthermore, they have shifted from a view of the state as the root of all evils to a view that comes close to Nicos Poulantzas': the state as a space contested by different social forces, which is partly open to grassroots demands and interventions as long as they have sufficient force to impose themselves, as seen for example in the creation of labour ministries or in the provision of public education and health as a means to institutionally integrate some typical working class demands.[8]

The strategy of the assault on the institutions indicates a politics that, in the words of Spanish activist Javier Toret, "is not about the traditional idea of moving out of the state, but instead [proposes] 'let's try to shape it'". This pragmatic and reformist attitude is well summed up in the words of Brazilian activist Pablo Ortellado:

> Our cause in 2001 was one for which there was no state to claim things from. It was a global process of organising to obstruct the process of liberalisation. But it did not have a very clear target. With these new movements such as 15-M in Spain, the protests in Brazil, or even Occupy, there is a government that is selected as a target, and which can make decisions. At the end if you look at the demands of these movements, they are demands for state policies. There is a contradiction between the rejection of institutions and the nature of these demands.

This re-orientation of the relationship of protest movements towards the state overcomes some of the evident shortcomings inherent in the politics of the anti-globalisation movement which, acting at the global level, lacked a clear interlocutor for its demands.

What are the reasons for this radical change in attitude and political strategy? Why have protest movements moved to a more pragmatic position vis-à-vis parties and the state?

To understand how the occupations have given way to the "assault on the institutions" one must take into account the mixed feelings of enthusiasm and disappointment among the participants, and the way in which it led many of the veterans of this protest wave to find new ways to mobilise on the various issues discussed during the occupations. Petros, a 34-year-old Greek activist, reports how many of the new participants were left "with a feeling of bitter disappointment" due to the rapid collapse of the mobilisation. Isham Christie, who was highly involved in communications and organising with Occupy in New York, similarly recounts the psychological blow he and many of his comrades felt after the movement fizzled out. "It took me three years. I am finally done getting over Occupy Wall Street. And it was for many people a huge process... It was like the most traumatic thing to get over in your entire life. Because it was not someone you know passing away. It is like I put all of my hopes, aspirations, and dreams into this movement, that I thought had so many possibilities, and then it was just gone again."

However, the events also provided some important resources for the ensuing mobilisations, in terms of accrued experience and a sense of solidarity. Christos, a Greek activist and supporter of the radical left Antarsya party, comments: "In a way it did not win anything. However, it gave a lot of experience to people who had participated." Furthermore, as argued by Tim Fitzgerald, an activist with Occupy in New York, it infused people with a sense of solidarity, inviting them "to look outside of their own political silos". Occupy activist Micah White sums up well the collective feeling among the veterans of the movement, saying that the 2011 upheaval had been a "constructive failure: it showed us how close we are".

From this experience participants also drew some painful lessons about the limits of spontaneous organisation and direct democracy. Many activists experienced a similar path to Isham Christie who recounts, "I was enthusiastic about horizontality and consensus. But after I saw what happened in Occupy Wall Street, and how it led us to paralysis, I realised that these ideas don't work as promised". These lessons inspired activists to experiment with more structured forms of organising, including through political parties. As Spanish activist Javier Toret explains, "this is a more organised phase of the 15-M movement," which involves "the construction of organisational structures that can allow us to sustain initiatives [over] time, avoiding [the problem of] temporary aggregations," as was the case with the squares' occupations.

On the other hand, however, this evolution is also the organic development of a series of tendencies that were already present in the populist spirit of the upheavals, and its reaffirmation of the principle of popular sovereignty. Germán Cano, a 44-year-old professor of philosophy and a member of the civic council of Podemos, points out that, "this turn was already coming out of 15-M, because people in the squares were already saying we need to change the institutions". This pragmatic attitude—the situation of social emergency calling for political realism and immediate solutions—led participants to discuss, from the start, the need for a radical reform of the state as a means to address the ebb of democracy, leading them to see the weakening of (institutional) representative democracy as a weapon in the hands of the oligarchy. Thus, the assault on the institutions is both a process of overcoming some of the most problematic tendencies inherent in the informal politics of the occupation, and a fulfilment of some of its goals, in particular regarding the question of popular sovereignty. The consequences of this strategic and psychological turn have been on display in both civil society campaigns and party politics that have emerged in the aftermath of 2011, both of which revolve around radical engagement with the state with a view to re-appropriating it away from the control of neoliberal elites.

A tide of civic renewal

The aftermath of the movement of the squares has been marked by an intense development of new civic campaigns and initiatives, which have built on the spirit of popular unity and solidarity invoked by the occupied squares of 2011, 2013 and 2016. Campaigns sustained by collectives and personal networks established during the occupations have taken aim at the state and its institutions, accusing them of unresponsiveness, demanding a halt to austerity politics, and calling for new policies to address inequality and extend citizens' democratic participation. At the core of these mobilisations was the project of a "politics of citizenship", aimed at the reconstruction of democratic society around the figure of the citizen as its basic pillar, and the depository of a series of rights—civil liberties, public services, welfare provisions—and responsibilities—participation as an active citizen, contribution to the community—towards the polity. For this reason I refer to this mobilisation in this section's title as a "tide of civic renewal", after the post-15-M mobilisations in Spain, the citizens' tides [mareas ciudadanas].

The effort to deepen the struggle has been manifested at three levels: in the development of single-issue campaigns that have focused attention on specific issues raised by these movements, such as housing, poverty, unemployment and public services; in the creation of alternative media projects aimed at voicing the concerns of "unrepresented" citizens; and in renewed demands for constituent assemblies, aiming at rewriting the fundamental law of the respective countries.

While the movement of the squares was dominated by a syncretic dynamic of confluence among different constituencies and different issues, its aftermath has witnessed an inverse process of diversification of campaign efforts, with various issue-specific initiatives taking their own partly independent paths. Activists have thus tried to respond to the diverse issues contained in the *cahiers de doléances*, or the lists of grievances compiled by protesters in the occupied squares, and to strategically pursue them one by one. Yet all these single-issue campaigns have maintained a connection with the unifying popular spirit of the movement, which has acted as an almost mythological backdrop for their efforts, reflecting the foundational imaginary associated with these upheavals and the strong memories and emotions associated with them.

After the departure of Mubarak, Egypt saw a flourishing of civil society campaigns, facilitated by the more democratic and pluralist climate that followed the fall of Mubarak. The various groups that had led the revolution,—the 6 April Youth Movement, Mohamed ElBaradei's National Association for Change, the leftist Justice and Freedom Movement, and members of the Muslim Brotherhood's youth wing—set up a Coalition of the Youth of the Revolution that attempted to coordinate mobilising efforts, and organised a series of new occupations of Tahrir Square in April, July, and November 2011. While some of these organisations participated in electoral ventures, for the most part they decided to keep out of electoral politics and chose the role as civil society guardians of a newborn Egyptian democracy. This aspiration, however, found itself at odds with the still incomplete revolution and the continuing presence of a "deep state" apparatus controlled by the Egyptian army, which pursued a "strategy of tension" that provoked a slew of new street confrontations and eventually managed to win Egyptian public opinion away from the revolution, setting the conditions for the coup d'état of 30 June 2013 and the presidency of General Abdel Fattah el-Sisi.

In the aftermath of the Indignados movement, Spain experienced an intense development of single-issue campaigns, raising questions of economic inequality and the lack of democracy. The inheritors of the Indignados were the Rodea el Congreso [Besiege the Congress] protests starting on 26 September 2012, and the Mareas Ciudadanas [Citizens' Tides]. These colour-coded protest movements, which began in late 2012 in Madrid and focused on the effects of budget cuts on different aspects of society, comprised the "green tide" for education, the "white tide" for public health, the "red tide" for the unemployed, and the "orange tide" in defence of social services. These campaigns mobilised ordinary citizens and public sector workers affected by cuts, often in conflict with trade unions, accused of not doing enough to stop cuts to public services, and thus prefiguring what some have described as "civic unionism", in which the citizens organise themselves directly to raise economic and political demands without the intermediation of trade unions.

Of all the issues raised in 2011 housing acquired a particularly important role, due to the connection of the economic crisis to the housing bubble, and the deleterious effects it had on the everyday life of many people faced with foreclosures and indebtedness. To deal with these issues, already in 2009—two years before 15-M—a group of activists launched the Plataforma de Afectados por la Hipoteca—PAH [Platform for People Affected by Mortgages], a movement taking direct action to stop evictions of the several thousand people in mortgage arrears. This initiative was motivated by the draconian Spanish housing legislation, which makes mortgagers responsible for paying loan instalments even after being evicted. The campaign made rapid strides, and thanks to the momentum from the 15-M, it gained the support of thousands of members, establishing over 100 branches throughout Spain. One of the founding members, Ada Colau, rose to national prominence after an emotional speech in the Spanish Congress on 5 February 2013, where she accused Spanish banks of being "cynical and criminal". She was elected mayor of Barcelona in 2015.

A similar trend towards diversification was witnessed in Greece in the aftermath of the Aganaktismenoi movement. An array of different campaigns sought to confront the manifold problems affecting Greek society at a time of profound economic crisis and austerity politics. The most notable phenomena have been the development of a community solidarity movement, providing basic services for an impoverished population increasingly deprived of state provisions; a wave of worker occupations of bankrupt factories, as in the case of the construction materials manufacturer Vio.Me in Thessaloniki; and episodes of mass civil disobedience like the no-pay campaign against a tax on property, charged via electricity bills. One of the most important organisations in the solidarity movement in Greece was Solidarity for All, founded in 2012, which aimed to coordinate and support various local solidarity initiatives. Its field of operation was wide and comprised such varied activities as social clinics, social pharmacies, free courses and tutorials, food banks, direct producer-consumer markets, and free legal support. The campaign was funded through popular donations along with 20 per cent of the salaries of Syriza MPs. As explained by one of its coordinators, 44-year-old Christos Giovanopoulos, the campaign "followed in the steps of the Aganaktismenoi movement and the networks it had created" to "create a new bottom-up politics," providing for the basic necessities of common people: food, shelter, health, and schooling.

In the US, the aftermath of Occupy Wall Street was less impressive than has been the case in Spain and Greece. Yet still, Occupy continued to serve as an inspiration for new mobilisations. Among the most notable offshoots were Strike Debt, Occupy Sandy, and Black Lives Matter. Strike Debt was a movement for debt resistance that emerged in 2012 after the end of the occupations. It was supported by a number of academics including Andrew Ross and David Graeber, and organised a rolling jubilee, which raised hundreds of thousands of dollars to (buy at knockdown price, and then) abolish the debt of people picked at random.[9] Occupy Sandy was instead a grassroots relief movement, which responded to the devastation wrought upon New York and New Jersey by Hurricane Sandy in October 2012 and delivered food, medicines, clothes, and blankets to people affected by the natural disaster. Arguably the most important successor of Occupy Wall Street has been the Black Lives Matter movement, which campaigns against police brutality towards the black population in the US. It was founded in July 2013 after outrage at the acquittal of George Zimmerman, responsible for the shooting of teenager Trayvon Martin, and proceeded to organise the demonstrations that led to the "Ferguson unrest" of August 2014, sparked by the police shooting of African-American Michael Brown. In subsequent years, protests triggered by the release of videos incriminating police agents have repeated themselves to growing frequency until the 2016 state of siege in Charlotte, North Carolina.

In the cases of Turkey and Brazil it is more difficult to clearly map out this spin-off process, as less time has elapsed since the 2013 upheavals. However, it is possible to detect some signs of a similar trend. In Turkey, after the Gezi protests the country experienced a wave of occupations, with the creation of social centres such as the "Don Quixote" in Istanbul, and an intensification of campaigns on LGBT issues, human rights, the Kurdish question, and the environment, the latter in opposition to megaprojects pushed forward by Erdoğan including the controversial Ilısu Dam in south-eastern Anatolia.

In Brazil, in the aftermath of the Movimento de Junho the momentum of the protests was mostly exploited by the political Right, campaigning against the governing PT and President Dilma Rousseff, who was accused of corruption in a number of cases, including one involving the national oil company Petrobras that ultimately led to her impeachment.[10] The right-wing mobilisation escalated in 2015, with between one to two million people taking part in the 15 March protests: the same, if not a greater number than participated in the Movimento de Junho, in a demonstration of deep-seated popular discontent toward the government. However, on the left-wing end of the political spectrum, the "June days" have also engendered new political and social activity, as seen in the intensification of protests about transportation by the Free Pass Movement, and the emergence of *"rolezinhos"* (from the Brazilian Portuguese locution *rolé*, to go around): flashmobs protesting against the racist attitude of shopping centres that bar entry to black people.[11]

Another significant development in the aftermath of the 2011–16 upheavals has been the emergence of a range of alternative media channels, aimed at breaking the monopoly of corporate news media, in order to provide citizens with sources of information that reflect their interests rather than those of political and economic oligarchies. Since 15 May 2011, the start date for the Indignados, Spain has seen a veritable blossoming of alternative media projects. These include online information sources such as *Diagonal*,[12] *Madrilonia*,[13] which pre-dated 15-M and grew thanks to its momentum, and *InfoLibre*,[14] in addition to various periodical print publications, such as *la Marea*,[15] a spin-off of failed daily newspaper *Publico*,[16] and humouristic magazines like *Mongolia*[17] which were established after the movement. Furthermore, an important phenomenon in Spain was the online TV programme *La Tuerka*,[18] founded in November 2010 shortly before the 15-M movement managed to capture an ever-growing public in its aftermath, which was the political launching pad for its main anchor-man, the current leader of Podemos, Pablo Iglesias. In Greece, a similar trend was seen in the creation of the political magazine *Unfollow*,[19] and in the establishment of alternative radio stations such as *Radio Bubble*, which provided coverage and analysis of the severe effects of the economic crisis and of political conflicts.[20]

In Turkey the Gezi uprising inspired the development of a number of new media channels, adding to existing alternative media, such as the satirical magazine *Penguen*.[21] These included video projects like Kamera Sokak[22] (Street Camera) and Çapul TV,[23] providing video coverage of the movement's activities, as well as Ötekilerin Postasi[24] (The Other Post), an online blog that was repeatedly targeted for censorship. In Brazil, the most famous alternative media emerging out of the protests of the Movimento de Junho has no doubt been the *Midia Ninja* project.[25] This initiative, launched by activists of the Fora do Eixo network of cultural organisers, provided live coverage of protest events and reported cases of police brutality, but was criticised by many activists because of the way it tried to present itself as the official voice of the movement and an inter-locutor for government. Also in the US and other countries hit by the Occupy wave there have been similar developments, best exemplified by the *Occupy Wall Street Journal*[26] in the US (closed in 2013), the *Occupied Times of London*[27] in the UK (still active as of 2016), as well as the media and online TV project *Novara Media*.[28] Finally the online political journal *ROAR Magazine*,[29] founded by activist and researcher Jerome Roos, played a key role as a global space for activist analysis and debate. These differ-ent projects, which can be seen as the contemporary equivalent of the anti-globalisation movement's alternative news sites like Indymedia, testify to the importance the movement has placed on responding to the crisis of representation in the broadest sense of the term, which was after all one of the root causes of the occupations.

Besides single-issue campaigns and alternative media, another interest-ing development and the clearest demonstration of the re-orientation of civil society campaigns towards the state is the development of a number of constituent assembly proposals, which have argued for a rewriting of the constitutional laws of the country. This effort has reflected the move-ment of the squares' ambition to act as a "constituent moment": a foun-dation of a new politics, and thus also of re-foundation of a democratic state, an aim which, as Hannah Arendt highlights, is a common theme of many revolutions.[30]

In Egypt a new constitution topped the list of demands raised by Tahrir activists, in order to rid the country of the remnants of dictator-ship and secure democracy. However, this aspiration was rapidly suffo-cated with the constitutional referendum of 19 March 2011, which conceded only small amendments to the existing document. Once in power, the Muslim Brotherhood went on to approve its own constitution despite facing growing public opposition, thus creating the conditions for the army to seize on popular discontent and regain power. In Brazil some activists have proposed a constituent assembly to pursue various reforms, including measures to prevent the interference of economic power in the electoral process and to ensure better representation for young people, workers, the LGBT community, and indigenous people in parliament. In Spain, from the early days of 15-M protesters denounced the deterioration of the institutions established by the 1978 constitution and asked for a number of important constitutional reforms, such as transitioning from a monarchy to a republic, the introduction of institutions of direct democracy, limits on mandates for politicians, and measures against corruption and embezzlement of public funds.

The Greek Aganaktismenoi assemblies in 2011 vocally demanded a new constitution "written by the people and not by the members of parliament."[31] Some of these demands would be included in the Thessaloniki programme adopted by Syriza in 2014, of which the fourth pillar was the promise to, "transform the political system to deepen democracy", though such commitments faded once Syriza entered government and was accused of becoming a tool of oligarchic power.

Occupy Wall Street also originated proposals to reform the constitution, though these were, for obvious reasons, strongly opposed by the anarchist section of the movement. The "99 Percent Declaration", initially proposed by a working group in New York, wanted to call for a new assembly for the redress of grievances, and proposed an amendment to the constitution to overturn the Supreme Court's decision in *Citizens United v. FEC* [2010], which had led to massive deregulation of campaign finance.[32] However, it never obtained the backing of the New York General Assembly. In the pamphlet *Republic, Lost*, academic Lawrence Lessig, the leading advocate of the Creative Commons "copyleft" system, called for a constitutional convention to address the corrupting influence of campaign funding on politics, but this proposal also failed to win the support of the movement's executive organs.[33]

No similar proposals for the drafting of a new constitution have been witnessed in Turkey in the aftermath of the Gezi protests of 2013. This is because the re-writing of the constitution has been, in recent years, a proposal advanced by President Erdoğan in an attempt to pass through authoritarian reforms aimed at strengthening the executive branch, so movements have instead focused on defending the guarantees in the existing constitution against Erdoğan's attack. Finally, in France discussions about a constituent process did emerge, most notably via movement intellectual Frédéric Lordon's proposal for a new constitution that would abolish private ownership of the means of production and establish the "property of use"; certainly not a very realistic prospect, but still a demonstration of the constituent aspirations of the movement.

These different initiatives illustrate the nature of this "assault on the institutions" strategy. While acting within the sphere of civil society, as have previous protest movements, these campaigns have not conceived of themselves as asserting the autonomy of civil society vis-à-vis the state, as it was the case with the anti-globalisation movement, but have been also aimed at a far-reaching transformation of state institutions, opening them up to emerging popular demands, and restoring and expanding citizens' rights and their associated public provisions.

The electoral turn

"*Que si, que si, que si nos representan*" ["They do, they do represent us"]: this chant, reversing the 2011 slogan of protesters in Puerta del Sol, "*Que no, que no, que no nos representan*" ["They don't represent us"], was heard in May 2014 during the celebrations for the spectacular electoral results achieved by Podemos in the European elections, where it secured 8 per cent of the popular vote and gained 5 MEPs just three months after its foundation. This linguistic reversal demonstrates the way in which the movement's vocal criticisms of political representatives has ultimately led not to an anarchistic wholesale rejection of representative politics, but rather to a populist drive to construct new forms of representation that could channel popular demands into the state.

The rise of Podemos is the most iconic example of the "electoral turn" that has seen activists shifting their focus from protest politics to electoral politics. The same trend is responsible for the electoral success of Syriza, rising to power in January 2015 on the back of the energy unleashed by the Aganaktismenoi; and for the growth of the Peoples' Democratic Party in Turkey, which has likewise tried to present itself as a political outlet for the Gezi movement. Similar dynamics have been seen in the US and the UK, with the rise within the establishment's Democratic and Labour parties, respectively, of radical left figures Bernie Sanders and Jeremy Corbyn, who have responded to the demand for a new progressive populist politics against rampant inequality raised by the movement of the squares.

Podemos [We Can] was founded in February 2014 by a core group of left-wing academics mostly based at the Complutense University of

Madrid, with strong connections with autonomist movements in Europe and Latin American populist politics. Leading figures included Pablo Iglesias, assistant professor of Political Science, who became famous as a regular presence on political talk shows; Juan Carlos Monedero, professor of Political Science at the same university; and Íñigo Errejon, a researcher working in the tradition of Ernesto Laclau and Chantal Mouffe's ideas on emancipatory populism,[34] as well as activists originating from the Trotskyist party Izquierda Anticapitalista, including Pablo Echenique and Teresa Rodríguez. After the impressive result in the European elections of May 2014 it continued to grow strongly, and after a good performance in the local elections of 2015, it won 20 per cent of the vote in the December 2015 elections that delivered a hung parliament. In the ensuing snap elections of June 2016, the alliance Unidos Podemos—encompassing Podemos and Izquierda Unida—proved however a partial disappointment, with their aggregate percentage of the vote falling.

Podemos' ideology was deeply informed by left-wing populism and by 2011's citizenism. It has drawn inspiration from the example of the Latin American populist Left, from Chilean President Salvador Allende to Venezuelan President Hugo Chávez, and in this vein the party presented itself as a force fighting for "popular and citizen unity". Other ideological influences included the Five Star Movement in Italy, a party led by the comedian Beppe Grillo and heavily organised online, with an eclectic policy platform combining demands for basic income and green technologies with xenophobic populist rants against migrants. Podemos has also drawn on the organisational spirit and direct democracy of the 15-M movement. This was seen in its structuring through local "circulos" ["circles" or local assemblies], operating very much like the assemblies of the 15-M movement, as well as in its creation of online discussions and decision-making platforms to deliberate on policies, roles, and candidates.

The most obvious difference between 15-M citizenism and Podemos' populism consists in the latter's abandonment of all pretences of leaderlessness, as seen in the pivotal role played by the highly charismatic and personalised leadership style of its secretary-general Pablo Iglesias. Iglesias has come to exercise what Germán Cano calls a "hyper-leadership," a highly vertical and centralised form of direction that has made use of the outreach opportunities of TV talk shows to compete in the national political arena. The presence of a charismatic leader has provided a way to overcome some of the issues of organisational dispersiveness and evanescence experienced by the 2011 mobilisations. However, it attracted vociferous criticism from some 15-M veterans. The leadership of Podemos, beginning with Pablo Iglesias, was soon accused of bypassing internal processes and overlooking the opinion of local circles. Critics noted how the system of online voting—initially seeming to provide an opportunity for strong grassroots control over the leadership— was progressively geared towards a plebiscitary model, in which party members were simply asked to support decisions already taken by the party's executive, with little room for authentic grassroots intervention.

Besides Podemos, Spain has also witnessed the emergence of local "municipalist" formations, in particular Barcelona en Comú and Ahora Madrid, which managed the impressive feat of winning control of the two largest cities in Spain in the mayoral elections of May 2015. These formations were more directly related to 15-M, counting many activists among members, including several who had been active in PAH before it, and as such decision-making processes followed the principles of horizontality and consensus. The municipalist vision of these formations, strongly influenced by the thought of anarchist activist Murray Bookchin,[35] is more libertarian than Podemos, with its focus on the urban level also informed by the idea that the city is a space which can be governed without hierarchy and centralisation. Thus, Podemos and the municipalist wave could be seen as the electoral projection of the two founding inspirations of citizenism: left-wing populism and neo-anarchism respectively. While Podemos' platform has revolved around the populist demand for full democratic sovereignty, the municipalist formations have instead focused on the pursuit of horizontality and the construction of participatory spaces at the local level.

Quite apart from the remarkable Spanish situation, where new political organisations emerged seemingly out of nowhere, is the case of the electoral rise of Syriza in Greece. As Yannis, a Greek Left activist argued shortly before the 2015 election that would see Syriza win, "the fact that now the radical Left is challenging for power is a direct product of the change of consciousness that was produced by the movements of the squares". However, Syriza cannot be considered a product of the movement, for the simple fact that it pre-dates it. Syriza, an acronym for the "Coalition of the Radical Left" [*Synaspismós Rizospastikís Aristerás*], was originally founded in 1991 as Synaspismós, from the Greek word for "coalition"; an alliance of Left and Green parties and various social movements, represented in the three flags in the party's logo: red, green, and purple respectively. The Aganaktismenoi protest and the prospects of electoral victory led to a push for unity within the party that, in 2013, under the leadership of the young MP Alexis Tsipras, resulted in the dissolution of the constituent parties and the creation of a unitary party.

Since the 2011 upheaval in which many of its activists had partici- pated as normal citizens, the party experienced an impressive escalation, managing to attract many disaffected voters from mainstream parties, and in particular from the former governing centre-left formation, the Panhellenic Socialist Movement (PASOK). Having received 16.8 per cent of the vote in the May 2012 elections, it topped close to 27 per cent in the following June elections, called after all attempts to form a govern- ment failed. In the European elections of May 2014, Syriza became the most popular Greek party, paving the way for its victory in the national elections of 25 January 2015, which led to a coalition government with the right-wing populist party ANEL.

Syriza's experience in power has, however, proven very turbulent. The negotiations initiated by charismatic Finance Minister Yanis Varoufakis with the Troika to re-negotiate Greece's rescue package soon demon- strated the stubbornness of Eurozone finance ministers and the German government, as they offered no serious concessions on the previous plan, and in particular no reduction to the public debt that had ballooned to over 170 per cent. The tug-of-war took a dramatic turn when, close to signing an agreement with the Troika, Tsipras called for a referendum on the new proposal, inviting voters to reject it. The referendum visibly worried the European elites and ended with 61 per cent voting *Oxi* [No] to the Troika's proposal. Tsipras, who had presented the move as neces- sary to give Greece the bargaining power to obtain greater latitude from European institutions, eventually ended up firing his finance minister, despised by the European elites, and "capitulating" in the early hours of 13 July 2015 to a third memorandum of agreement that imposed severe conditions on economic policy, including another forced round of priva- tisation that targeted strategic assets such as railways, ports, and airports, and imposed a straitjacket on public spending. Tsipras' surrender to the European institutions also provoked a split inside Syriza, with the inter- nal faction Left Platform, led by Panagiotis Lafazanis, eventually splitting to create the new party Popular Unity [Laïkí Enótita] party. The prime minister called snap elections in September 2015 in which Syriza managed to return to government. Tsipras faced rising popular discontent, as the government proceeded to apply the new memorandum and enforce harsh austerity measures,[36] the likes of which it had vehemently denounced while in opposition.

In the case of the US, the most remarkable electoral spinoff of the 2011 protests was the impressive, though ultimately unsuccessful, performance of Senator Bernie Sanders in the 2016 Democratic Party primaries. The first inklings of a possible electoral translation of some of the energy of Occupy came in 2013, as some Occupy veterans based in Detroit, including Justin Wedes, had engaged in an unsuccessful attempt to launch a new self-defined "populist" party, jokingly named the After Party. The same year Socialist Party candidate and former Occupy activist Kshama Sawant was elected as councillor in Seattle in 2013.

These developments were, however, incomparable with the veritable earthquake unleashed by the remarkable performance of septuagenarian Vermont Senator Sanders in the Democratic primaries in 2015 and 2016, where he challenged establishment favourite Hillary Clinton by riding a wave of growing popular discontent, especially among the young. Despite a much lower campaign budget than Clinton, Sanders carried over twenty states, mostly in the country's north. In the spring of 2016 he seemed very close to upsetting the predictions that had from the start positioned Clinton as the presumptive nominee. But faced with a lack of grassroots momentum in southern states and the strong support for Clinton by the Party's non-elected "super-delegates," he eventually had to abandon his campaign in June 2016. The surprising (relative) success was fuelled by the support of activist networks established during the Occupy protests, as demonstrated by the many Occupy veterans swelling the campaign's ranks, but also by Sanders tapping into Occupy's typical populist themes, particularly in his tirade against the super-wealthy 1 per cent.[37]

The nomination of Hillary Clinton over Bernie Sanders as the Democratic candidate in the US election is, in fact, widely seen as having set the conditions for the victory of Donald Trump. It deprived the Democrats of a left-wing populist option to oppose right-wing populism, at a time at which it was apparent that a populist candidate would have prevailed over an establishment figure.

Another surprising surge for a radical candidate in the aftermath of the movement has taken the form of the far left MP Jeremy Corbyn, elected as leader of the British Labour Party in September 2015. The sexagenarian Corbyn, a campaigning politician deeply involved in anti-war and anti-austerity protests and therefore a long-time fringe figure within the party, rose as rank outsider in the leadership contest to finish with improbably overwhelming support: 59 per cent of party members cast their vote for him. A factor in the impressive "Corbyn surge" was the influx of a new generation of young people—many of whom had been radicalised during the student protests of 2010 and the Occupy protests—who swelled party ranks by hundreds of thousands. While parts of Corbyn's discourse harked back to old leftist ideas of socialism and the state-managed economy, others contained a democratic populist element, which drew the ire of his opponents such as former Prime Minister Tony Blair, and which bore resemblance to the Occupy movement's discourse, as seen in his denunciation of "grotesque inequality" and frequent attacks against "the Establishment". Corbyn has managed to create widespread enthusiasm among people opposed to the neoliberal agenda, and this has enabled him to fend off repeated attacks from the Blairite wing of the Labour Party.

In Brazil and Turkey, the aftermath of the movements of 2013 have also seen the rise of new political formations that have tried to lay claim to their mantle.

In the case of Turkey, this process found its main outlet in the People's Democratic Party, or HDP (Halkların Demokratik Partisi). Like Syriza, the HDP is a coalition party comprising various small leftist parties, including the pro-Kurdish Peace and Democracy Party (BDP), with whom the party is often closely identified. In the aftermath of the Gezi movement, the HDP tried to capitalise upon the public opinion that supported the Gezi protests. In the local elections of 2013, the first important electoral test for President Erdoğan after the protests, the HDP's results were mixed, with only an estimated 7 per cent voting for the left-wing party across the country, but its support doubled in the June 2015 elections. This made it the third largest party in Turkey and contributed to depriving Erdoğan of a majority, though he regained this in the ensuing November elections. The political situation in Turkey has however been marked by growing political authoritarianism and instability, culminating in the failed coup d'état attempt of 15 July 2016, launched by a section of the army and followed by a government campaign of repression and arrests.

More complex and ambiguous is the connection between the Movimento de Junho and electoral politics in Brazil. The mobilisation contributed to weakening the popular consensus behind the Partido dos Trabalhadores (PT) and President Dilma Rousseff—both of which were enjoying a peak of popularity before the protests—and demonstrated the extent of the lack of representation felt by large sections of the electorate. In the 2014 presidential elections Marina Silva, candidate of the Green formation Rede Sustentabilidade and the Brazilian Socialist Party (PSB), whose emphasis on transparency, sustainable development and civic participation resonated with many themes of the 2013 mobilisations, tried to appeal to this wave of discontent. She initially managed to gather an impressive momentum, but the chances of her candidature soon deflated due to inconsistencies in her policies and her alliance with some sectors of the banking industry.[38]

Of all the cases covered in this book, Egypt provides the bleakest picture of the risks involved in the post-mobilisation phase, and in the turn towards electoral politics. The revolutionary forces did not manage to translate their capacity for street mobilisation into electoral prowess, ending up being marginalised in the transition phase, which, after an uneasy temporary alliance, led to full-blown conflict between the Islamists and the Army. The seeds were sown during the parliamentary elections of 2011–12, which saw a triumph of the Islamists, with the Muslim Brotherhood gaining 37.5% of the vote and the Salafist al-Nour bloc 27.8%, while the revolutionary youth coalition, The Revolution Continues Alliance, supported by many Tahrir activists, scored a miserly 2.8%. The victory hastened the path to power of the Muslim Brotherhood, whose candidate Mohamed Morsi triumphed in the first free presidential elections in Egypt on 24 June 2012, with 51.73% in the run-off against the old regime's candidate, Ahmed Shafik.

The Muslim Brotherhood's time in government, after over eighty years in existence, most of which it spent as a clandestine organisation, did not last for long. Wracked by divisions with its Salafist allies, and by criticisms from the revolutionary youth, whilst still boycotted by the so-called "deep state"—the magistrates, public administration officials, and an army apparatus still loyal to the old regime—the first post-revolutionary government was faced with a powerful wave of opposition. The anti-government mobilisation peaked in the enormous demonstrations of 30 June 2013, which were followed by a military coup on 3 July, led by the minister of defence, General Abdel Fattah el-Sisi. Sisi soon mounted a widespread campaign of repression against the Islamists and then against secular activists, killing thousands of protesters, sending tens of thousands of political opponents to prison, and presiding over hundreds of forced disappearances, a practice reminiscent of the horrors of the Videla and Pinochet dictatorships in Argentina and Chile.

The electoral turn that developed in the aftermath of the 2011 and 2013 upheavals has, then, produced varied results, with some countries succeeding more than others in translating the resolve of the occupied squares of 2011 into electoral politics. Many of these political ventures have produced disappointments, as seen in Syriza's capitulation to the Troika, the dismal performance of the Podemos-Izquierda Unida alliance in the 2016 Spanish elections, the defeat of Bernie Sanders, and the way it opened the way to Trump's victory in the US elections, and the problems encountered by Jeremy Corbyn in the aftermath of Brexit. However, the very fact that for movement veterans the electoral option has once again become appealing constitutes a remarkable turnaround, given the long dominance of an anti-statist and anti-party attitude within protest movements and the radical Left. The general assemblies' denunciations regarding lack of representation have not translated into an anarchistic rejection of representative democracy (that "nobody can represent us"), but have instead eventually found accommodation in the demand for a fairer, more participatory system of political representation. The populist commitment to the principle of popular sovereignty has thus taken primacy over the neo-anarchist tenet of horizontality, most clearly seen in the left-wing populist politics pursued by the likes of Podemos, Sanders and Corbyn.

This turn can be understood as a response to the present situation of protracted social emergency, that demands progressive forces in society avail themselves of all possible tools to achieve systemic change and therefore cannot allow themselves the luxury of eschewing electoral methods. However, electoral pursuits have also generated notable disappointments, as seen in the criticism levelled against Pablo Iglesias and Alexis Tsipras, amid accusations from some veterans of the squares that party politics has taken energy away from protest movements. These developments highlight the need for a two-pronged strategy, combining the pursuit of electoral politics as a pragmatic means to push for concrete demands raised by these movements, with the development of new grass-roots campaigns, that might both provide popular support for the implementation of radical policies by allied political parties and candidates, and also act as a check on them.

CONCLUSION

AFTER THE DEMOCRATIC AWAKENING

Si Se Puede! [Yes We Can!]
Slogan of Plataforma de Afectados por la Hipoteca (PAH)
and the Indignados

The beginning is here.

Occupy Wall Street poster

"We were asleep, we woke up." This sentence, inscribed on a plaque in Puerta del Sol, central Madrid, on the first anniversary of the 15 May 2011 demonstration—one of the hotspots of the movement of the squares—sums up the meaning of this protest wave for its supporters: a moment of democratic awakening after a long phase of political sleep; a renewed hope after years of apathy and resignation. Mobilising millions of people, who embraced this protest wave and made it their own, and involving them in great rituals of popular union like those celebrated in the occupied squares of Tahrir, Puerta del Sol and Syntagma, these movements ushered in a sense of collective hope and a new political culture, informed by a spirit of inclusiveness and unity, and a mix of pragmatism and ingenuity.

At the heart of this upheaval and of its "new politics" often discussed by activists, there was a collective dream with a familiar name and a contested history: democracy. Combining neo-anarchist and neo-populist criticisms of existing forms of democracy, and desiring a more direct intervention of citizens in all the decisions affecting them, protesters called for a "real" democracy precisely because they felt current political arrangements were

233

trampling upon, if not the name, certainly democracy's substance. To this end they pursued a project of radical democracy, seeing in a culture of active and direct participation in politics the necessary antidote to the concentration of power in the hands of the oligarchy.

As can be appreciated in the course of this book, this politics of radical citizenship and the connected call for a re-democratisation of society from the bottom-up created both great enthusiasms and equally great disappointments; it provoked both euphoria and bitter depression, as is often the case with great historical upheavals. At the height of the protest wave, in the months between the late spring and winter of 2011, it seemed that the uprising would never stop (*esto no para*): the prevailing feeling among many activists was that the status quo would crumble under the people's pressure; that the democratic revolution was going to prevail over the neoliberal *ancien régime*. However, after the spring came the winter. The movements vanished with almost the same speed with which they emerged, defeated by police raids or imploding through internal fatigue and bickering. The protest encampments were either evicted or abandoned due to internal exhaustion, the assemblies became dysfunctional and dwindled until they almost vanished, and the enthusiastic political conversations on social media abated.

Due to these shortcomings, some have argued that the revolutions of 2011 ended in defeat. While the Egyptian movement effectively abandoned Tahrir only when the state caved in to its main demand and Mubarak was removed from power, all other *acampadas* around the world failed to hold fast to their promise to leave only when their demands were met and the "regime" was gone. In almost all cases the powerful stayed in government, and continued in much the same fashion as before the protests. In fact, in places like Greece and Spain the protests hastened the fall of centre-left governments, and the rise to power of the Right. In Brazil the movement opened the terrain for a rightist mobilisation against the left-wing government. In the US, while Occupy understood that the coming political battle was anti-establishment in character, between the 99 per cent and the 1 per cent, it was ultimately Donald Trump who managed to cast himself as the vanquisher of the liberal elite. Ironically also, in Egypt—the first and only country in which the take-the-square strategy delivered on its own stated aims of regime change—the movement has found itself in dire straits, with the army once again seizing power in the military coup of 3 July 2013, in the strongest reminder of the risks of a backlash of the old system inherent in all revolutionary phases.

While the democratic dream that was nurtured in the squares may seem to have perished, this is not the case. Like many other movements in history, through extinguishing itself in a burst of motion it has left behind powerful traces; a scent of possibility after many years in which popular movements were forced to be on the defensive and any discussion of radical change to the neoliberal order was easily ridiculed. Ultimately it is short-sighted to measure the impact of protest movements simply in terms of their immediate political or economic repercussions. As argued by Alain Touraine, the main mission of social movements in the present era revolves around the introduction of new values and worldviews to society, a contribution whose effects can only be measured in the mid to long term.[1] When one approaches the movement of the squares from this perspective their huge impact on contemporary society becomes truly apparent.

The emergence of the movement of the squares has revolutionised the political landscape of the countries it affected. This has been seen in the change of political discourse and common sense, in the way in which the question of economic inequality has become centre-stage, and in the development of new social campaigns and the rise of new radical candidates and political parties. From Podemos to the municipal movements taking power in Madrid and Barcelona, from Syriza's election in Greece to the revival of leftist politics in the US and the UK, the progressive political camp has never been so vibrant for many decades. All these political developments would not have emerged were it not for the movement of the squares, and their political agenda owes much to the discussions that took place in the popular assemblies. Despite their disappointments and shortcomings they can be seen as the first inklings of a new egalitarian and progressive politics for the twenty-first century, whose worldview and methodology largely derive from the protest wave of 2011.

These developments—whose importance is starting to be recognised even by the most sceptical commentators—testify how, far from being an inconsequential protest wave, the movement of the squares constitutes one of the most important political events of recent decades, and possibly the beginning of a new progressive political cycle. Concluding the trajectory of this study, I wish to reflect on the content and form of the new politics that has emerged out of the movement of the squares: the nature and prospects for citizenism and its politics of radical citizenship; and the new organisational culture that has been developed by the movement of the squares, with particular reference to the contentious debate about the relationship between participation and representation.

From autonomy to radical citizenship

Key in the spirit of the movement of the squares was its reclamation of the idea of citizenship, long associated with liberal or conservative views, but now reclaimed as a radical banner by protesters. As we have seen in the course of this book, the imaginary and language of citizenship informed myriad aspects of the movement of the squares, from their collective identity, with its reference to the subject of the citizen and the citizenry, to the vision of a better and more democratic society, centring on a recuperation of citizenship rights, seen as the best countermeasure against the nefarious influence of economic and political oligarchies. The politics of radical citizenship is key to understanding the change of paradigm introduced by the movement of the squares vis-à-vis previous protest waves, and in particular the neo-anarchist alternative movements and their politics of autonomy.

For a start, the discourse of citizenship served as an inclusive source of collective identity and a remedy for a society in which class identities no longer seemed to provide strong grounds for mass mobilisation, and in which alternative forms of factional identity, based on notions of race, gender, and life-style—those proposed by the identity politics of the new social movements—often appeared to contribute to fragmentation and thus ultimately the oligarchic strategy of divide and rule. The movement of the squares departed from the postmodern glorification of diversity and autonomy and its suspicion of all forms of collective unity, which were underlying themes for many neo-anarchist movements. It showed that there can be unity in diversity; that struggling for cultural recognition, to use the language of Axel Honneth and Nancy Fraser,[2] should not stop us from pursuing unifying struggles for economic and political justice. Its underlying rationale in the present times of social emergency was to prioritise reaching across traditional social divides, to unite different constituencies against the plight affecting everybody, regardless of their identity or positionality.

This reclaiming of the notion of the citizen was far from just a rhetorical change. Rather it reflected the radically different attitude towards the state harboured by the occupation movements vis-à-vis neo-anarchist movements. As expressed by the notion of the "politics of autonomy," neo-anarchists demanded autonomy against what they saw as the penetration of state and other large-scale institutions in everyday life. In parallel with the opposite end of the political spectrum, where the neoliberal position criticises the State as inefficient and illegitimate, neo-anarchists mostly understood liberation as liberation from the state, and in this vein they pursued the construction of "autonomous spaces" in society. As we have seen, theirs was the conflict of the "society against the state" to use the terms of Pierre Clastres,[3] or a "politics of exodus", a term self-ascribed to Italian Marxist autonomists such as Paolo Virno;[4] turning away from the State and towards self-organised ways of life.

While some theorists as David Graeber, Mark Bray, and others have argued that the movement of the squares was fundamentally anarchist in character, this does not correspond to the facts. Its dominant urge was in fact not the typical anarchist precept of doing away with the state—seen as the root of all evil—but was instead the pursuit of radical reform and re-appropriation of the state, seen as a necessary structure for social cohesion. As evidenced by the content of their resolutions and declarations, popular assemblies called for what can be best described as a radical "opening up" of the state, reclaiming it as a structure serving the political community and its individual members. This was most clearly seen in the manifold demands for new political rights and new institutions of popular participation including referenda, online votes, and constitutional processes aimed at closing the gap between citizens and decision-making. It is true that the procedures of popular assemblies were neo-anarchist in character, as seen in their adoption of consensus and appeals to horizontality, but their substance was ultimately neo-populist, demanding a reassertion of popular sovereignty via a more empowered citizenry.

Citizenism also reflects a different view of protest and political conflict than that harboured by neo-anarchists. Like neo-anarchism, citizenism sees social change as coming from a radical contestation of existing power structures, but also sees this contestation as leading to the construction of alternative power structures. Thus one could say that citizenism has taken the good sense from the left-libertarianism of post-'68 movements, as seen in its foregrounding of the citizen over the People, and the bottom-up participatory processes versus top-down logics of command, while disposing of its most problematic elements: its tendency towards countercultural escapism; its primitivist communitarian utopianism; its all-too-facile rejection of bureaucracy and institutions; and its quasi-religious obsession with personal behaviour and ethics.

To sum up, the movement of the squares blazed an opposing path to that trodden by post-'68 anti-authoritarian movements: instead of an outward pivot away from the state and towards community and society, a forward march from society to the state. Rather than simply fomenting countercultural opposition to the power of governments and corporations, the movement of the squares operated using the populist method of re-appropriating state institutions in the interests of popular sovereignty; instead of seeing itself simply as a means to oppose existing power structures, the movement and its spinoffs eventually sought to constitute new forms of power at all levels of government: municipal, regional, national, supranational, as expressed in the idea of the "assault on the institutions".

The motivations for this turnaround derive from the changing conditions in the aftermath of the 2008 financial crisis, times of unprecedented political and geo-political instability. The neo-anarchist criticism of the State and of its bureaucracies originated at a time, between the late 1960s and 1970s, when totalitarianism still abounded in the Eastern bloc and a number of military dictatorships in Southern Europe and Latin America, and even in nominally democratic countries an interventionist "Moloch-State" and its "authoritarian statism", described by Nicos Poulantzas, truly seemed destined to dominate all recesses of society.[5] In the present era of globalisation and financialisation, the state appears less the almighty and blood-thirsty Leviathan and more a weak, neoliberal failed husk; one incapable of maintaining a minimum of consensus and legitimacy. What is remarkable is how, instead of giving further creed to the anti-statist view of a politics of autonomy, the crisis of the neoliberal order has ended up giving a new lease of life to the traditional populist demand for a radical reclamation of public institutions, in the recognition that these institutions originate in the history of popular struggles and therefore need to be defended and reverted to the control of their citizens.

The transition from the politics of autonomy to the politics of radical citizenship can also be seen as reflecting a more general shift in society's value-system in the aftermath of the Great Recession, with a foregrounding of the value of collective solidarity, often celebrated by populists, over the value of individual freedom dear to neo-anarchists. The direct experience of extreme economic inequality—today part of the everyday life of growing numbers of people since the crisis—and the perception of living in a dangerous situation of social emergency have discredited not just the market gospel of entrepreneurialism and upward mobility, but also the neo-anarchist imaginary of autonomy and self-management that constituted the contestational response to neoliberal hegemony. It is true that these movements have also displayed individualist elements, as seen for example in their appeal to the citizen rather than to the people, reflecting a multitude of individual grievances. However, the occupations have also been the stage where these individualist tendencies have been transcended in the name of collective unity as seen in the rituals of popular communion and their effort to re-construct forms of collective solidarity, reflecting the awareness that many issues citizens face in everyday life cannot be resolved individually but necessitate a systemic political change, only achievable through collective action and institutional intervention.

Reflecting its characteristic pragmatism, the movement of the squares fleshed out the content of this politics of radical citizenship in a number of concrete policies that were widely discussed in the occupied squares, contrary to the stereotype of this protest wave as lacking in clear demands. If anything the movement of the squares was not just a protest movement but also a "proposal movement", that issued a variety of policies to "redress" present grievances. As we saw in Chapter 2 there was a clear consensus around a number of issues including: political reform to allow for more direct participation of ordinary citizens through referenda, popular initiatives, and online democracy; a reform of the financial system to prevent a repetition of "too big to fail" banks being bailed out by governments; a guarantee of the right to privacy, freedom of expression, assembly and association; limits to free markets and free trade; higher taxation for the rich and the suppression of fiscal havens; measures to prevent and punish political corruption; and the provision of the means for a decent life for every citizen, including public housing, health, education, and a guaranteed minimum income for all.

This political platform, which has since gone on to inform many of the political spinoffs of the movement of the squares from Podemos to Bernie Sanders, will no doubt appear far too moderate to radical left militants, who still cling to the nineteenth-century ideologies of communism or anarchism and their messianic and teleological vision of a total doing-away with capitalism and/or the state. Citizenism is not necessarily anti-capitalist in the strict sense,[6] but it is certainly anti-plutocratic, seeking to target big capital, banks, corporations, hedge fund managers, and speculators, while remaining mostly supportive towards small business and the self-employed. Furthermore, it is anti-authoritarian but certainly not anti-statist, since it sees the state as something to be radically reformed rather than destroyed, a structure to be liberated from the elites presently quartered in it, and occupied by ordinary citizens. In some respects citizenism's political platform and its demands for social rights resemble the old social-democratic vision of "social citizenship", even though in its emphasis on participatory practices and direct democracy it also sounds a ringing criticism of the passivity and bureaucratism of the social-democratic project. Some of its aspects might even appear conservative to some because of the defensive emphasis on the need to preserve public institutions and protect citizens against the onslaught of financial markets, or even as manifestations of a middle class egotistical urge to defend privilege.

However, these criticisms seem to overlook the way in which citizenism has provided a resonant response to the challenges of the present historical conjuncture, which can only be described as radical in its political consequences. First, it is evident that many of the policies proposed by these movements, and since adopted by connected organisations, parties and candidates, while appearing moderate and even common sense, will nonetheless be seen by oligarchic power structures as an existential threat. Furthermore, this policy platform has effectively managed to articulate the competing desires of different constituencies in a broad popular coalition, in a way that has few precedents in recent protest movements and unlocks new political opportunities for social change from the grassroots. Ultimately, as the movement of the squares demonstrated, a radical politics in the present times of organic crisis is not necessarily one that "demands the impossible," to use a famous 1968 slogan, one that contents itself with issuing radical declarations of principle, in the recognition that they will probably never be actualised, but a politics capable of harnessing sufficient power to change the balance of forces and transform society for the better.

This pragmatic political attitude, one of the distinguishing characteristics of the movement of the squares, explains why this protest cycle engendered new parties with mass support such as Podemos, a once-in-a-generation event, in one of the most powerful waves of radical Left electoral politics in many decades. Some of these electoral riffs on the movement of the squares have certainly led to bitter disappointment, as most clearly seen in the case of Syriza's capitulation to the Troika. However, what is important in a long-term perspective is the fact that the movement of the squares has reasserted in the radical imagination the idea that electoral politics and parties constitute a necessary component of political change, an attitude that many pre-2011 movements would have considered tantamount to betrayal.

All in all, citizenism has been a highly productive turn in protest culture, one that has allowed protest movements to develop a narrative matching the requirements of the present historical conjuncture. Nonetheless citizenism also contains two risks of which we should take heed: the assimilation of social movements in the state, and a national entrenchment of radical politics.

Firstly, adopting a strategy of radical intervention in the state raises the risk that these protest movements might end up becoming political movements rather than social movements; formations that are eventually destined to organise as parties and to be integrated into the State apparatus, thus diminishing their capacity for cultural criticism and contestation, which was the prime element of many post-industrial movements. This danger has become apparent with the rise of new political formations and the way they have been accused of depriving social movements of their erstwhile energy with many of their leading activists now turned politicians. In this new political phase, activists will need to find ways to juggle "struggle and government": contestation against institutions, and administration within institutions, in ways that are productive at both levels. Thus, new protest movements directing their criticism at the political spinoffs of the movement of the squares, which can already be seen in countries like Greece and Spain, should act as a necessary check against possible oligarchic tendencies in these new formations, and the ever-present risks of moral and political involution.

Secondly, the focus on the national level of citizenism raises serious problems of efficacy and legitimacy. While it is true that it is necessary to revisit and reclaim the national as a political space—erroneously overlooked by the anti-globalisation movement—it is also important to take into account that many of the power structures responsible for economic and political inequality operate at a supranational level, and therefore they also need to be confronted at that level. There is a mismatch between the strong national framework of the movement of the squares and its politics of citizenship, and the reality of a globally interconnected world, in which many economic and political phenomena necessarily escape control by the nation-state. Furthermore, there is a risk that when encased in national space the discourse of citizenship might be used by other actors as a means of exclusion towards migrants and other non-citizens, as seen for example in Donald Trump's discourse and in the Brexit referendum campaign. It is thus important that while maintaining a footing in national space, protest movements also retain a sense of the global scale of their struggle, to address issues such as climate change, fiscal havens and global trade, which transcend national space.

Between participation and representation

A key issue for debate in the aftermath of the movement of the squares is the question of organisation; the nature and dynamics of the structures of collective action. Reflecting their indebtedness to the organisational practices of the anti-globalisation movement, and more generally to the libertarian spirit which imbued post-'68 movements—the criticism of bureaucratism and the view that the personal is political—the movement of the squares espoused a strong participatory ethos and an equally strong "anti-organisations" spirit. It laid claim to horizontality and participation versus verticality and representation, and pursued a practice of "liquid organising", striving for informality and spontaneity, against the negative background of ossified formal organisations and institutions in times of post-democracy and its "crisis of representation."[7] While the content of citizenism has been strongly populist in character, its organisational form has been adamantly libertarian and neo-anarchist in inspiration.

A libertarian organisational ethos was seen everywhere in this protest wave, from the consensus procedures adopted in protest assemblies to the use of social media as participatory and collaborative platforms, and the communitarian experience of protest camps. These practices of participatory mass action earned the 2011 upheavals much of its allure, contributing to making ordinary people feel that this was a movement they could make their own. Yet a certain obsession with horizontality also led to some of the most perilous quandaries of this protest wave, along with its fragility and lack of strategic direction.

The movements of 2011 and since shared a common tendency towards evanescence. Popular assemblies shrank with almost the same rapidity with which they first grew to unprecedented heights; the movements followed the protest camps into oblivion; and online platforms moved from being a stage for enthusiasm to pits of bickering among various activist factions. As I have argued in this book, such a rapid pattern of explosion and implosion can be read as the result of a crisis of growth; the inability of these movements to integrate the masses of newcomers within the movement's ranks. Due to the lack of any formalised structure of membership and direction that could act as a "backbone" to sustain the movement in the long run, and beyond the occupations of specific sites, these movements ultimately failed in crystallising the extraordinary energy they had accumulated at their climax.

The movement of the squares was also hampered by the contradiction between the notion of leaderlessness proposed by these movements, and the *de facto* persistence of various forms of leadership. Leaders and leading groups organically emerged in online discussions, protest camps, and the assemblies. If anything this protest wave was a formidable training ground or "incubator" for a new generation of political leaders and organisers, who have gone on to form new parties and campaigns descended from the 2011 wave. This emergent leadership was nevertheless met with suspicion, contradicting, as it does, the imaginary of horizontality. Paradoxically, the claim to leaderlessness has often ended up serving as a smokescreen for movement leaders to avoid scrutiny and accountability, as seen in the fights emerging among various collectives, especially around the control of social media accounts.

The idea of horizontality has its own positive value, as a manifestation of the radically libertarian and egalitarian spirit that informed this protest wave, and it contributed to a not insignificant amount of the success of these movements, particularly their public image of openness and inclusiveness. However, adopting the imaginary of horizontality in full runs the risk not only of obfuscating the organic emergence of centres of leadership and organisational structures, but also of condemning protest movements to an eternal embryonic state that, if artificially protracted, invariably translates into organisational asphyxia, as the movement's fragile informal structures cannot cope with the growing body of participants. In this veritable "infatuation with beginnings", liquidity or ephemerality—elements that pervade social experience in the age of social media—are seen as a state to be preserved *ad libitum*, since everything that is solid is necessarily hierarchical, and hence authoritarian, alienating, and anti-democratic.

All of this points to a deeper tendency in contemporary protest culture, one which needs to be carefully scrutinised and criticised if we are to move beyond the current predicament: "the cult of participation". The cult of participation describes a situation in which "to live for the moment is the prevailing passion, to live for yourself, not for your predecessors or posterity."[8] In this context, the personal experience of participants—their longing for a sense of community, their search for compensation for the loneliness and alienation of contemporary society, and their own transformational journey—becomes in itself the ultimate aim of the protest movement. The cult of participation problematically conflates utopia and praxis, ends and means; the world we want to build and the ways in which we can build it. Collective action runs the risk of becoming merely therapeutic rather than emancipatory, and its nature more ethical and quasi-religious instead of political.

This tendency, which reflects the uncanny resonance between neo-anarchism and neo liberalism in their common reflection of individualistic narcissistic tendencies, considers all moves towards formalisation as necessarily equating to ossification and sclerotisation rather than, for example, maturation. However, this suspicion of collective organisations actually runs counter to the evidence gleaned from the history of protest movements. Many protest movements started in an informal manner, similar to that seen at the inception of the movement of the squares, only to progressively acquire more formalised and stable structures.[9] Consider the history of the labour, feminist, or environmental movements and the trend appears undeniable: the progressive formalisation of practices, and their integration into the institutional sphere.[10] Furthermore, neither was the movement of the squares completely deprived of organisations, as seen in the role of the 6 April Youth Movement in Egypt, ¡Democracia Real Ya! in Spain, Convergence des Luttes in France, and the Movimento Passe Livre in Brazil in acting as initial "bullhorns" for movements which they nevertheless did not manage, or often even attempt to direct after they took the squares.

The challenge in the aftermath of 2011 is to overcome this obsession with participation as the higher good and devise hybrid organisational structures that combine the spontaneous and participatory character of assemblies and horizontal democracy with the sustainability and scalability of more formalised and democratic organisational and leadership structures. For too long these logics were seen as at loggerheads. One had either to choose a grassroots participatory politics with plenty of democratic legitimacy and no efficacy, or opt for an institutional and electoral politics, with some efficacy but no democratic legitimacy; either the politics of horizontality, or the politics of verticality. A democratic politics in the twenty-first century requires, however, both elements. What needs to be developed is a new blueprint of participatory representation in which participation and representation, grassroots intervention in decision-making and leadership, might find a viable compromise, and organisational forms that are both democratic and efficient may be devised.

New organisations that have emerged in the aftermath of the 2011 protests have already been working in this direction, especially in the Spanish context, with electoral formations such as Podemos and Barcelona en Comú combining participatory practices such as local circles, citizens' assemblies and various forms of online participation with more vertical and formalised elements, starting with the presence of publicly recognised leaders. These organisations are attempting, in different ways, to marry the participatory ethos of the movement of the squares with a more strategic coordination of collective efforts, and have achieved impressive outcomes in this regard. Perhaps in them we are witnessing the birth of a new organisational form befitting the liquid social experience of a digital society, and they may progressively substitute the worn-out organisational models inherited from industrial society.

This is obviously not to say that protest movements ultimately need to become parties, as has been suggested by Marxist scholar Jodi Dean in reference to Occupy Wall Street.[11] Protest movements are different from and can never be represented by any specific political party. Furthermore, they will always retain an element of impromptu informality since they are sites in which new sensibilities, new demands, and new collectivities—not yet fully formed—emerge. More modestly, this author advocates for protest movements not to see formalisation and leadership as a betrayal of their founding values, but rather as an organic process of development, which is fundamental to the contribution protest movements make to society at large, and the latter's capacity to regenerate itself morally and politically. As the movements of 2011 have reminded us, popular politics starts from the squares, from those occasions in which people gather together and self-organise. But if this collective effort is to achieve systemic change, of the kind that is necessary to improve material conditions for the majority of the population, it cannot stop at the squares, but needs to construct more sophisticated organisational structures that may sustain people-power between necessarily ephemeral peaks of protest mobilisation.

The beginning is here

In conclusion, it can be affirmed that the movement of the squares was a Janus-faced event, a historical watershed which marked both an end (of neoliberal hegemony) and a beginning,[12] as the "year zero" for a new progressivism in the twenty-first century, moving past a long phase of disappointment for the Left and progressive protest movements, marked by the defeat of the labour movement, the fall of the Soviet bloc, and the triumph of neoliberal capitalism.

The occupied squares of 2011 were thus not just the realisation of an anti-representational democracy beyond institutions, as some anarchist activists believed, but also a prophecy of the democracy to be. They were not just a destituent moment denouncing the illegitimacy of the neoliberal regime, but also a constituent moment, a sort of civic ritual and collective oath taken by indignant citizens to revive the age-old democratic project and reclaim political institutions. Though the 2011 protests eventually expired, their vision continues to be pursued in street demonstrations, in communities, and public spaces, and increasingly also in the arena of institutional politics.

The obstacles to be overcome in the development of this progressive politics are daunting, and any approximation, never mind realisation, of the aims of democratic renewal and social justice called for in the occupied squares will undoubtedly be a bumpy ride, as befits all political beginnings. The drama of the Greek government's negotiations with the European Council in 2015 and the ultimate capitulation of Tsipras to the latter are a cautionary tale, demonstrating that any threat of democratic "regime change" is going to be met with formidable resistance. Furthermore, the rise of the xenophobic populist right wing—the Front National in France, Golden Dawn in Greece and the victory of Donald Trump in the US elections—show that citizenism and the left-wing populism of Podemos and Sanders still have a long way to go to win the battle for hegemony in the post-neoliberal era. Finally geo-political instability, from ISIS to tensions between the West and Russia, the war in Syria, and the connected refugee crisis, can favour a politics of fear instead of the politics of hope proposed by the occupation movement. The risk remains that the organic crisis of neoliberal politics may be resolved in a regressive rather than progressive direction, possibly also ushering in authoritarian phenomena thought to have been consigned to the dustbin of history.

Faced with these challenges, the generation of 2011, and its multiple social and political spinoffs, will need to not lose contact with the sense of possibility that was manifested in the occupied squares. It will need to stay true to the spirit of inclusivity, unity, and pragmatic ingenuity those events so movingly conjured. Only time will tell if, once this necessary build-up of moral and political resolve has run its course, the new politics that has arisen from the movement of the squares will achieve more democratic societies: a world in which extreme economic inequality is overcome and ordinary people can regain control of their collective destiny. What can be affirmed with confidence in the meantime is that the movement of the squares has set propitious conditions for this systemic change, through gathering immense popular enthusiasm and producing a contagious sense of possibility, summed up in what will remain this movement's most representative slogan, the 15-M (and formerly Obama's) rallying cry: "Yes we can!"

APPENDIX

This book is based on research conducted between 2011 and 2016 in a number of countries in which the "movement of the squares" spread and grew: Egypt, Tunisia, Spain, Greece, Brazil, Turkey, the US, the UK and France. The research design was informed by the principles of grounded theory (GT), whereby the researcher develops a theory starting with the empirical data, which is progressively coded and organised so as to develop a model of the phenomenon analysed.[1] The starting questions were: what is new about these movements? How do they compare with previous movements and the anti-globalisation movement in particular? How do they reflect the change in the economic and political situation? And what kind of political and organisational logic underpins them?

To address these questions I adopted a mixed methods approach enlisting different data sources which could provide me with a holistic understanding of these movements and of their discourse and practices: in-depth semi-structured interviews with organisers and participants; participant observations of protest events; and analysis of archival documents and social media material. I selected six of the aforementioned countries—Egypt, Spain, Greece, Brazil, Turkey and the US—as core case studies on which more extensive and in-depth research was conducted, with 15–25 in-depth interviews per country, and used the other countries as less intensive background case studies with around five interviews per country, for a total of 140 personal interviews. On top of this, I utilised fifty interviews with anti-globalisation autonomist activists that I had conducted for my doctoral research in Italy, Germany and France. These interviews, plus the observations conducted for that project, provided me with a suitable term of comparison to ascertain the continuities and novelty of the movement of the squares.

Interviewees were recruited in two stages: firstly through direct contact in the squares and other protest events, or via social media, and secondly through snowball sampling:[2] by asking the first group of interviewees to put me in contact with other movement participants with an eye to maintaining balance in terms of gender, age, social background, and levels of involvement in the movement. Around half of the interviewees were highly involved people or organisers and the other half ordinary participants. Interviews were conducted either in person or by phone. They were semi-structured, with some basic topics covered in each, such as the background of the interviewee and the nature of their involvement in the movement in question, before exploring questions of a broader nature—the organisational logic of the movement, horizontality, the presence or absence of leaders, etc.—or questions that the interviewee was likely to be particularly qualified to talk about. I left the interviewees the decision of whether they wished to be anonymous.

Observations were conducted in the occupied squares and a number of connected events, such as meetings, demonstrations, and various debates. After each observation I took 2–4 pages of notes describing what I had seen during each session, usually followed by some reflections on the significance and implications of the events recorded. In total I gathered field note descriptions of twenty-four protest sites and events across various countries. This data was particularly useful in exploring the lived action of these movements such as the protest camps, the assemblies, and the demonstrations.

As part of the archival research, I collected an extensive database of social movement documents, which amounted to a total of twenty official resolutions, declarations, manifestos of general assemblies, and manifestos of key protest groups, including ¡Democracia Real Ya! in Spain, the 6 April Youth Movement in Egypt, True Democracy Now in Greece, the Movimento Passe Livre in Brazil, and Taksim Solidarity in Turkey, as well as "about" pages on activist websites. Furthermore, I collected a database of key social media messages chosen from leading Facebook and Twitter activist channels in each of the countries, to gather a sense of the discourse developed on social media and their role in mobilising people.

The different data sources hereby discussed had specific purposes in the overall research schema. Movement documents and social media messages were particularly important for investigating the ideology and identity of the movement of the squares. Observations shone light on how different forms of organisation and protest tactics functioned. Interviews provided the participants' perspectives, as well as the organisers' insider views, allowing an exploration of issues of experience, identity, and behaviour within these protest movements.

Research data was coded following a bottom-up open-coding procedure,[3] with larger categories progressively emerging out of basic categories and then being organised into an overarching narrative. The concept of citizenism emerged organically out of this analysis as a means to condense the various trends that had been identified, including the reclaiming of popular identity; the crossover between neo-anarchist and populist themes; and the strategy of active engagement with the state.

The interpretation developed in this book has limitations in its applicability to each of the specific case studies, with some countries more closely corresponding to this ideal-type than others. However, arguably this is the case with all generalisations, whose value is in providing a general abstract model against which concrete empirical cases can be compared and understood. A list of all interviewees, along with the select movement documents analysed in this book, follows.

LIST OF INTERVIEWEES

US—Occupy Wall Street

	Name	Age	City	Profession
1	Malav Kanuga	32	New York	Researcher
2	Linnea	23	New York	Student
3	Caiti	22	New York	Student
4	Mark	25	San Diego	Travel writer
5	Noah	28	New York	Student
6	Richard	42	New York	Community organiser
7	Elizabeth	46	New York	Teacher
8	Thanu	27	New York	Student
9	Julian	25	New York	Teacher
10	David	34	New York	IT designer
11	James	22	New York	Unemployed
12	Andrew	26	New York	Event organiser
13	Shawn Carrié	23	New York	Unemployed
14	Laura	27	New York	Student
15	Emily Kokernak	36	New York	Fundraiser
16	Patrick Gill	32	New York	Unemployed
17	Stephanie Jane	27	New York	Filmmaker
18	Kalle Lasn	70	Vancouver	*Adbusters* main editor
19	Cari	32	Iceland	Activist
20	Michael Premo	30	New York	Community organiser
21	Tim Fitzgerald	30	New York	IT developer
22	Micah White	35	New York	Journalist/activist
23	Joan Donovan	41	Los Angeles	Researcher
24	Isham Christie	34	New York	Union organiser

Egypt—Revolutionary movement

	Name	Age	City	Profession
1	Hannah El-sissi	25	Cairo	Student
2	Marwa Hussein	32	Cairo	Journalist
3	Ahmed Samih	38	Cairo	Human rights activist
4	Nour Ayman Nour	25	Cairo	Musician and activist
5	Kamal	28	Cairo	Employee
6	Mohammed 'Mido'	22	Cairo	Journalist
7	Nora Rafea	25	Cairo	NGO worker
8	Nora Shalaby	32	Cairo	Archaeologist
9	Sally Zohney	27	Cairo	NGO worker
10	Mahmoud Al-Banna	42	Cairo	Architecture student
11	Mustafa Shamaa	21	Cairo	Student
12	Ahmed Sabry	41	Cairo	Architect
13	Osama Hunna	42	Cairo	Unemployed
14	Abdallah	26	Cairo	Accountant
15	Salma Hegab	21	Cairo	Student
16	Mohammed El-Agati	43	Cairo	NGO worker
17	Ahmed Sharquawi	22	Zagazig	Student
18	Khaled	24	Cairo	Teacher
19	Carlos Latuff	43	Rio de Janiero	Activist/cartoonist
20	Ali Hamad	22	Cairo	Tourism worker
21	Ahmed Maher	41	Cairo	Activist/engineer
22	Israa Abdelfattah	39	Cairo	Activist
23	Mahmoud Salem	40	Cairo	Blogger/activist
24	Ahmed	32	Cairo	IT worker

Spain—15-M movement

	Name	Age	City	Profession
1	Laura Blanco	28	Madrid	Researcher
2	Taiz	28	Madrid	Unemployed
3	Luis Ordóñez	37	Madrid	Self-employed
4	Sofia de Roa	32	Madrid	Journalist
5	Segundo Gonzales	24	Madrid	Student
6	Asun Villar	48	Madrid	Unemployed
7	Aitor Tinoco	28	Barcelona	Unemployed
8	Gregorio Herrero	72	Malaga	Retired
9	Feliz Herrero	70	Malaga	Retired

10	Fabio Gandara	27	Madrid	Architecture student
11	Pablo Gallego	23	Madrid	Unemployed
12	Pablo Rey Mantoz	32	Madrid	Researcher
13	Ana Turull	27	Barcelona	Architect
14	Vicente Martin	30	Barcelona	Unemployed
15	Jorge Izquierdo	38	Barcelona	IT worker
16	Helena Candelas	40	Madrid	Unemployed
17	Teresa Marcos	26	Madrid	Web designer
18	Carmen Haro Barba	24	Madrid	Researcher
19	Marina	28	Madrid	Designer
20	Francisco	30	Madrid	Teacher
21	Leonidas Martin	38	Madrid	Lecturer/artist
22	Javier Toret	37	Barcelona	Researcher
23	Marta Franco	32	Madrid	Community manager
24	Klaudia Alvarez	37	Barcelona	Designer/lecturer
25	Germán Cano	44	Madrid	University lecturer
26	Sara Bienzobas	30	Madrid	Video producer

Greece

	Name	*Age*	*City*	*Profession*
1	Dimitris	24	Athens	Student
2	Krinis	42	Athens	Researcher
3	Erasmos	40	Athens	Student
4	Georgios	46	Athens	Unemployed
5	Nikos	27	Athens	Unemployed
6	Eleni	32	Athens	Teacher
7	Sissy	58	Athens	Politician
8	Tzortzis	28	Athens	Student
9	Anastasios	27	Athens	Student
10	Anastasia	29	Athens	Student
11	Christos	31	Athens	Student
12	Nikos	32	Athens	Office worker
13	Yannis	27	Athens	Activist
14	Petros	34	Athens	Activist
15	Christos Giovanopoulos	44	Athens	Activist/researcher
16	Babis Christakopulos	40	Athens	Activist/journalist

Turkey

	Name	Age	City	Profession
1	Örsan Şenalp	40	Amsterdam	Organiser
2	Mehmet	32	Istanbul	–
3	Sarphan Uzunoğlu	30	Istanbul	Lecturer
4	Aytaç	27	Istanbul	Student
5	Neşe	26	Istanbul	Student
6	Arzu	29	Istanbul	–
7	Selçuk	34	Istanbul	Organiser
8	Özlem	33	Istanbul	Activist
9	Devrim	27	Istanbul	Student
10	Harun	34	Istanbul	Activist/researcher
11	Ayşegül	29	Istanbul	–
12	Diyar	34	Izmir	Researcher
13	Dominic	28	London	–
14	Mika	32	Istanbul	Activist
15	Kazim	31	Istanbul	–
16	Önder	28	Istanbul	–

Brazil

	Name	Age	City	Profession
1	Paique Duques	28	Brasilia	Student
2	Pablo Ortellado	40	São Paulo	Lecturer
3	Andre Basseres	32	Rio de Janeiro	Teacher
4	Ivana Bentes	44	Rio de Janeiro	Lecturer
5	Stefania	27	Rio de Janeiro	Journalist
6	Leandro	42	São Paulo	Artist
7	Rodrigo Nunes	37	Rio de Janeiro	Researcher
8	Barbara	23	Rio de Janeiro	Student
9	Thaís	22	São Paulo	Student
10	Mariana	27	São Paulo	Student
11	Bernardo	35	São Paulo	Journalist
12	Pedro	32	Rio de Janeiro	Researcher
13	Pepe Martin	32	Porto Alegre	Organiser
14	Bruno	41	Rio de Janeiro	Lecturer

Further interviews (UK, Tunisia, France)

	Name	Age	City	Profession
1	Tim	28	London	Student
2	Bernard Goyer	24	London	Student

LIST OF INTERVIEWEES

3	Kirsten Forkert	32	London	Lecturer
4	James Haywood	23	London	Student
5	John Jordan	43	London	Activist
6	Brian	23	London	Student
7	Shimri Zameret	33	London	Student
8	Steve Reid	33	London	Activist
9	Ahmed	24	Tunis	Student
10	Mohammed	42	Tunis	Accountant
11	Haithem	28	Tunis	Lecturer
12	Hamza	23	Tunis	Student
13	Ismail	27	Tunis	Worker
14	Fathma Rigi	26	Tunis	Employee
15	Ibrahim	32	Tunis	Employee
16	Baki Youssoufou	37	Paris	Web developer/campaigner
17	Loubna	25	Paris	Unemployed
18	Selyne	32	Paris	Unemployed
19	Oliver	42	Paris	–
20	David	24	Paris	Student

SELECTED MOVEMENT DOCUMENTS

Coalition of the Youth of the Revolution: Invitation to Save the Revolution, Friday, 16 April 2011. http://www.tahrirdocuments.org/2011/04/coalition-of-youth-revolution-invitation-to-save-the-revolution-friday, last accessed 12 Sep 2016.

Consensus of the Assembly of the Occupation of Puerta del Sol, Madrid, 20 May 2011. https://15mpedia.org/wiki/Archivo:Propuestas_movimiento_15M.pdf, last accessed 12 Sep 2016.

Declaration of minimum consensus of the Assembly of Barcelona. https://15mpedia.org/wiki/Acampada_Barcelona#Demanda_de_m.C3.ADnimos, last accessed 12 Sep 2016.

Manifesto of ¡Democracia Real Ya! http://www.democraciarealya.es/manifiesto-comun, last accessed 12 Sep 2016.

Proposals of ¡Democracia Real Ya! http://www.democraciarealya.es/documento-transversal, last accessed 12 Sep 2016.

Declaration of the Occupation of New York City, 29 September 2011, with minor amendments on 1 October 2011. http://www.nycga.net/resources/documents/declaration, last accessed 12 Sep 2016.

Occupy Wall Street's Statement of Autonomy, passed by the General Assembly at Occupy Wall Street, 10 November 2011, and passed revision by the General Assembly at Occupy Wall Street, 3 March 2012. http://www.nycga.net/resources/documents/statement-of-autonomy, last accessed 12 Sep 2016.

Occupy Wall Street's Principles of Solidarity. http://www.nycga.net/resources/documents/principles-of-solidarity, last accessed 12 Sep 2016.

99 Percent Declaration, first drafted and published on 7 October 2011 and announced to the NYCGA on 15 October 2011. https://sites.google.com/site/the99percentdeclaration/

Resolutions of the People's Assembly of Syntagma Square, 2 June 2011. http://www.metamute.org/community/your-posts/updates-greek-squares-and-peoples-assemblies, last accessed 12 Sep 2016.

Manifesto of True Democracy Now Greece, published on 24 May 2011. http://www.realdemocracy.gr, last accessed 12 Sep 2016.

Resolution of the People's Assembly of Syntagma Square 14 October 2011. https://acampadabcninternacional.wordpress.com/2011/10/15/resolution-of-the-people%E2%80%99s-assembly-of-syntagma-square-14102011, last accessed 12 Sep 2016.

Taksim Solidarity statement, 5 June 2013. http://www.timdrayton.com/a59.html

Press Release from Taksim Solidarity, 12 June 2013. http://www.jadaliyya.com/pages/index/12192/taksim-solidarity-statement_to-the-press-and-citizn, last accessed 12 Sep 2016.

Founding manifesto of the Anarchist Federation of Rio de Janeiro [Manifesto de Fundação da Federação Anarquista do Rio de Janeiro]. https://anarquismorj.wordpress.com/textos-e-documentos/manifesto-de-fundacao-da-federacao-anarquista-do-rio-de-janeiro, last accessed 12 Sep 2016.

Nuit Debout, Minutes of the Popular Assembly of Place de la République, 8 April 2016. https://nuitdebout.fr/memoire-commune-paris/wp-content/uploads/sites/13/2016/05/CR_AP_Nuit_Debout_08042016.pdf, last accessed 12 Sep 2016.

NOTES

INTRODUCTION

1. *V for Vendetta* is a dystopian science-fiction movie, directed by James McTeigue and written by the Wachowski Brothers, based on the popular comic: Alan Moore and David Lloyd, *V for Vendetta* (New York: Vertigo/DC Comics, 2005).

2. Lewis Call, "A is for Anarchy, V is for Vendetta: Images of Guy Fawkes and the Creation of Postmodern Anarchism," *Anarchist Studies* 16, no. 2 (2008): 154.

3. The Narodniks were a nineteenth-century Russian movement which campaigned against the serfdom of the peasantry. See Franco Venturi, *Roots of Revolution: A History of the Populist and Socialist Movements in Nineteenth Century Russia* (New York: Knopf, 1960).

4. John Charlton, *The Chartists: The First National Workers' Movement* (London: Pluto Press, 1997).

5. Charles Postel, *The Populist Vision* (Oxford: Oxford University Press, 2007).

6. See for example John P. McCormick, *Machiavellian Democracy* (Cambridge: Cambridge University Press, 2011).

7. In recent years the term citizenism has been widely discussed in Spain, though we yet lack a clear definition of the term. See for example Ricard Zapata-Barrero, "Democracia y multiculturalidad: el 'ciudadanismo' como argumentación política." *Sistema: Revista de ciencias sociales* 203 (2008): 171–195. Lorenzo Casellas López and Jorge Rocha Cuesta, "Del culturalismo al ciudadanismo." *Intervención Psicosocial* 18, no. 1 (2009): 5–18. For a polemical contrast of citizenism and anti-capitalism see Carlos Taibo, "The Spanish Indignados: A movement with two souls." *European Urban and Regional Studies* 20, no. 1 (2013): 155–158, esp. p. 157: "The *ciudadanista* proposal [...] aspires to address external authorities—parties, institutions—with the aim of making them modify specific attitudes and politics. As a result, and by definition, it does not contest capitalism itself, it does not consider problems in terms of class and it

tends to dilute its demands in a more diffuse way." In the United States some have used the term "citizenism" to mean a politics favouring current citizens against migrants. This is obviously not the meaning of the term I operate with in this book: appealing to citizenship does not necessarily mean excluding those who are not citizens already. An anonymous 2001 text published in French as "The Citizenist Impasse," and published in English by the Not Bored collective (http://www.notbored.org/citizenism.html, last accessed 12 Sep 2016), polemically discussed citizenism as a problematic political orientation represented in the anti-globalisation movement by figures such as *Le Monde Diplomatique*'s Ignacio Ramonet, which saw democracy as a force against capitalism, framed the citizen as the basis of politics, and called for a strengthening of state power against capitalism. This version comes quite close to my understanding of citizenism.

8. See for example Stany Grelet, "Un moment constituent," *Vacarme* 3 (2002): 15–17. The Nuit Debout activist and scholar Frederic Lordon has attacked citizenism in a speech: http://www.fakirpresse.info/frederic-lordon-nous-n-apportons-pas-la-paix, last accessed 12 Sep 2016.

9. Karl Marx, *The Eighteenth Brumaire of Louis Bonaparte* (Moscow: Progress Publishers, 1977), p. 10.

10. Hannah Arendt refers to citizenship as the "right to have rights." Hannah Arendt, *The Origins of Totalitarianism* (New York: Harcourt, Brace & World, 1966), new edition, p. 299.

11. The term libertarian populism has been recently introduced in the US in reference to the politics of right-wing libertarian Rand Paul, and the way he has tried to integrate his libertarianism with more populist anti-corporate messages. See for example Conn Carroll, "What is libertarian populism?" *The Washington Examiner* (8 Aug 2013). http://www.washingtonexaminer.com/what-is-libertarian-populism/article/2534045, last accessed 12 Sep 2016. Citizenism, conversely, is a left-wing libertarian populist ideology, which does not necessarily see the state as the enemy.

12. Here I am adopting Alain Touraine's scheme of analysis of protest movements involving the I-O-T triad: Identity, Opposition, and Totality; that is, the way in which social movements influence the entirety of society through their values and meanings. Alain Touraine, *The Voice and the Eye: An Analysis of Social Movements* (Cambridge: Cambridge University Press, 1981), pp. 80–83. Also see Alain Touraine, *The Self-Production of Society* (Chicago: University of Chicago Press, 1977).

13. Deborah Hardoon, Deborah Ayele and Ricardo Fuentes-Nieva, "An Economy for the 1%," Oxfam Briefing Paper. *Oxfam* (2016). https://www.oxfam.org/sites/www.oxfam.org/files/file_attachments/bp210-economy-one-percent-tax-havens-180116-en_0.pdf, last accessed 12 Sep 2016.

14. Margaret Somers and Olin Wright have argued that under neoliberalism

citizenship has been privatised and contractualised, thus assuming a character similar to the one of market exchanges. Margaret R. Somers and Olin E. Wright, *Genealogies of Citizenship: Markets, Statelessness, and the Right to Have Rights* (Cambridge: Cambridge University Press, 2008), p. 2.

15. Imaginary in this context describes the space of political thought, invention and imagination navigated by protesters and social movements. See Cornelius Castoriadis, *The Imaginary Institution of Society* (Cambridge, MA: MIT Press, 1987).

16. Paul Mason, *Why It's Kicking Off Everywhere: The New Global Revolutions* (London: Verso, 2012), pp. 38, 173.

17. Pippa Norris, *Democratic Deficit: Critical Citizens Revisited* (New York: Cambridge University Press, 2011).

18. Real democracy was a term often heard in this protest wave, including in the name of the Spanish group ¡Democracia Real Ya!

19. Thus far few works have explored this protest wave from a global perspective. The only two works that stand out in this respect are Marina Sitrin and Dario Azzellini, *They Can't Represent Us!: Reinventing Democracy from Greece to Occupy* (London: Verso, 2014) and Donatella Della Porta, *Social Movements in Times of Austerity: Bringing Capitalism Back into Protest Analysis* (Cambridge: Polity Press, 2014).

20. With respect to this Brazil is an outlier, since there were no public square occupations like the other countries. But as we shall see in Chapter 6, the mass flooding of large thoroughfares like the Avenida Paulista in Sao Paulo played a similar symbolic and functional role.

21. Blair Taylor, "From alterglobalization to Occupy Wall Street: Neoanarchism and the new spirit of the left," *City* 17, no. 6 (2013): 729–747.

22. David Graeber, "Occupy and anarchism's gift of democracy," *The Guardian* (15 Nov 2011). http://www.theguardian.com/commentisfree/cifamerica/2011/nov/15/occupy-anarchism-gift-democracy, last accessed 12 Sep 2016.

23. Mark Bray, *Translating Anarchy: The Anarchism of Occupy Wall Street* (Winchester: Zero Books, 2013).

24. Michael Kazin, "Anarchism Now: Occupy Wall Street Revives an Ideology," *New Republic* (7 Nov 2011).

25. Sitrin and Azzellini, *They Can't Represent Us!*

26. Süreyyya Evren, "Gezi Resistance in Istanbul: Something in Between Tahrir, Occupy and a Late Turkish 1968," *Anarchist Studies* 21, no. 2 (2013).

27. Raúl Zibechi, "Debajo y detrás de las grandes movilizaciones," *OSAL Observatório Social de América Latina* 14, no. 34 (2013).

28. Alain Badiou and Gregory Elliott, *The Rebirth of History: Times of Riots and Uprisings* (London: Verso, 2012).

29. See for example Slavoj Žižek, "Occupy Wall Street: what is to be done next?" *The Guardian* (20 Apr 2013). http://www.theguardian.com/commentisfree/ cifamerica/2012/apr/24/occupy-wall-street-what-is-to-be-done-next, last accessed 12 Sep 2016. Also relevant is Žižek's book on the 2011 uprisings: Slavoj Žižek, *The Year of Dreaming Dangerously* (London: Verso, 2012).

30. Alain Badiou, "The Communist Hypothesis," *New Left Review* 49 (2008): 29–42.

31. Badiou, *The Rebirth of History*, p. 5.

32. Francis Fukuyama, *The End of History and the Last Man* (New York: Free Press, 1992).

33. See for example Badiou, *The Rebirth of History*, p. 40.

34. Jodi Dean expresses suspicion at the "democracy" discourse in her previous work. In particular see Jodi Dean, *Democracy and Other Neoliberal Fantasies: Communicative Capitalism and Left Politics* (Durham: Duke University Press, 2009).

35. See Jodi Dean, *The Communist Horizon* (London: Verso, 2012), Jodi Dean, *Crowds and Party* (London: Verso, 2016).

36. Alain Badiou, *Being and Event* (London: A&C Black, 2007).

37. Lance W. Bennett, *The Logic of Connective Action: Digital Media and the Personalization of Contentious Politics* (Cambridge: Cambridge University Press, 2013).

38. See for example A. Monterde, J. Toret, E. Serrano and A. Calleja-López, "De las redes y las plazas al espacio institucional: Movimiento-red 15M e iniciativas electorales emergentes," *Empiria: revista de metodología deficiencias sociales* (2015), A. Monterde, A. Calleja-López, M. Aguilera, X. E. Barandiaran, and J. Postill, "Multitudinous identities: a qualitative and network analysis of the 15M collective identity," *Information, Communication & Society*, 18, no. 8 (2015): 930–950.

39. Paolo Gerbaudo, *Tweets and the Streets: Social Media and Contemporary Activism* (London: Pluto Press, 2012).

40. Manuel Castells, *Networks of Outrage and Hope: Social Movements in the Internet age* (Cambridge: Polity, 2012), p. 233.

41. Jeffrey S. Juris, "Reflections on #Occupy Everywhere: Social media, public space, and emerging logics of aggregation," *American Ethnologist* 39, no. 2 (2012): 259–279.

42. This definition of populism draws upon the large body of scholarship on populism and in particular the work of Ernesto Laclau, Margaret Canovan, Yves Meny, Yves Surel, Cas Mudde, Daniele Albertazzi and Duncan McDonnell: Cas Mudde, *Populist Radical Right Parties in Europe* 22, no. 8, (Cambridge: Cambridge University Press, 2007); Daniele Albertazzi and Duncan McDonnell, *Twenty-First Century Populism: The Spectre of Western*

European Democracy (Basingstoke, Hampshire: Palgrave Macmillan, 2008); Ernesto Laclau, *On Populist Reason* (London: Verso, 2005); Margaret Canovan, *Populism* (New York: Harcourt Brace Jovanovich, 1981); Yves Mény and Yves Surel, *Democracies and the Populist Challenge* (Basingstoke, Hampshire: Palgrave Macmillan, 2002).

43. Cas Mudde has described the populist zeitgeist as a phase in which populist politics increasingly goes mainstream. Cas Mudde, "The Populist Zeitgeist," *Government and Opposition* 39, no. 4 (2004): 542–563.

44. Joseph A Schumpeter, *Capitalism, Socialism and Democracy* (New York: Harper, 1950), pp. 236–7.

45. Jacques Rancière, *Hatred of Democracy* (London: Verso, 2006), p. 96.

46. Alexis de Tocqueville, *Democracy in America: And Two Essays on America* (London: Penguin, 2003).

47. Antonio Gramsci, Quintin Hoare and Geoffrey Nowell-Smith, *Selections from the Prison Notebooks of Antonio Gramsci*, (London: Lawrence & Wishart, 1972).

48. On the individualism of the present era see Ulrich Beck, *Individualization: Institutionalized Individualism and Its Social and Political Consequences*, vol. 13 (Sage: 2002), Z. Bauman, *The Individualized Society* (London: John Wiley & Sons, 2013).

49. Laclau, *On Populist Reason*, p. 100.

50. Gustave Le Bon, *The Crowd: A Study of the Popular Mind* (London: Fisher, 1897).

51. Geoffrey Pleyers and Alain Touraine, *Alter-Globalization: Becoming Actors in the Global Age* (Cambridge, UK: Polity, 2010), Jeffrey S. Juris, *Networking Futures: The Movements Against Corporate Globalization* (Durham, NC: Duke University Press, 2008).

52. The Tute Bianche [White Overalls] were an Italian direct action group of a Marxist autonomist bent that used civil disobedience tactics at various counter-summit protests.

53. The idea of "political opportunities" and "political opportunity structure" was introduced by Sidney Tarrow to indicate the "consistent—but not necessarily formal or permanent—dimensions of the political struggle that encourage people to engage in contentious politics." Different political conditions can create more or less favourable political opportunities for social movements. See Sidney G. Tarrow, *Power in Movement* (New York: Cambridge University Press, 1998).

54. Michael Hardt and Antonio Negri, *Multitude: War and Democracy in the Age of Empire* (New York: Penguin Press, 2004). Michael Hardt and Antonio Negri, *Empire* (Cambridge, MA: Harvard University Press, 2000).

55. Pierre Clastres, *Society Against the State: Essays in Political Anthropology* (New York: Zone Books, 1987).

56. Destituent, as contrasted with constituent, is a term used by Giorgio Agamben

and other Italian political philosophers to express the way in which certain political processes—mobilisations, events, etc.—can act as a "negative moment" of criticism, and subsequent overthrowing, of the present state of things. See Giorgio Agamben and Stephanie Wakefield, "What is a destituent power?" *Environment and Planning D: Society and Space* 32, no. 1 (2014): 65–74.

1. MOVEMENTS IN THE CRISIS OF NEOLIBERALISM

1. Resolution of the People's Assembly of Syntagma Square, Athens, 27 May 2011.
2. Gramsci, Hoare and Nowell-Smith, *Selections from the Prison Notebooks of Antonio Gramsci*, p. 556.
3. Colin Crouch has referred to this "zombie" state of neoliberalism in a recent book: Colin Crouch, *The Strange Non-Death of Neoliberalism* (Cambridge, UK: Polity, 2011). A similar argument has been put forward in John Quiggin, *Zombie Economics: How Dead Ideas Still Walk Among Us* (Princeton: Princeton University Press, 2012). On its prospects, also see the work of Philip Mirowski, who argues neoliberalism is far from dead: Philip Mirowski, *Never Let a Serious Crisis Go to Waste: How Neoliberalism Survived the Financial Meltdown* (London: Verso, 2013).
4. My argument here draws on my previous analysis in Paolo Gerbaudo, "Protest Diffusion and Cultural Resonance in the 2011 Protest Wave," *The International Spectator* 48, no. 4 (2013): 86–101.
5. The 30 November 1999 Seattle protests are considered a foundational event of the anti-globalisation movement. The protests saw the participation of around 40,000 people and succeeded in shutting down a meeting of the World Trade Organisation, which was discussing a new round of market liberalisations.
6. Castells, *Networks of Outrage and Hope*.
7. The expression comes from a Chinese proverb often used by Mao Zedong in his writings.
8. For an overview of the Arab Spring, see Gilbert Achcar, *The People Want: A Radical Exploration of the Arab Uprising* (Berkeley: University of California Press, 2013) and Marc Lynch, *The Arab Uprising: The Unfinished Revolutions of the New Middle East* (New York: PublicAffairs, 2012).
9. The 6 April Youth Movement is a protest movement founded in 2008 that campaigns for democracy and social justice. It takes its name from the date on which organisers had planned a protest in support of a strike of textile workers in the industrial town of Mahalla el-Kobra. For an overview of the various groups involved in the Tahrir mobilisation see Tarek Masoud, "The Road to (and from) Liberation Square," *Journal of Democracy* 22, no. 3 (2011): 20–34.

10. The 30 June 2013 protests surpassed the record set by the 2011 revolution, with several million people taking to the squares. However, the high turnout was also due to the fact that people knew the army and the police were backing the protests and therefore there would be no consequences for participants. If 30 June 2013 was a second revolution, rather than a coup d'etat, as claimed by its apologists, then it would be the first one, in which no tear gas or bullets were fired, and none of the anti-government protesters were wounded or killed by police.

11. Stéphane Hessel, *Indignez-vous!* (Montpellier: Indigène, 2010). For the English translation: Stéphane Hessel and Marion Duvert, *Time for outrage!* (New York: Twelve, 2011).

12. On 1 October 2011 700 protesters were arrested during a march on Brooklyn Bridge, causing public outrage. See Paul Harris, "Occupy Wall Street protesters arrested on Brooklyn Bridge," *The Guardian* (2 Oct 2011). https://www.theguardian.com/world/2011/oct/02/occupy-wall-street-protesters-brooklyn-bridge, last accessed 12 Sep 2016.

13. The Movimento Passe Livre—Free Fare Movement is a popular movement founded in 2005 that advocates for universal free access to public transportation. See this account in Portuguese: Marcela de Andrade Gomesand Kátia Maheirie, "Passe livre já: participação política e constituição do sujeito," *Revista Psicologia Política* 11, no. 22 (2011): 359–375.

14. A good overview of the movement is provided in Pablo Ortellado, "Reflections on The Free Fare Movement and Other 'New Social Movements'," *Mediações-Revista de Ciências Sociais* 18, no. 2 (2013): 110–117.

15. The World Bank, World Development Indicators. 2016. Youth Unemployment [Data file]. http://data.worldbank.org/indicator/NY.GDP.MKTP.KD.ZG, last accessed 12 Sep 2016.

16. The World Bank, World Development Indicators. 2016. Unemployment [Data file]. http://data.worldbank.org/indicator/SL.UEM.TOTL.ZS, last accessed 12 Sep 2016.

17. The World Bank, World Development Indicators. 2016. Youth Unemployment [Data file]. http://data.worldbank.org/indicator/SL.UEM.1524.ZS, last accessed 12 Sep 2016.

18. On the relationship between neoliberalism and economic inequality see Göran Therborn, *The Killing Fields of Inequality* (Cambridge: Polity, 2013), Thomas Piketty and Arthur Goldhammer, *Capital in the Twenty-First Century* (Cambridge, MA: The Belknap Press of Harvard University Press, 2014), and Joseph E. Stiglitz, *The Price of Inequality: How Today's Divided Society Endangers Our Future* (New York: W.W. Norton & Co, 2012).

19. The founding texts of neoliberalism include: Friedrich August Hayek and Bruce Caldwell, *The Road to Serfdom: Text and Documents—The Definitive Edition*

(London: Routledge, 2014), Friedrich August Hayek, *Individualism and Economic Order* (Chicago: University of Chicago Press, 1948), and Milton Friedman, *Capitalism and Freedom* (Chicago: University of Chicago Press, 2009).

20. David Harvey, 2005. *A Brief History of Neoliberalism* (Oxford: Oxford University Press, 2005).

21. Guy Standing, *The Precariat: The New Dangerous Class* (London: A&C Black, 2011). Also see Alex Foti, "Mayday Mayday: Euro flex workers time to get a move on," *Republicart.net* 4 (2005) for an activist account of the precariat.

22. Alexander Kentikelenis, Marina Karanikolos, Aaron Reeves, Martin McKee and David Stuckler, "Greece's health crisis: From austerity to denialism." *The Lancet* 383, no. 9918 (2014): 748–753.

23. FT View, "The risks and rewards of Osborne's austerity," *Financial Times* (21 July 2015). http://www.ft.com/cms/s/0/675b99c4-2f9b-11e5-91ac-a5e17d9b4cff.html#axzz4Cmuh7ri3

24. Yen Ap Hope, Business Writer, "4 in 5 in USA face near-poverty, no work." *USA Today* (28 July 2013). http://www.usatoday.com/story/money/business/2013/07/28/americans-poverty-no-work/2594203, last accessed 12 Sep. 2016. The article is based on the research by M. R. Rank, T. A. Hirschi, & K. A. Foster, *Chasing the American Dream*: Understanding What Shapes Our Fortunes (New York: Oxford University Press, 2014).

25. Hardoon, Ayele and Fuentes-Nieva, "An Economy for the 1%." https://www.oxfam.org/sites/www.oxfam.org/files/file_attachments/bp210-economy-one-percent-tax-havens-180116-en_0.pdf, last accessed 12 Sep 2016.

26. Larry M. Bartels, *Unequal Democracy: The Political Economy of the New Gilded Age* (New York: Russell Sage Foundation, 2008).

27. One of the best accounts of the US People's Party is Postel, *The Populist Vision*.

28. Neo-feudalism is a term that has been used by a number of writers and editorialists including Evgeny Morozov.

29. OECD, "Trust in government and in political parties in European OECD member countries," in *Government at a Glance 2013* (Paris: OECD Publishing, 2013). DOI: http://dx.doi.org/10.1787/gov_glance-2013-graph6-en, last accessed 12 Sep 2016.

30. Institute for Democracy and Electoral Assistance, "Voter turnout" [Data file] (2016). http://www.idea.int/vt/index.cfm, last accessed 12 Sep 2016.

31. Anna Manchin, "Trust in Government Sinks to New Low in Southern Europe," *Gallup* (30 Oct 2013). http://www.gallup.com/poll/165647/trust-government-sinks-new-low-southern-europe.aspx, last accessed 12 Sep 2016.

32. Edelman Trust Barometer, "Edelman Trust Barometer Global Results," (2012). http://trust.edelman.com/trust-download/globalresults, last accessed 12 Sep 2016.

33. See Simon Tormey, *The End of Representative Politics* (Malden, MA: Polity, 2015), p. 17, and Russell, J. Dalton, *Democratic Challenges, Democratic Choices:*

The Erosion of Political Support in Advanced Industrial Democracies (Oxford: Oxford University Press, 2004).

34. Ibid.
35. Colin Crouch, *Post-democracy* (Cambridge: Polity, 2004).
36. Wolfgang Streeck, "The Crises of Democratic Capitalism," *New Left Review* 71 (2011): 5–29.
37. Rancière, *Hatred of Democracy*, pp. 81–82.
38. Ibid., p. 80. Étienne Balibar, *Citizenship* (Cambridge: Polity, 2015), pp. 5, 171.
39. Wendy Brown, *Undoing the Demos: Neoliberalism's Stealth Revolution* (New York: Zone Books, 2015).
40. Somers and Wright, *Genealogies of Citizenship*.
41. Anderson Antunes, "The Cost Of Corruption In Brazil Could Be Up To $53 Billion Just This Year Alone," *Forbes* (28 Nov 2013). http://www.forbes.com/sites/andersonantunes/2013/11/28/the-cost-of-corruption-in-brazil-could-be-up-to-53-billion-just-this-year-alone/#cb2c05a610bb, last accessed 12 Sep. 2016.
42. Citizens United v. Federal Election Commission was a US Supreme Court ruling which lifted restrictions on electoral campaign funding. Richard L. Hasen, "'Citizens United' and the illusion of coherence," *Michigan Law Review* (2011): 581–623.
43. Jack Abramoff, *Capitol Punishment: The Hard Truth About Washington Corruption From America's Most Notorious Lobbyist* (Washington, DC: WND Books, 2011).
44. Raphael Spuldar, "Brazilian police target protesters—and journalists," *Index on Censorship* (2013). https://www.indexoncensorship.org/2013/06/brazilian-police-target-protesters-and-journalists, last accessed 12 Sep. 2016.
45. The best account of "Datagate," sparked by Edward Snowden's revelations, is in Glenn Greenwald, *No Place to Hide: Edward Snowden, the NSA, and the US Surveillance State* (London: Hamish Hamilton, 2014).
46. Donatella Della Porta and Massimiliano Andretta, "Protesting for Justice and Democracy: Italian Indignados?" *Contemporary Italian Politics* 5, no. 1 (2013): 23–37.
47. Hanspeter Kriesi, "New Social Movements and the New Class in the Netherlands," *American Journal of Sociology* (1989): 1078–1116.
48. Here the analogy is with post-industrial parties, capable of appealing to more diverse constituencies than industrial parties. Otto Kirchheimer, "The Transformation of the Western European Party Systems," *Political Parties and Political Development* (1966): 177–200.
49. Al-Jazeera, "Protesters flood Egypt streets" (2 Feb 2011). http://www.aljazeera.com/news/middleeast/2011/02/20112113115442982.html, last accessed 12 Sep 2016.
50. RTVE, "Más de seis millones de españoles han participado en el Movimiento 15M" ["More than six million people participated in the 15M movement"],

(6 Aug 2011). http://www.rtve.es/noticias/20110806/mas-seis-milloneses-panoles-han-participado-movimiento-15m/452598.shtml, last accessed 12 Sep 2016.

51. Patricia Rey Mallen, "Brazil's Protests Get More Violent, Reach Brasilia And Threaten The Confederation Soccer Cup," IBTimes (17 June 2013). http://www.ibtimes.com/brazils-protests-get-more-violent-reach-brasilia-threaten-confederation-soccer-cup-1310179#, last accessed 12 Sep 2016.

52. Public Issue, "Αγανακτισμένων Πολιτών," [The Movement of Indignant Citizens] (June 2011). http://www.skai.gr/files/1/PDF/aganaktismenoi.pdf, last accessed 12 Sep 2016.

53. G1, "Protestos Pelo País Têm 1,25 Milhão de Pessoas, Um Morto E Confrontos," *Globo*, Brasil (21 June 2013). http://g1.globo.com/brasil/noti-cia/2013/06/protestos-pelo-pais-tem-125-milhao-de-pessoas-um-morto-e-confrontos.html, last accessed 12 Sep 2016.

54. Peter Yeung, "Violent scenes break out in France as tens of thousands pro-test controversial labour reform," *The Independent* (9 Apr 2016). http://www.independent.co.uk/news/world/europe/nuit-debout-violent-scenes-break-out-in-france-as-tens-of-thousands-protest-controversial-labour-a6976746.html, last accessed 12 Sep 2016.

55. Edith Honan and Ed McCallister, "Anti-Wall St protesters march through New York," *Reuters* (16 Oct 2011). http://uk.reuters.com/article/us-usa-wallstreet-protests-ny-idUSTRE79F05F20111016, last accessed 12 Sep 2016.

56. Jackie Smith, "The World Social Forum and the challenges of global democ-racy," *Global Networks* 4, no. 4 (2004): 413–421.

57. Fernando Garea, "Apoyo a la indignacio del 15-M," *El Pais* (5 June 2011). http://politica.elpais.com/politica/2011/06/05/actualidad/1307231940_787459.html

58. Fernando Garea, "El 15-M mantiene la simpatía ciudadana dos años después," *El Pais* (18 June 2013). http://politica.elpais.com/politica/2013/05/18/actualidad/1368894896_892384.html, last accessed 12 Sep 2016.

59. Public Issue, "Αγανακτισμένων Πολιτών" [The Movement of Indignant Citizens], *Skai* (June 2011). http://www.skai.gr/files/1/PDF/aganaktis-menoi.pdf, last accessed 12 Sep 2016.

60. Datafolha, "8 em 10 brasileiros apoiam protestso," *Folha de S. Paulo*, (29 June 2013). http://www1.folha.uol.com.br/fsp/cotidiano/116497-8-em-cada-10-brasileiros-apoiam-protestos.shtml, last accessed 12 Sep 2016.

61. Pew Research Centre, "Turks Divided on Erdogan and the Country's Direction," (30 July 2014). http://www.pewglobal.org/2014/07/30/turks-divided-on-erdogan-and-the-countrys-direction, last accessed 12 Sep 2016.

62. Jeff Zeleny and Megan Thee-Brean, "New Poll Finds a Deep Distrust of Government," *New York Times* (25 Oct 2011). http://www.nytimes.com/2011/10/26/us/politics/poll-finds-anxiety-on-the-economy-fuels-volatility-

in-the-2012-race.html, last accessed 12 Sep 2016.; Harry J. Enten, "Occupy Wall Street's People Power loses popularity," *The Guardian* (14 May 2012). http://www.theguardian.com/commentisfree/cifamerica/2012/may/14/occupy-wall-street-people-power-popularity, last accessed 12 Sep 2016.

63. Odoxa, "60% des Français soutiennent le mouvement 'Nuit Debout'," iTELE (9 Apr 2016). http://www.itele.fr/france/video/60-des-francais-soutiennent-le-mouvement-nuit-debout-160621, last accessed 12 Sep 2016.

64. Mason, *Why It's Kicking Off Everywhere*, p. 72.

65. Robert Frank, *Falling Behind: How Rising Inequality Harms the Middle Class* (Berkeley: University of California Press, 2013).

66. For a news media mention of the "new poor" see Jonathan Freedland, "Thanks to David Brent we cannot see the new poor," *The Guardian* (13 Dec 2013). http://www.theguardian.com/commentisfree/2013/dec/13/britain-working-poor-squeezed-middle-culture, last accessed 12 Sep 2016.

67. David K. Shipler, *The Working Poor: Invisible in America* (New York: Knopf, 2004).

68. Universal class is a concept introduced by Karl Marx to express the way in which the fight of the proletariat is a universal fight for the emancipation of humanity. See Karl Marx, *Economic and Philosophic Manuscripts of 1844* (New York: International Publishers, 1964), p. 34.

2. ANARCHISM, POPULISM, DEMOCRACY

1. Poem XV. Pablo Neruda and Ilan Stavans, *The Poetry of Pablo Neruda* (New York: Farrar, Straus and Giroux, 2003).

2. On the relationship between social movements and democratisation see Charles Tilly, *Democracy* (Cambridge: Cambridge University Press, 2007), and Donatella Della Porta, *Mobilizing for Democracy: Comparing 1989 and 2011* (Oxford/New York: Oxford University Press, 2014).

3. Crouch, *Post-Democracy*.

4. Brown, *Undoing the Demos*.

5. The idea that we live in a post-ideological society goes back to Daniel Bell and Jean-François Lyotard, *The End of Ideology: On the Exhaustion of Political Ideas in the Fifties* (Glencoe, IL: Free Press, 1960), and Jean-François Lyotard, *The Postmodern Condition: A Report on Knowledge* (Minneapolis: University of Minnesota Press, 1984).

6. The utility of the notion of ideology for my analysis of protest culture relies in its indication of an action-oriented system of ideas that structures the worldview and guides the action of participants. Therefore I do not subscribe to the negative view of ideology as connected with Marx's "false consciousness", leading subaltern groups to accept the ideas of the ruling class, but in the neutral sense proposed by Gramsci, who saw ideology as an array of

conceptions that allow social and political groups to organise themselves. Gramsci, Hoare and Nowell-Smith, *Selections from the Prison Notebooks of Antonio Gramsci*.

7. "Caste", referring here to corrupt political elites, is a term introduced by the Five Star Movement and then utilised by the Indignados.

8. Wendy Brown, "We Are All Democrats Now…" *Theory & Event* 13, no. 2 (2010).

9. For a discussion of different types of direct democracy see Russell J. Dalton, Wilhelm P. Burklin and Andrew Drummond, "Public opinion and direct democracy," *Journal of Democracy* 12, no. 4 (2001): 141–153.

10. Marina Sitrin, *Everyday Revolutions: Horizontalism and Autonomy in Argentina* (London: Zed Books, 2012).

11. The discussion in this chapter mainly relies on a selection of movement documents, including resolutions and declarations of popular assemblies, all listed in the Appendix.

12. I develop the notion of "liquid organising" in my previous book *Tweets and the Streets*, to describe organisational practices which attempt to sidestep formalised or "solid" structures. Here the reference is obviously to Zygmunt Bauman's theory of present society as a liquid society. Zygmunt Bauman, *Liquid Modernity* (Cambridge, UK: Polity Press, 2000).

13. Neo-anarchism is a term used by various scholars and activists. See for example Manuel Castells, "Neo-anarchism," *La Vanguardia* (21 May 2005), and Blair Taylor, "From alterglobalization to Occupy Wall Street: Neoanarchism and the new spirit of the left," *City*. 17, no. 6 (2013): 729–747. Among the scholarly works that discuss the postmodern revival of anarchism are Simon Critchley, *Infinitely Demanding: Ethics of Commitment, Politics of Resistance* (London: Verso, 2014), and Saul Newman, *The Politics of Postanarchism* (Edinburgh: Edinburgh University Press, 2010).

14. For a definition one can refer to Kropotkin's famous entry on Anarchism for Encyclopaedia Britannica. He defines anarchism as "the name given to a principle or theory of life and conduct under which society is conceived without government—harmony in such a society being obtained, not by submission to law, or by obedience to any authority, but by free agreements concluded between the various groups, territorial and professional, freely constituted for the sake of production and consumption, as also for the satisfaction of the infinite variety of needs and aspirations of a civilized being." Pyotr Alexseyevich Kropotkin, *Anarchism: A Collection of Revolutionary Writings* (Mineola, NY: Dover Publications, 2002). On the history of early anarchism see George Woodcock, *Anarchism: A History of Libertarian Ideas and Movements* (New York: New American Library, 1962) and Peter Marshall, *Demanding the Impossible: A History of Anarchism* (Oakland, CA: PM Press, 2009).

15. The term "new social movements" has been used by Alain Touraine, Alberto Melucci and Jürgen Habermas, among others, to describe the new "identity movements" that emerged in the aftermath of the 1968 revolts. Alain Touraine, *The Voice and the Eye: An Analysis of Social Movements* (Cambridge: Cambridge University Press, 1981), Alberto Melucci, *Challenging Codes: Collective Action in the Information Age* (Cambridge: Cambridge University Press, 1996), and Jürgen Habermas, "New Social Movements," *Telos* 1981, no. 49 (1981): 33–37.

16. David Graeber, "Occupy Wall Street's anarchist roots," *Al Jazeera English* (29 Nov 2011). http://www.aljazeera.com/indepth/opinion/2011/11/2011112872835904508.html, last accessed 12 Sep 2016.

17. Raúl Zibechi, "Autonomy in Brazil: below and behind the June uprising," *ROAR Magazine* (21 Nov 2013). http://roarmag.org/essays/raul-zibechi-brazilian-uprisings, last accessed 12 Sep 2016.

18. David Graeber, *The Democracy Project: A History, a Crisis, a Movement* (New York: Spiegel & Grau, 2013), p. 154.

19. Daniel Guérin and Paul Sharkey, *No Gods, No Masters* (Edinburgh: AK Press, 2005).

20. Kriesi, "New Social Movements and the New Class in the Netherlands."

21. Herbert Marcuse, *One-Dimensional Man: Studies in the Ideology of Advanced Industrial Society* (Boston: Beacon Press, 1964).

22. Exodus is a term used by Italian autonomists to express the refusal of labour, the disengagement from capital and the state, and the construction of autonomous spaces. See, for example, Paolo Virno and Michael Hardt, *Radical Thought in Italy: A Potential Politics* (Minneapolis, MN: University of Minnesota Press, 1996).

23. There has been much debate about the nature of alternative and international communities emerging out of the post-'68 protest movements. Rosabeth Moss Kanter, *Commitment and Community: Communes and Utopias in Sociological Perspective* (Boston: Harvard University Press, 1972), also see Raul Vaneigem, *The Revolution of Everyday Life* (Seattle: Left Bank Books, 1983).

24. Herbert P. Kitschelt, "Left-Libertarian Parties: Explaining Innovation in Competitive Party Systems," *World Politics* 40, no. 02 (1988): 194–234.

25. The best English source on Marxist autonomism is Steve Wright, *Storming Heaven: Class Composition and Struggle in Italian Autonomist Marxism* (London: Pluto Press, 2002).

26. Hardt and Negri, *Empire*, p. 350.

27. The biological term "rhizome" has been part of the imaginary of the anti-authoritarian Left since its discussion by Gilles Deleuze and Felix Guattari in opposition to the hierarchical structure of the tree. Gilles Deleuze and Félix Guattari, *A Thousand Plateaus: Capitalism and Schizophrenia* (Minneapolis: University of Minnesota Press, 1987).

28. Nick Witheford, "Autonomist Marxism and the Information Society," *Capital and Class* (1994): 85–125.

29. In France there is the term *anarcho-autonomie*, and in Greece the similar expression αναρχο—αυτονομοί. Obviously there are differences between anarchist and autonomist groups, but at the risk of eliding these nuances, in the present analysis they are treated as part of a common stream.

30. Amory Starr, *Naming the Enemy: Anti-Corporate Movements Confront Globalization* (London: Zed Books, 2000).

31. For an extended discussion of the anti-globalisation or "alter-globalisation" movement see Juris, *Networking Futures*, and Pleyers and Touraine, *Alter-Globalization*.

32. Richard Barbrook and Andy Cameron, "The Californian Ideology," *Science as Culture* 6, no. 1 (1996): 44–72.

33. Marina Sitrin and Dario Azzellini, *Occupying Language* (New York: Zuccotti Park Press, 2012), p. 80.

34. Cornelius Castoriadis, "Power, Politics, Autonomy," in Axel Honneth (ed), *Cultural-Political Interventions in the Unfinished Project of Enlightenment* (Cambridge, MA: MIT Press, 1992), pp. 269–298.

35. Alain Touraine, Michel Wieviorka and François Dubet, *The Workers' Movement* (Cambridge: Cambridge University Press, 1987).

36. George Katsiaficas, *The Subversion of Politics: European Autonomous Social Movements and the Decolonization of Everyday Life* (Oakland, CA: AK Press, 2006).

37. Sheila Rowbotham, *Women in Movement: Feminism and Social Action* (New York, NY: Routledge, 1992).

38. E. F. Schumacher, *Small is Beautiful: Economics as if People Mattered* (New York: Harper & Row, 1973).

39. Cristina Flesher Fominaya, "Autonomous Movements and the Institutional Left: Two Approaches in Tension in Madrid's Anti-globalization Network," *South European Society & Politics* 12, no. 3 (2007): 335–358.

40. Sitrin, *Everyday Revolutions*.

41. Marina Sitrin, *Horizontalism: Voices of Popular Power in Argentina* (Edinburgh: AK Press, 2006).

42. Wini Breines, *Community and Organization in the New Left, 1962–1968: The Great Refusal* (New York, NY: Praeger, 1982).

43. David Graeber, "The New Anarchists," *New Left Review* 13 (2002): 61–73. For a similar discussion see Barbara Epstein, "Anarchism and the Anti-Globalization Movement," *Monthly Review* 53, no. 4 (2001): 1.

44. Antonio Negri, *Insurgencies: Constituent Power and the Modern State* (Minneapolis: University of Minnesota Press, 1999).

45. Daniele Albertazzi and Duncan McDonnell, *Twenty-First Century Populism: The Spectre of Western European Democracy* (Basingstoke, Hampshire: Palgrave Macmillan, 2008), p. 3. For a similar definition of populism as an anti-estab-

lishment and anti-elite ideology see Margaret Canovan, "Trust the people! Populism and the two faces of democracy," *Political Studies* 47, no. 1 (1999): 2–16.

46. Gerbaudo, *Tweets and the Streets*.

47. Charles Postel, "Occupy: A populist response to the crisis of inequality," *Eurozine* (7 Nov 2012). http://www.eurozine.com/articles/2012-11-07-postel-en.html

48. Joe Lowndes and Dorian Warren, "Occupy Wall Street: A Twenty-First Century Populist Movement?" *Dissent* (21 Oct 2011). https://www.dissentmagazine.org/online_articles/occupy-wall-street-a-twenty-first-century-populist-movement, last accessed 12 Sep 2016.

49. Alexandros Kioupkiolis and Giorgios Katsambekis, *Radical Democracy and Collective Movements Today: The Biopolitics of the Multitude versus the Hegemony of the People* (Farnham: Ashgate, 2014), Íñigo Errejón, "El 15-M como discurso contrahegemónico," *Encrucijadas-Revista Crítica de Ciencias Sociales* 2 (2011): 120–145.

50. See for example Paul A. Taggart, *Populism* (Buckingham: Open University Press, 2000).

51. Albertazzi and McDonnell, *Twenty-First Century Populism*.

52. Rancière and Corcoran, *Hatred of Democracy*, p. 52.

53. Venturi, *Roots of Revolution*.

54. Charlton, *The Chartists*.

55. Postel, *The Populist Vision*.

56. See for example Pyotr Alexseyevich Kropotkin, *Selected Writings on Anarchism and Revolution* (Cambridge, MA: M.I.T. Press, 1970).

57. Two titles are particularly relevant for understanding the popular fronts in the US and in Europe: Chris Vials, *Realism for the Masses: Aesthetics, Popular Front Pluralism, and U.S. Culture, 1935–1947* (Jackson: University Press of Mississippi, 2009) and Julian Jackson, *The Popular Front in France: Defending Democracy, 1934–38* (Cambridge: Cambridge University Press, 1988).

58. This is a key argument made by Laclau and Mouffe in their influential *Hegemony and Socialist Strategy*. Ernesto Laclau and Chantal Mouffe, *Hegemony and Socialist Strategy: Towards a Radical Democratic Politics* (London: Verso, 1985).

59. Michael Kazin, *The Populist Persuasion: An American History* (New York, NY: BasicBooks, 1995).

60. Luke March, "From Vanguard of the Proletariat to Vox Populi: Left-populism as a 'Shadow' of Contemporary Socialism," *SAIS Review* 27, no. 1 (2007): 63–77.

61. On Latin American socialist neo-populism see Barry Cannon, *Hugo Chávez and the Bolivarian Revolution: Populism and Democracy in a Globalised Age* (Manchester: Manchester University Press, 2009).

62. The Latin American socialist-populist pink wave was negotiating a period of deep crisis at the time of writing (mid-2016), with several populist governments being ousted and the Nicolás Maduro government in Venezuela taking an authoritarian turn and jailing political opponents.

63. Laclau, *On Populist Reason*.

64. Ernesto Laclau, "Populism: What's in a Name?" *Populism and the Mirror of Democracy* (2005), p. 48.

65. Kazin, *The Populist Persuasion*.

66. Cristóbal Rovira Kaltwasser, "The Ambivalence of Populism: Threat and Corrective for Democracy," *Democratization* 19, no. 2 (2012): 184–208.

67. Jean-Jacques Rousseau, *The Social Contract* (Harmondsworth: Penguin, 1968).

68. John P. McCormick, "Machiavelli Against Republicanism: On the Cambridge School's 'Guicciardinian Moments'," *Political Theory* 31, no. 5 (2003): 615–643.

69. Austin Ranney, *The Doctrine of Responsible Party Government: Its Origin and Present State* (Urbana: University of Illinois Press, 1954).

70. Tocqueville, *Democracy in America*, p. 287.

71. Philip Pettit, *Republicanism: A Theory of Freedom and Government* (Oxford: Oxford University Press, 1999).

72. Kevin Inston, *Rousseau and Radical Democracy* (London: Continuum, 2010).

73. For a criticism of the way in which sovereignty has been used as a fiction to sustain representative democracy see Edmund S. Morgan, *Inventing the People: The Rise of Popular Sovereignty in England and America* (New York: Norton, 1988).

74. Hanna Fenichel Pitkin, *Representation* (New York: Atherton Press, 1969), p. 174.

75. Schumpeter, *Capitalism, Socialism and Democracy*.

76. Robert A. Dahl, *Polyarchy: Participation and Opposition* (New Haven: Yale University Press, 1971).

77. John P. McCormick, "The Contemporary Crisis of Democracy and the Populist Cry of Pain," *Berliner Zeitschrift für Sozialwissenschaft* (2017, forthcoming).

78. Mény and Surel, *Democracies and the Populist Challenge*.

79. Robert H. Dix, "Populism: Authoritarian and Democratic," *Latin American Research Review* (1985): 29–52.

80. Achcar, *The People Want*.

81. Melucci, *Challenging Codes*, p. 49.

82. Will Kymlicka and Wayne Norman, "Return of the Citizen: A Survey of Recent Work on Citizenship Theory," *Ethics* 104, no. 2 (1994): 352–381.

83. Here I am referring to Alain Touraine's discussion of the central conflict of society as a key element of social movements. Alain Touraine, *The Voice and the Eye: An Analysis of Social Movements* (Cambridge: Cambridge University Press, 1981), pp. 81–82.

84. For a similar discussion of the connection between populism and oligarchic power see Marco D'Eramo, "Populism and the New Oligarchy," *New Left Review* 82 (2013): 5–28.

85. This anti-oligarchic stance is not completely new. For example, one can recognise it in C. Wright Mills' discussion of "power elites". However, in the context of the squares this orientation acquired an unprecedented level of centrality, due to the perception of a situation of "financial dictatorship", in which the financialised economy was seen as bringing oligarchic power to its extremes.

86. Owen Jones, *The Establishment: And How They Get Away With It* (London: Penguin, 2014), pp. 4–5.

87. Alain Touraine, *The Post-Industrial Society, Tomorrow's Social History: Classes, Conflicts and Culture in the Programmed Society* (New York: Random House, 1971).

88. Theodore Roszak, *The Making of a Counter Culture: Reflections on the Technocratic Society and its Youthful Opposition* (Garden City, NY: Doubleday, 1969).

89. Bray, *Translating Anarchy*.

90. The original in Spanish is "*El pueblo debe ser rescatado y los banqueros desahuciados*".

91. Declaration of the Occupation of New York City.

92. Naomi Klein, *The Shock Doctrine: The Rise of Disaster Capitalism* (New York: Metropolitan Books/Henry Holt, 2007).

93. The classic text that sets this vision of activism against multinationals and consumer culture is Naomi Klein, *No Logo: No Space, No Choice, No Jobs* (New York: Picador, 2002).

94. The term plutocracy is a fusion of the Greek etymons "*plutos*" [wealth] and "*cracy*" [power].

95. Manifesto of ¡Democracia Real Ya!, see Appendix for full reference.

96. The Gilded Age was an era of US history characterised by rapid technological capitalist development, with the growing inequality a key factor in the rise of the People's Party. Some authors have described the present era as a second Gilded Age. See, for example, Larry M. Bartels, *Unequal Democracy: The Political Economy of the New Gilded Age* (New York: Russell Sage Foundation, 2008), and Paul Louis Street, *They Rule: The 1% vs. Democracy* (Boulder, CO: Paradigm Publishers, 2014).

97. Emma Goldman, *Anarchism and Other Writings* (Denver, CO: Frederick Ellis, 2005).

98. Crouch, *Post-Democracy*.

99. Michael Dobbs, *House of Cards* (Sony Pictures, 2014).

100. US Day of Rage was an activist group who took inspiration from the protests of the same name in the Arab World, and wanted to organise similar actions to protest against the influence of money upon politics.

101. Richard S. Katz and Peter Mair, "Changing Models of Party Organization and Party Democracy: The Emergence of the Cartel Party," *Party Politics* 1, no. 1 (1995): 5–28.

102. Manifesto of ¡Democracia Real Ya!. See Appendix, see Appendix for full reference.

103. Beliefs about the Illuminati and the Bilderberg Group are among the most popular conspiracy theories, in each case asserting that these are secret societies that control the economy and global politics. For an introduction to conspiracy theories see Jovan Byford, *Conspiracy Theories: A critical introduction* (Basingstoke, Hampshire: Palgrave Macmillan, 2011).

104. Clare Birchall, *Knowledge Goes Pop: From conspiracy theory to gossip* (Oxford: Berg, 2006).

105. Charles Morrow Wilson, *The Commoner: William Jennings Bryan* (Garden City, NY: Doubleday, 1970).

106. This vagueness makes the idea of real democracy an "empty signifier" in the sense proposed in Ernesto Laclau, "Why do empty signifiers matter to politics," *Emancipation(s)*, 36 (1996), 46.

107. Rousseau, *The Social Contract*.

108. Declaration of the Occupation of New York City. See Appendix.

109. 27 May 2011 communiqué of the Syntagma assembly. See Appendix.

110. Sitrin and Azzellini, *They Can't Represent Us!*

111. Manifesto of ¡Democracia Real Ya!, see Appendix for full reference.

112. Occupy Wall Street declaration. See Appendix.

113. Hannah Arendt, *On Revolution* (London: Penguin Books, 1970).

114. This list of recurrent policies is based on a review of assembly resolutions and protest manifestoes listed in the Appendix. The list is non-inclusive and not all countries proposed all of these demands.

115. Hilary Wainwright, *Reclaim the State: Experiments in Popular Democracy* (London: Verso, 2003).

3. THE 99 PER CENT AND THE INDIGNANT CITIZEN

1. The "We Are the 99 Percent" blog was an important channel of communication for the Occupy Wall Street movement, which hosted a collective conversation about the effects of the crisis. http://wearethe99percent.tumblr.com, last accessed 12 Sep 2016.

2. Hardt and Negri, *Multitude*.

3. My understanding of the meaning of popular identity draws on Laclau's work on populism as a discursive form. Laclau, *On Populist Reason*.

4. Rancière, *Hatred of Democracy*, p. 52.

5. Touraine, *The Voice and the Eye*.

6. Hardt and Negri, *Multitude*.

7. Deleuze and Guattari, *A Thousand Plateaus*.

8. Hardt and Negri, *Empire*.

9. Marcos and Juana Ponce de Leon, *Our Word is Our Weapon: Selected Writings* (New York: Seven Stories Press, 2001).

10. Ibid.

11. Wu Ming, "From the Multitudes of Europe," Dalle moltitudini d'Europa in marcia contro l'Impero e verso Genova (19–21 luglio 2001). http://www.wumingfoundation.com/italiano/Giap/giapxgenova.html; http://www.wumingfoundation.com/english/giap/Giap_multitudes.html, last accessed 12 Sep 2016.

12. "El Sup" is an endearing diminutive of Marcos' military title "*Subcommandante*" [Sub-commander].

13. Goldman, *Anarchism and Other Writings*.

14. Mills, *The Power Elite*.

15. Roszak, *The Making of a Counter Culture*.

16. The classic account of the German Autonomen is Geronimo, *Feuer und Flamme: zur Geschichte und Gegenwart der Autonomen: ein Abriss* (Berlin: Edition ID-Archiv, 1992).

17. The term "Lumpenproletariat" stands to designate the so-called underclass; those who are below the working class and often engage in criminal activities to survive. Marx famously wrote about this social grouping with disdain, also due to its support for Napoleon III in the events of 1848 in France. See Marx, *The Eighteenth Brumaire of Louis Bonaparte*.

18. Stephen A. Kent, *From Slogans to Mantras: Social protest and religious conversion in the late Vietnam War era* (Syracuse, NY: Syracuse University Press, 2001).

19. The spiritual turn of the post-'68 movements has been discussed by a number of authors, most notably Christopher Lasch. See his *The Culture of Narcissism: American life in an age of diminishing expectations* (WW Norton & Company, 1991).

20. Andrew A. King and Floyd Douglas Anderson, "Nixon, Agnew, and the 'silent majority': A case study in the rhetoric of polarization," *Western Speech* 35, no. 4 (1971): 243–255.

21. Leo Ferre, *Les Anarchistes* (1969). https://www.youtube.com/watch?v=_1PcOsbJbLI, last accessed 12 Sep 2016.

22. Joseph Stiglitz, "Of the 1%, by the 1%, for the 1%," *Vanity Fair* (31 Mar 2011). http://www.vanityfair.com/news/2011/05/top-one-percent-201105, last accessed 12 Sep 2016.

23. Jenny Pickerill and John Krinsky, "Why does Occupy Matter?" *Social Movement Studies* 11, no. 3–4 (2012): 279–287.

24. Kate Khatib, Margaret Killjoy and Mike McGuire, *We Are Many: Reflections on movement strategy from occupation to liberation* (Oakland, CA: AK Press, 2012).

25. Translated from the French expression, "*Ils ont les Milliards nous sommes des*

Millions," used in a banner in the 9 April 2016 demonstrations and widely adopted by the movement.

26. The best account of Anonymous, its discourse, and its practice is offered by Gabriella Coleman in *Hacker, Hoaxer, Whistleblower, Spy: The Many Faces of Anonymous* (London/New York: Verso, 2014).

27. One of the most relevant examples of this transhistorical conflict between the many and the few are the plebeian mobilisations in ancient Rome, discussed by Machiavelli in his *Discourses on Livy* (Harmondsworth: Penguin Books, 1970).

28. On intersectionality see Kimberlé Crenshaw, "Mapping the Margins: Intersectionality, identity politics, and violence against women of color," *Stanford Law Review* (1991): 1241–1299; and Leslie McCall, "The Complexity of Intersectionality," *Signs* 30, no. 3 (2005): 1771–1800.

29. The idea of "constitutive outside" is discussed among other sources in Chantal Mouffe, *Dimensions of Radical Democracy: Pluralism, citizenship, community* (London: Verso, 1992), pp. 225–239.

30. Percy Bysshe Shelley, Geoffrey Matthews, and Kelvin Everest, *The Poems of Shelley* (London: Routledge, 2014).

31. Eric J. Hobsbawm, *Primitive Rebels: Studies in archaic forms of social movement in the 19th and 20th centuries* (New York: W.W. Norton, 1965).

32. "Occupy Wall Street Poster Adopts Imagery From Tiananmen Square (PHOTO)," Huffington Post (17 Nov 2011). http://www.huffingtonpost.com/2011/11/17/occupy-wall-street-poster-art_n_1100048.html, last accessed 12 Sep 2016.

33. ¡Democracia Real Ya!, "Porque somos más, toma la calle". https://www.youtube.com/watch?v=1SAfFFpGF3E&list=PL037B639366E326E3, last accessed 12 Sep 2016.

34. Jeffrey S. Juris, Michelle Ronayne, Firuzeh Shokooh-Valle, and Robert Wengronowitz, "Negotiating Power and Difference within the 99%," *Social Movement Studies* 11, no. 3–4 (2012): 434–440.

35. Konstantin Kilibarda, "Lessons from #Occupy in Canada: Contesting space, settler consciousness and erasures within the 99%," *Journal of Critical Globalisation Studies* 5 (2012): 24–41.

36. Zygmunt Bauman, *The Individualized Society* (Cambridge, UK: Polity Press, 2001); Ulrich Beck and Elisabeth Beck-Gernsheim, *Individualization: Institutionalized Individualism and its Social and Political Consequences* (London: SAGE, 2002).

37. Antonio Gramsci described common sense as that "chaotic aggregate of disparate conceptions" in Gramsci, Hoare and Nowell-Smith, *Selections from the Prison Notebooks of Antonio Gramsci*, p. 422.

38. "*O kadar haklıyız ki, aklımı oynatıcam haklılıktan*" ["We are so right that I am

going to lose my mind because of righteousness/rightfulness"]. https:// twitter.com/DejaNoir/status/342358227238912000, last accessed 12 Sep 2016.

39. "*1. gün teröristtik, 2. gün provakatör, 3. gün gösterici... 4. gün HALK olduk.*" ["First day we were terrorists, the second day provocateurs, the third day protesters, and the fourth day we became the people."] https://twitter.com/ KulYavani/status/340890526054223872, last accessed 12 Sep 2016.

40. Zenhaus, "Occupy Wall Street Together. We are the 99%" poster, (9 December 2011). https://commons.wikimedia.org/wiki/File:Occupy_Wall_Street_ Together.svg, last accessed 12 Sep 2016.

41. Alex Foti, *Anarchy in the EU* (Milan: Agenzia X, 2009).

42. Graeme Chesters and Ian Welsh, *Complexity and Social Movements: Multitudes at the Edge of Chaos* (London: Routledge, 2006).

43. Laclau, "Why do empty signifiers matter to politics," p. 46.

44. These elements of collective identity reflect the fluid character of the contemporary activist experience described by Kevin McDonald, though in contrast to McDonald I contend that they remain manifestations of collective identity. Kevin McDonald, "From Solidarity to Fluidarity: Social movements beyond 'collective identity'—The case of globalization conflicts," *Social Movement Studies* 1, no. 2, (2002): 1474–2837; Kevin McDonald, *Global Movements* (Oxford: Blackwell, 2006).

4. FROM THE GLOBAL TO THE NATIONAL

1. This thesis was most famously proposed by Hardt and Negri in their best-selling *Empire* (Cambridge, MA: Harvard University Press, 2001).

2. The continuing importance of the nation has been highlighted by a series of authors: see Manuel Castells, *End of Millennium: The Information Age—Economy, Society, and Culture* 3. (London: John Wiley & Sons, 2010), p. 335; Craig Calhoun, *Nations Matter: Culture, History and the Cosmopolitan Dream* (London: Routledge, 2007).

3. Mario Pianta and Paolo Gerbaudo, "In Search of European Alternatives: Anti-Austerity Protests in Europe," in Mary Kaldor and Sabine Selchow (eds), *Subterranean Politics in Europe* (Basingstoke, Hampshire: Palgrave Macmillan, 2015), pp. 31–59.

4. Pleyers and Touraine, *Alter-Globalization.*

5. Hardt and Negri, *Empire.*

6. The term "precarians" refers to individual members of the Precariat.

7. Paolo Gerbaudo, "Navigating the Rebel Archipelago: Orientation, Space and Communication in the 'Autonomous Scene'," Doctoral Dissertation, Goldsmiths, University of London, 2010.

8. Date: Wed, 8 Oct 2008. From: Alex Foti. Subject: <nettime> a to-do list. To: nettime-l@kein.org.

9. Hakim Bey, *T.A.Z.: The Temporary Autonomous Zone, Ontological Anarchy, Poetic Terrorism* (Brooklyn, NY: Autonomedia, 1991).

10. Marc Bassets, "Spain's New Patriots," *Dissent* (Summer 2015). https://www. dissentmagazine.org/article/marc-bassets-podemos-patriotism-spain, last accessed 12 Sep 2016.

11. Todd Gitlin, *Occupy Nation: The Roots, the Spirit, and the Promise of Occupy Wall Street* (New York: It Books, 2012).

12. "Summit-hopping" is the strategy of utilising the enemy's events (the various global summits) as rallying points.

13. Tarrow, *Power in Movement*, pp. 37–56.

14. Kriesi, "New Social Movements and the New Class in the Netherlands."

15. Gregorio Herrero kindly made his protest diary available for use in this research.

16. Oliver Cyran, "Mississippi: rightwing, white and poor," *Le Monde Diplomatique* (7 June 2012). http://mondediplo.com/2012/06/07mississipi, last accessed 12 Sep 2016.

17. Nancy Fraser, "Special Section—Transnational Public Sphere. Transnationalizing the Public Sphere: On the Legitimacy and Efficacy of Public Opinion in a Post-Westphalian World," *Theory, Culture & Society* 24, no. 4 (2007): 7–30.

18. Walden F. Bello, *De globalization: Ideas for a New World Economy* (London: Zed Books, 2003).

19. Paul Smith, "Flowback, or the End of Globalization," *IIM Kozhikode Society & Management Review* 3, no. 1 (2014): 1–9.

20. Barry K. Gills, *Globalization in Crisis* (London: Routledge, 2011).

21. Benedict Anderson, *Imagined Communities: Reflections on the Origin and Spread of Nationalism* (London: Verso Book, 2006).

22. Isaiah Berlin, Henry Hardy and Patrick L. Gardiner, *The Sense of Reality: Studies in Ideas and their History* (New York: Farrar, Straus and Giroux, 1997), p. 251.

23. Johann Gottfried Herder, Ernest A. Menze and Karl Menges, *Johann Gottfried Herder: Selected Early Works, 1764–1767. Addresses, Essays, and Drafts—Fragments on Recent German Literature* (University Park, PA: Pennsylvania State University Press, 1992).

24. Emmanuel Joseph Sieyès, *What is the Third Estate?* (New York: Praeger, 1964).

5. SOCIAL MEDIA AND CITIZENS' MOBILISATION

1. Wael Ghonim, *Revolution 2.0—The Power of the People is Greater than the People in Power: A Memoir* (Boston: Houghton Mifflin Harcourt, 2012).

2. See Bennett, *The Logic of Connective Action.*

3. Paolo Gerbaudo, "The persistence of collectivity in digital protest," *Information, Communication & Society* 17, no. 2 (2014): 264–268.

4. I have developed this notion elsewhere: Paolo Gerbaudo, "Populism 2.0: Social media activism, the generic internet user and interactive direct democracy," *Social Media, Politics and the State: Protests, Revolutions, Riots, Crime and Policing in the Age of Facebook, Twitter and YouTube* New York: Routledge, 2014, pp. 67–87.

5. The notion of aggregation can be opposed to networking as proposed in Jeffrey Juris, "Reflections on #Occupy Everywhere: Social media, public space, and emerging logics of aggregation," *American Ethnologist* 39, no. 2 (2012): 259–279.

6. This part of the argument draws upon previous research conducted by the author, and in particular my book *Tweets and the Streets.*

7. Indymedia. https://www.indymedia.org.uk/

8. On the concept of open publishing please see Victor W. Pickard, "Assessing the Radical Democracy of Indymedia: Discursive, Technical, and Institutional Constructions," *Critical Studies in Media Communication*, vol. 23, no. 1 (2006): 19–38.

9. Riseup. https://mail.riseup.net/

10. Aktivix. https://aktivix.org

11. Autistici. https://www.autistici.org/

12. Inventati. https://www.inventati.org/

13. Nadir. https://www.nadir.org/

14. Bey, *T.A.Z.*

15. Ibid.

16. The World Bank, "World Development Indicators: Internet users per 100 people," [Data file], (2016). http://data.worldbank.org/indicator/IT.NET. USER.P2, last accessed 12 Sep 2012.

17. Manuel Castells, *Communication Power* (Oxford, UK: Oxford University Press, 2009).

18. Astra Taylor, *The People's Platform: Taking Back Power and Culture in the Digital Age* (New York: Metropolitan Books, 2014).

19. "Datagate" was a public scandal leaked by US systems analyst Edward Snowden, who revealed the reality of mass internet surveillance programmes waged by the NSA in the US and GCHQ in the UK, with the collaboration of other security agencies worldwide.

20. https://www.facebook.com/anarchistmemes.org, last accessed 12 Sep 2016.

21. https://www.facebook.com/10.posta, last accessed 12 Sep 2016.

22. Geert Lovink, *Networks Without a Cause: A Critique of Social Media* (Cambridge, UK: Polity Press, 2011).

23. The possibility of creating new social networks and data-services has been recently discussed in conferences and seminars by a number of scholars, including Trebor Scholz.

24. The argument here runs along the lines to that of Jeffrey Juris in his "Reflections on #Occupy Everywhere".

25. https://www.facebook.com/ElShaheeed, last accessed 12 Sep 2016.

26. https://www.facebook.com/shabab6april, last accessed 12 Sep 2016.

27. https://www.facebook.com/AsociacionDRY, last accessed 12 Sep 2016.

28. https://www.facebook.com/juventudsinfuturo, last accessed 12 Sep 2016.

29. https://twitter.com/OccupyWallStNYC, last accessed 12 Sep 2016.

30. https://twitter.com/OccupyWallSt, last accessed 12 Sep 2016.

31. https://www.facebook.com/OccupyWallSt?fref=photo, last accessed 12 Sep 2016.

32. https://www.facebook.com/OccupyTogether

33. I introduce the notion of "generic internet user" in Gerbaudo, "Populism 2.0," p. 67.

34. Ethan Zuckerman, "The Cute Cat Theory Talk at ETech," (8 March 2008). http://www.ethanzuckerman.com/blog/2008/03/08/the-cute-cat-theory-talk-at-etech, last accessed 12 Sep 2016.

35. Gramsci, Hoare and Nowell-Smith, *Selections from the Prison Notebooks of Antonio Gramsci*, p. 731.

36. Ghonim, *Revolution 2.0*, p. 143.

37. Paolo Gerbaudo, "Rousing the Facebook Crowd: Digital Enthusiasm and Emotional Contagion in the 2011 Protests in Egypt and Spain," *International Journal of Communication* 10 (2016): 254–273.

38. I have elsewhere discussed the role of internet memes and their adoption as protest avatars: Paolo Gerbaudo, "Protest Avatars as Memetic Signifiers: Political profile pictures and the construction of collective identity on social media in the 2011 protest wave," *Information, Communication & Society* 18, no. 8 (2015): 916–929.

39. Ghonim, *Revolution 2.0*, p. 15.

40. The idea of the "wisdom of the crowd" derives from the unprecedented speed information can be exchanged via systems as complex as the internet. See James Surowiecki, *The Wisdom of Crowds* (New York: Anchor Books, 2005).

41. Evgeny Morozov, "The Brave New World of Slacktivism," *Foreign Policy* 19, no. 5 (2009).

42. Mason, *Why It's Kicking Off Everywhere*; Castells, *Networks of Outrage and Hope*.

43. Gerbaudo, *Tweets and the Streets*, pp. 139–145.

44. Parmy Olson narrates the role played by influential hacktivists within Anonymous in *We Are Anonymous: Inside the Hacker World of Lulzsec, Anonymous, and the Global Cyber Insurgency* (New York: Little, Brown and Co, 2012). Gabriella Coleman also discusses the presence of hubs and key groups within the movement in *Hacker, Hoaxer, Whistleblower, Spy: The Many Faces of Anonymous* (London: Verso, 2014).

45. My argument is informed by Jo Freeman's discussion of the tyranny of structurelessness, according to which the apparent absence of leaders often conceals the presence of informal elites. Jo Freeman, "The Tyranny of Structurelessness," *Berkeley Journal of Sociology* 17 (1972): 151–164.

46. Paolo Gerbaudo, "Social media teams as digital vanguards: the question of leadership in the management of key Facebook and Twitter accounts of Occupy Wall Street, Indignados and UK Uncut," *Information, Communication & Society* (2016): 1–18.

47. While at the inception of these movements, some teams simply operated by giving everybody in the group the login details for Facebook and Twitter pages, in most cases they shifted to using social media management systems in order to streamline content production and management. However, this shift also entailed the creation of a hierarchy of control over the content produced.

48. "The Justine Tunney Debacle & OccupyWallSt.org." http://occupywall-street.net/story/justine-tunney-debacle-occupywallstorg, last accessed 12 Sep 2016.

6. THE CAMP AND THE AGORA

1. Pickard, "Assessing the Radical Democracy of Indymedia," pp. 19–38.

2. Charles Tilly, *Contentious Performances* (Cambridge: Cambridge University Press, 2008).

3. Ibid., p. 16.

4. Ibid., p. 15.

5. Charles Tilly, *Regimes and Repertoires* (Chicago: University of Chicago Press, 2006).

6. Charivari, also called rough music, was a collective ritual in which a group of people would make noises by pounding on pots and pans, often as a means of social coercion towards individuals seen as violating community norms.

7. Charles Tilly, "Major Forms of Collective Action in Western Europe 1500–1975," *Theory and Society* 3, no. 3 (1976): 365–375.

8. See for example Tim Jordan, *Activism!: Direct Action, Hacktivism and the Future of Society* (London: Reaktion Books, 2002).

9. For a description of the small group politics of collectives and affinity groups see David Graeber, *Direct Action: An Ethnography* (Edinburgh: AK Press, 2009).

10. Richard J. F. Day describes these protest forms as "branded tactics" in *Gramsci is Dead: Anarchist Currents in the Newest Social Movements* (London: Pluto Press, 2005).

11. Joss Hands, *@ is for Activism: Dissent, Resistance and Rebellion in a Digital Culture* (London: Pluto, 2011).

12. Michael Sorkin, *Variations on a Theme Park: The New American City and the End of Public Space* (Basingstoke: Macmillan, 1992); Don Mitchell, *The Right to the City: Social Justice and the Fight for Public Space* (New York: Guilford Press, 2003); Robert D. Putnam, *Bowling Alone: The Collapse and Revival of American Community* (New York: Simon and Schuster, 2001).

13. Emile Durkheim, *The Elementary Forms of the Religious Life* (New York: Free Press, 1912/1965).

14. Rousseau, *The Social Contract*, p. 133.

15. Kemalists are the followers of modern Turkey's founder and first president, Kemal Atatürk. Umut Azak, *Islam and Secularism in Turkey: Kemalism, Religion and the Nation State* (London: I.B. Tauris, 2010).

16. Unlike most other movements, the Occupy Wall Street camp accepted money donations, which were used to buy food, clothing, equipment, and even travel cards for homeless people, though this led to some serious internal suspicions about how such funds were managed. In the other camps protesters instead categorically refused any donations, reasoning that this would corrupt the movement or create serious infighting.

17. Jehane Noujaim, *The Square*.

7. THE PEOPLE'S PARLIAMENT

1. http://www.nycga.net/wp-content/uploads/2011/10/occupy.pdf, last accessed 12 Sep 2016.

2. Sitrin and Azzellini, *They Can't Represent Us!*

3. Francesca Polletta, *Freedom is an Endless Meeting: Democracy in American Social Movements* (Chicago: University of Chicago Press, 2002).

4. Nicos Ar. Poulantzas, *State, Power, Socialism* (London: NLB, 1978).

5. Robert Michels, *Political Parties: A sociological study of the oligarchical tendencies of modern democracy* (New Brunswick, NJ: Transaction Publishers, 1999).

6. Barbara Epstein, *Political Protest and Cultural Revolution: Nonviolent direct action in the 1970s and 1980s* (Berkeley: University of California Press, 1991).

7. Graeber, *The Democracy Project*, p. 211.

8. Epstein, *Political Protest and Cultural Revolution*, p. 3.

9. Graeber, "The New Anarchists," pp. 61–74.

10. Marianne Maeckelbergh, *The Will of the Many: How the Alterglobalisation Movement is Changing the Face of Democracy* (London: Pluto Press, 2009), p. 37.

11. Ibid., p. 50.
12. *World Social Forum: A Users' Manual* (Centro de Estudos Sociais, 2004).
13. Lew Daly, "God's Economy," *The Financial Times* (8 Jan 2010). http://www. ft.com/cms/s/2/ca65e0a0-fbe0-11de-9c29-00144feab49a.html, last accessed 12 Sep 2016.
14. Juris, *Networking Futures*.
15. Maeckelbergh, *The Will of the Many*, p. 37.
16. In Egypt, Turkey and especially Brazil, assemblies were far less systematic than in Greece, Spain and the US. In Taksim Square large popular assemblies were only celebrated during the last days of the occupation. In Brazil assemblies were held during the protests, but they never had the importance and centrality ascribed to public squares during the 2011 movements, also due to the lack of protest camps in this wave of protest. In Egypt, there were no assemblies in the square or in similar spaces, even though the aspiration for popular democracy could be seen in less formalised meetings and discussions that took place during the revolution.
17. Graeber, *The Democracy Project*.
18. Passed by the General Assembly at Occupy Wall Street on 10 November 2011, and revised by the General Assembly on 3 March 2012.
19. Declaration of Syntagma Square.
20. "Lista de Comisiones Y Grupos de Trabajo—15Mpedia." https://15mpedia. org/wiki/Lista_de_comisiones_y_grupos_de_trabajo, last accessed 12 Sep 2016.
21. Bray, *Translating Anarchy*.
22. This attitude reflects a suspicion of groups and fragmentation, a strong current in these movements. This position resonates with Rousseau's argument in *The Social Contract* that, "if groups, sectional associations are formed at the expense of the larger association […] we might then say that there are no longer as many votes as there are men, but only as many votes as there are groups".
23. Document of the facilitation team of Puerta del Sol. See Appendix.
24. David Graeber, "Enacting the Impossible: On Consensus Decision Making," *Occupied Wall Street Journal* (29 Oct 2011). http://occupywallst.org/article/ enacting-the-impossible, last accessed 12 Sep 2016.
25. Bray, *Translating Anarchy*.
26. This declaration came during the debate about the internal organisation of Podemos, with Monedero arguing that the party risked becoming like the 15-M movement: "*Si seguimos con estos discursos puede suceder que ocurra como con el 15-M, éramos radicalmente democráticos, pero radicalmente inoperativos.*" ["If we continue with this talk it is possible we will end up like the 15-M movement: radically democratic, but radically inoperative."] "Las Bases de Podemos Se

Enfrentan a Sus Fundadores Para Exigir Democracia Interna http://polit-ica.elpais.com/politica/2014/06/09/actualidad/1402295920_514605.html, last accessed 12 Sep 2016.

27. Polletta, *Freedom is an Endless Meeting*.
28. Bray, *Translating Anarchy*, pp. 91–93.
29. Antonio Machado and Robert Bly, *Times Alone: Selected Poems of Antonio Machado* (Middletown, CN: Wesleyan University Press, 1983).

8. THE ASSAULT ON THE INSTITUTIONS

1. See for example "El Asalto a Las Instituciones: ¿es Lo Mismo 'Sí, Podemos' Que Podemos?" https://www.diagonalperiodico.net/la-plaza/21608-asalto-instituciones-es-lo-mismo-si-podemos-podemos.html, last accessed 12 Sep 2016.
2. John Holloway, *Change the World Without Taking Power* (London: Pluto Press, 2010).
3. Ibid., pp. 17–18.
4. Neil Harding, *Leninism* (Durham, N@Citation: Duke University Press, 1996).
5. Hardt and Negri, *Empire*.
6. Hardt and Negri, *Multitude*.
7. Fraser, "Transnationalizing the Public Sphere," pp. 7–30.
8. Poulantzas, *State, Power, Socialism*, pp. 123–127.
9. "Strike Debt!—Debt Resistance for the 99%." http://strikedebt.org, last accessed 12 Sep 2016.
10. "Brazil's Lower House of Congress Votes for Impeachment of Dilma Rousseff," *The New York Times* (18 April 2016). http://www.nytimes.com/2016/04/18/world/americas/brazil-dilma-rousseff-impeachment-vote.html?_r=0, last accessed 12 Sep 2016.
11. Bernardo Gutiérrez, "Rolezinhos, Las Flashmobs Raciales Y Consumistas Que Desconciertan a Brasil." Eldiario.es. http://www.eldiario.es/turing/redes_sociales/Brasil-rolezinho-flashmob-vemprarua_0_220128482.html, last accessed 12 Sep 2016.
12. http://www.diagonalperiodico.net/
13. http://www.madrilonia.org/
14. http://www.infolibre.es/
15. http://www.lamarea.com/
16. http://www.publico.es/
17. http://www.revistamongolia.com/
18. http://www.latuerka.net/
19. http://unfollow.com.gr/
20. http://www.radiobubble.gr/
21. http://www.penguen.com/

22. https://www.facebook.com/KameraSokak, last accessed 12 Sep 2016.

23. http://capul.tv/

24. http://otekilerinpostasi.org/

25. https://ninja.oximity.com/

26. http://occupiedmedia.us/

27. https://theoccupiedtimes.org/

28. http://novaramedia.com/

29. https://roarmag.org/

30. Arendt, *On Revolution*.

31. "Στόχοι του κινήματος/Συζητήσεις," (27 May 2011). real-democracy.gr, last accessed 12 Sep 2016.

32. "The 99% Declaration.org Takes Occupy Grievances to the Next Phase." http://www.dailykos.com/story/2011/12/7/1043045/-, last accessed 12 Sep 2016.

33. Lessig, *Republic, Lost*.

34. Ernesto Laclau has been the most important proponent of a revision of populism as a political logic, wresting it from right-wing ownership to demonstrate its progressive and emancipatory potential. Laclau's writings on this issue include *On Populist Reason*, "Populism: What's in a Name?" and *Politics and Ideology in Marxist Theory: Capitalism, Fascism, Populism* (London: NLB, 1977).

35. Murray Bookchin, "Libertarian Municipalism: An Overview," *Society and Nature* 1, no. 1 (1992): 102.

36. "Greek MPs approve toughest austerity measures yet amid rioting," *The Guardian* (8 May 2016). http://www.theguardian.com/world/2016/may/08/rioters-take-to-the-streets-ahead-of-greek-austerity-vote, last accessed 12 Sep 2016.

37. "Occupy Wall Street Rallying for Bernie in New York." https://content.jwplatform.com/previews/7u0dYpL6, last accessed 12 Sep 2016.

38. "7 Motivos Pelos Quais Marina Silva Não Representa a 'nova Política'," CartaCapital. http://www.cartacapital.com.br/blogs/carta-nas-eleicoes/marina-silva-nao-representa-a-nova-politica-7849.html, last accessed 12 Sep 2016.

CONCLUSION: AFTER THE DEMOCRATIC AWAKENING

1. Touraine, *The Voice and the Eye*.

2. Nancy Fraser and Axel Honneth, *Redistribution or Recognition?: A Political-Philosophical Exchange* (London: Verso, 2003).

3. Clastres, *Society Against the State*.

4. Paolo Virno, "Virtuosity and Revolution: The political theory of exodus," in Hardt and Virno, *Radical Thought in Italy*, pp. 189–210.

5. Poulantzas, *State, Power, Socialism*.

6. This point is also made by Carlos Taibo, though he is negative in his political evaluation. Carlos Taibo, "The Spanish Indignados: A movement with two souls," *European Urban and Regional Studies* 20, no. 1 (2013): 155–158.
7. Simon Tormey, *The End of Representative Politics* (Malden, MA: Polity, 2015).
8. Christopher Lasch, *The Culture of Narcissism: American life in an age of diminishing expectations* (New York: Norton, 1978), p. 5.
9. See for example Herbert Blumer, "Social movements," in Barry McLaughlin, *Studies in Social Movements: A social psychological perspective* (New York, NY: Free Press, 1969), pp. 8–29.
10. There are different stages in the development of social movements, moving from spontaneity towards progressive formalisation and institutionalisation, see Debra C. Minkoff, "The Sequencing of Social Movements," *American Sociological Review* (1997): 779–799. The labour movement produced trade unions, cooperatives, and social-democratic and communist parties; the feminist movement women's associations, lobbies, and advocacy groups fighting for female equality; and the environmental movement, while embracing many libertarian and anti-bureaucratic ideas, still spawned numerous NGOs and organised Green Parties in most Western countries.
11. This thesis is proposed in two of Jodi Dean's recent works: *The Communist Horizon* and *Crowds and Party*.
12. Arendt, *On Revolution*.

APPENDIX

1. Anselm Strauss and Juliet Corbin, "Grounded theory methodology," in Norman K. Denzin and Yvonna S. Lincoln, *Handbook of Qualitative Research* (Thousand Oaks: Sage Publications, 1994), pp. 273–285.
2. Patrick Biernacki and Dan Waldorf, "Snowball Sampling: Problems and techniques of chain referral sampling," *Sociological Methods & Research* 10, no. 2 (1981): 141–163.
3. Anselm L. Strauss and Juliet M. Corbin, *Basics of Qualitative Research: Grounded Theory Procedures and Techniques* (Newbury Park, CA: Sage Publications, 1990).

BIBLIOGRAPHY

Abramoff, Jack. 2011. *Capitol Punishment: The Hard Truth About Washington Corruption from America's Most Notorious Lobbyist*. Washington, DC: WND Books.

Achcar, Gilbert. 2013. *The People Want: A Radical Exploration of the Arab Uprising*. Berkeley: University of California Press.

Albertazzi, Daniele, and Duncan McDonnell. 2008. *Twenty-First Century Populism: The Spectre of Western European Democracy*. Basingstoke, Hampshire [UK]: Palgrave Macmillan.

Anderson, Benedict. 2006. *Imagined Communities: Reflections on the Origin and Spread of Nationalism*. London: Verso.

Arendt, Hannah. 1970. *On Revolution*. London: Penguin.

———— 1973. *The Origins of Totalitarianism*. New York: Mariner Books.

Azak, Umut. 2010. *Islam and Secularism in Turkey: Kemalism, Religion and the Nation State*. London: I.B. Tauris.

Badiou, Alain. 2007. *Being and Event*. London: Continuum.

———— "The Communist Hypothesis." *New Left Review* 49 (2008): 29–42.

———— 2012. *The Rebirth of History*. London: Verso.

Balibar, Etienne. 2015. *Citizenship*. Cambridge: Polity.

———— "Propositions on citizenship." *Ethics* 98, no. 4 (1988): 723–730.

Bartels, Larry M. 2008. *Unequal Democracy: The Political Economy of the New Gilded Age*. New York: Russell Sage Foundation.

Berlin, Isaiah, Henry Hardy, and Patrick L. Gardiner. 1997. *The Sense of Reality: Studies in Ideas and their History*. New York: Farrar, Straus and Giroux.

Biernacki, Patrick and Dan Waldorf. "Snowball Sampling: Problems and Techniques of Chain Referral Sampling." *Sociological Methods & Research* 10, no. 2 (1981): 141–163.

Birchall, Clare. 2006. *Knowledge Goes Pop: From Conspiracy Theory to Gossip*. Oxford: Berg.

Bookchin, Murray. "Libertarian Municipalism: An Overview." *Society & Nature*, vol. 1, no. 1 (1992): 102.

BIBLIOGRAPHY

Byford, Jovan. 2011. *Conspiracy Theories: A Critical Introduction*. Basingstoke, Hampshire: Palgrave Macmillan.

Bauman, Zygmunt. 2000. *Liquid Modernity*. Cambridge, UK: Polity Press.

——— 2001. *The Individualised Society*. Cambridge, UK: Polity Press.

Bell, Daniel. 1962. *The End of Ideology: On the Exhaustion of Political Ideas in the Fifties*. Cambridge, MA: Harvard University Press.

Beck, Ulrich, and Beck-Gernsheim, Elisabeth. 2002. *Individualization: Institutionalised Individualism and its Social and Political Consequences*. London: Sage.

Bello, Walden F. 2003. *De-Globalization: Ideas for a New World Economy*. London: Zed.

Bennett, W. Lance, and Alexandra Segerberg. 2013. *The Logic of Connective Action: Digital Media and the Personalisation of Contentious Politics*. Cambridge: Cambridge University Press.

Bey, Hakim. 1991. *T.A.Z.: The Temporary Autonomous Zone, Ontological Anarchy, Poetic Terrorism*. Brooklyn, NY: Autonomedia.

Bray, Mark. 2013. *Translating Anarchy: The Anarchism of Occupy Wall Street*. London: Zed Books.

Breines, Wini. 1982. *Community and Organization in the New Left, 1962–1968: The Great Refusal*. New York, NY: Praeger.

Brown, Wendy. "We Are All Democrats Now…" *Theory & Event* 13, no. 2 (2010).

——— 2015. *Undoing the demos: neoliberalism's stealth revolution*. New York: Zone Books.

Calhoun, Craig J. 1994. *Social Theory and the Politics of Identity*. Oxford, UK: Blackwell.

Call, Lewis. "A is for Anarchy, V is for Vendetta: Images of Guy Fawkes and the Creation of Postmodern Anarchism." *Anarchist Studies* 16, no. 2 (2008): 154.

Cannon, Barry. 2009. *Hugo Chávez and the Bolivarian Revolution: Populism and Democracy in a Globalised Age*. Manchester: Manchester University Press.

Canovan, Margaret. 1981. *Populism*. New York: Harcourt Brace Jovanovich.

Castells, Manuel. 2004. *The Network Society: A Cross-Cultural Perspective*. Cheltenham: Edward Elgar Pub.

——— 2009. *Communication Power*. Oxford: Oxford University Press.

——— 2012. *Networks of Outrage and Hope: Social Movements in the Internet Age*. Cambridge, UK: Polity.

Castoriadis, Cornelius. 1992. "Power, politics, autonomy," in Honneth, Axel (ed). *Cultural-Political Interventions in the Unfinished Project of Enlightenment*. Cambridge, MA: MIT Press, pp. 269–298.

Charlton, John. 1997. *The Chartists: The First National Workers' Movement*. London: Pluto Press.

Chesters, Graeme and Ian Welsh. 2006. *Complexity and Social Movements: Multitudes at the Edge of Chaos*. London: Routledge.

Clastres, Pierre. 1987. *Society Against the State: Essays in Political Anthropology*. New York: Zone Books.

Coleman, Gabriella. 2014. *Hacker, Hoaxer, Whistleblower, Spy: The Many Faces of Anonymous*. London/New York: Verso.

Crouch, Colin. 2004. *Post-Democracy*. Malden, MA: Polity.

———— 2011. *The Strange Non-Death of Neo-Liberalism*. Cambridge/UK: Polity.

Dahl, Robert A. 1971. *Polyarchy: Participation and Opposition*. New Haven: Yale University Press.

Dalton, Russell J. 2004. *Democratic Challenges, Democratic Choices: The Erosion of Political Support in Advanced Industrial Democracies*. Oxford: Oxford University Press.

Day, Richard J. F. 2005. *Gramsci is Dead: Anarchist Currents in the Newest Social Movements*. London: Pluto Press.

Dean, Jodi. 2012. *The Communist Horizon*. London: Verso.

———— 2009. *Democracy and other Neoliberal Fantasies: Communicative Capitalism and Left Politics*. Durham: Duke University Press.

Deleuze, Gilles and Félix Guattari. 1987. *A Thousand Plateaus: Capitalism and Schizophrenia*. Minneapolis: University of Minnesota Press.

Della Porta, Donatella (ed). 2008. *Another Europe: Conceptions and Practices of Democracy in the European Social Forums*. London: Routledge.

———— 2006. *Globalization From Below: Transnational Activists and Protest Networks*. Minneapolis: University of Minnesota Press.

———— 2014. *Mobilising for Democracy: Comparing 1989 and 2011*. Oxford: Oxford University Press.

———— 2015. *Social Movements in Times of Austerity: Bringing Capitalism Back into Protest Analysis*. Cambridge, UK: Polity Press.

Della Porta, Donatella and Massimiliano Andretta. "Protesting for Justice and Democracy: Italian Indignados?" *Contemporary Italian Politics* 5, no. 1 (2013): 23–37.

Denzin, Norman K. and Yvonna S. Lincoln. 1994. *Handbook of Qualitative Research*. Thousand Oaks, CA: Sage Publications.

D'Eramo, Marco. "Populism and the New Oligarchy." *New Left Review* 82 (2013): 5–28.

Dix, Robert H. "Populism: Authoritarian and Democratic." *Latin American Research Review* (1985): 29–52.

Durkheim, Emile. 1912/1965. *The Elementary Forms of the Religious Life*. New York: Free Press.

Epstein, Barbara. 1991. *Political Protest and Cultural Revolution: Nonviolent Direct Action in the 1970s and 1980s*. Berkeley: University of California Press.

———— 2001. "Anarchism and the anti-globalization movement." *Monthly Review* 53, no. 4: 1.

Feigenbaum, Anna, Fabian Frenzel and Patrick McCurdy. 2013. *Protest Camps*. London: Zed Books.

Flesher Fominaya, Cristina. "Autonomous Movements and the Institutional Left: Two Approaches in Tension in Madrid's Anti-Globalization Network." *South European Society & Politics* 12, no. 3 (2007): 335–358.

———— 2014. *Social Movements and Globalization: How Protests, Occupations and Uprisings are Changing the World*. Basingstoke, Hampshire: Palgrave Macmillan.

Foti, Alex. 2009. *Anarchy in the EU*. Milan: Agenzia X.

Frank, Robert H. 2007. *Falling Behind: How Rising Inequality Harms the Middle Class*. Berkeley: University of California Press.

Fraser, Nancy and Axel Honneth. 2003. *Redistribution or Recognition?: A Political-Philosophical Exchange*. London: Verso.

Fraser, Nancy. "Special Section—Transnational Public Sphere: Transnationalizing the Public Sphere, On the Legitimacy and Efficacy of Public Opinion in a Post-Westphalian World." *Theory, Culture & Society* 24, no. 4 (2007): 7–30.

Freeman, Jo. 1972. "The Tyranny of Structurelessness." *Berkeley Journal of Sociology* 17: 151–164.

Friedman, Milton. 2009. *Capitalism and Freedom*. Chicago: University of Chicago Press.

Fukuyama, Francis. 1992. *The End of History and the Last Man*. New York: Free Press.

Gerbaudo, Paolo. 2010. *Navigating the Rebel Archipelago: Space, Communication and Participation in the Autonomous Scene*. (Unpublished doctoral dissertation). Goldsmiths College, London.

———— 2012. *Tweets and the Streets: Social Media and Contemporary Activism*. London: Pluto Press.

———— 2013. "Protest Diffusion and Cultural Resonance in the 2011 Protest Wave." *The International Spectator* 48, no. 4: 86–101.

———— "The Persistence of Collectivity in Digital Protest." *Information, Communication & Society* 17, no. 2 (2014): 264–268.

———— 2014. "Populism 2.0: Social Media Activism, the Generic Internet User, and Interactive Direct Democracy," in Daniel Trottier and Christian Fuchs (eds). *Social Media, Politics and the State: Protests, Revolutions, Riots, Crime and Policing in the Age of Facebook, Twitter and YouTube*. New York: Routledge.

Geronimo. 1992. *Feuer und Flamme: zur Geschichte und Gegenwart der Autonomen: ein Abriss*. Berlin: Edition ID-Archiv.

Ghonim, Wael. 2012. *Revolution 2.0—The Power of the People is Greater than the People in Power: A Memoir*. Boston: Houghton Mifflin Harcourt.

Gills, Barry K. 2011. *Globalization in Crisis*. London: Routledge.

Gitlin, Todd. 2012. *Occupy Nation: The Roots, the Spirit, and the Promise of Occupy Wall Street*. New York: It Books.

BIBLIOGRAPHY

Graeber, David. "The New Anarchists." *New Left Review* 13, Second Series (2002): 61–74.

———— 2009. *Direct Action: An Ethnography*. Edinburgh: AK Press.

———— "Occupy Wall Street's Anarchist Roots." *Al Jazeera English* (2011).

———— 2013. *The Democracy Project*. New York: Random House.

Gramsci, Antonio, Quintin Hoare and Geoffrey Nowell-Smith. 1972. *Selections from the Prison Notebooks of Antonio Gramsci*. London: Lawrence & Wishart.

Guérin, Daniel. 1970. *Anarchism: From Theory to Practice*. New York: Monthly Review Press.

Guérin, Daniel and Paul Sharkey. 2005. *No Gods, No Masters*. Edinburgh: AK Press.

Goldman, Emma. 2005. *Anarchism and Other Writings*. Denver, CO: Frederick Ellis.

Greenwald, Glenn. 2014. *No Place to Hide: Edward Snowden, the NSA, and the US Surveillance State*. London: Hamish Hamilton.

Habermas, Jürgen. 1981. "New social movements." *Telos* 1981, no. 49 (1981): 33–37.

Hall, Stuart. "The Rediscovery of Ideology: Return of the Repressed in Media Studies." *Cultural Theory and Popular Culture: A Reader* (1982): 111–41.

Hands, Joss. 2011. *@ is for Activism: Dissent, Resistance and Rebellion in a Digital Culture*. London: Pluto Press.

Harding, Neil. 1996. *Leninism*. Durham, NC: Duke University Press.

Hardt, Michael and Antonio Negri. 2000. *Empire*. Cambridge, MA: Harvard University Press.

———— 2005. *Multitude: War and Democracy in the Age of Empire*. New York: Penguin Books.

Harvey, David. 2005. *A Brief History of Neoliberalism*. Oxford: Oxford University Press.

Hayek, Friedrich August and Bruce Caldwell. 2014. *The Road to Serfdom: Text and Documents, The Definitive Edition*. London: Routledge.

Hayek, Friedrich August. 1948. *Individualism and Economic Order*. Chicago: University of Chicago Press.

Herder, Johann Gottfried, Ernest A. Menze and Karl Menges. 1992. *Johann Gottfried Herder: Selected Early Works, 1764–1767. Addresses, Essays, and Drafts, Fragments on Recent German Literature*. University Park, PA: Pennsylvania State University Press.

Hessel, Stéphane and Marion Duvert. 2011. *Time for Outrage!* New York: Twelve.

Hobbes, Thomas and J. C. A. Gaskin. 1998. *Leviathan*. Oxford: Oxford University Press.

Hobsbawm, Eric J. 1965. *Primitive Rebels: Studies in Archaic Forms of Social Movement in the 19th and 20th Centuries*. New York: W.W. Norton.

Holloway, John. 2010. *Change the World Without Taking Power*. London: Pluto Press.

Inston, Kevin. 2010. *Rousseau and Radical Democracy*. London: Continuum.

Invisible Committee. 2009. *The Coming Insurrection*. Semiotext(e).

Jackson, Julian. 1988. *The Popular Front in France: Defending Democracy, 1934–38*. Cambridge: Cambridge University Press.

Jenkins, Henry. 2006. *Convergence Culture: Where Old and New Media Collide*. New York: New York University Press.

Jones, Owen. 2015. *The Establishment: And How They Get Away With It*. London: Penguin.

Jordan, John. 1998. "The Art of Necessity: The Subversive Imagination of Anti-Road Protest and Reclaim the Streets," in McKay, G. (ed.). *DiY Culture: Party and Protest in Nineties Britain*. London: Verso.

Jordan, Tim. 2002. *Activism!: Direct Action, Hacktivism and the Future of Society*. Focus on Contemporary Issues. London: Reaktion Books.

Juris, Jeffrey S. "The New Digital Media and Activist Networking within Anti-Corporate Globalisation Movements," *Annals AAPS*, (2005): 597.

———— 2008. *Networking futures: the movements against corporate globalization*. Durham, N.C.: Duke University Press.

———— 2012. "Reflections on #Occupy Everywhere: Social media, public space, and emerging logics of aggregation." *American Ethnologist* 39, no. 2 259–279.

Juris, Jeffrey S., Michelle Ronayne, Firuzeh Shokooh-Valle and Robert Wengronowitz. "Negotiating Power and Difference within the 99%." *Social Movement Studies* 11, no. 3–4 (2012): 434–440.

Kaltwasser, Cristóbal Rovira. 2012. "The ambivalence of populism: threat and corrective for democracy." *Democratization* 19, no. 2: 184–208.

Kanter, Rosabeth Moss. 1972. *Commitment and Community: Communes and Utopias in Sociological Perspective*. Cambridge, MA: Harvard University Press.

Katsiaficas, George. 2006. *The Subversion of Politics: European Autonomous Social movements and the Decolonization of Everyday Life*. Oakland, CA: AK Press.

Katz, Richard S. and Peter Mair. "Changing models of party organization and party democracy the emergence of the cartel party." *Party Politics* 1, no. 1 (1995): 5–28.

Kazin, Michael. 1995. *The Populist Persuasion: An American History*. New York: Basic Books.

Kent, Stephen A. 2001. *From Slogans to Mantras: Social Protest and Religious Conversion in the late Vietnam War Era*. Syracuse, NY: Syracuse University Press.

Khatib, Kate, Margaret Killjoy and Mike McGuire. 2012. *We Are Many: Reflections on Movement Strategy from Occupation to Liberation*. Oakland, CA: AK Press.

Kilibarda, Konstantin. "Lessons from #Occupy in Canada: Contesting space, settler consciousness and erasures within the 99%." *Journal of Critical Globalisation Studies* 5 (2012): 24–41.

King, Andrew A. and Floyd Douglas Anderson. "Nixon, Agnew, and the 'silent majority': A case study in the rhetoric of polarization." *Western Speech* 35, no. 4 (1971): 243–255.

BIBLIOGRAPHY

Kioupkiolis, Alexandros and Giorgios Katsambekis. 2014. *Radical Democracy and Collective Movements Today: The biopolitics of the multitude versus the hegemony of the people*. Farnham: Ashgate.

Kirchheimer, Otto. "The Transformation of the Western European Party Systems." *Political Parties and Political Development*. (1966): 177–200.

Kitschelt, Herbert P. "Left-libertarian parties: Explaining innovation in competitive party systems." *World Politics* 40, no. 2 (1988): 194–234.

Klein, Naomi. 2000. *No Logo: No Space, No Choice, No Jobs*. New York: Picador.

―――― 2007. *The Shock Doctrine: The Rise of Disaster Capitalism*. New York: Metropolitan Books/Henry Holt.

Kriesi, Hanspeter. 1989. "New Social Movements and the New Class in the Netherlands." *American Journal of Sociology* (1989): 1078–1116.

Kropotkin, Pyotr Alexseyevich. 2002. *Anarchism: A Collection of Revolutionary Writings*. New York: Courier Corporation.

Kymlicka, Will and Wayne Norman. "Return of the Citizen: A Survey of Recent Work on Citizenship Theory." *Ethics* 104, no. 2 (1994): 352–381.

Laclau, Ernesto. 1977. *Politics and Ideology in Marxist Theory: Capitalism, Fascism, Populism*. London: NLB.

―――― "Why do empty signifiers matter to politics." *Emancipation(s)*, 36 (1996): 46.

―――― 2005. *On Populist Reason*. London: Verso.

Laclau, Ernesto and Chantal Mouffe. 1985. *Hegemony and Socialist Strategy: Towards a Radical Democratic Politics*. London: Verso.

Lasch, Christopher. 1991. *The Culture of Narcissism: American Life in an Age of Diminishing Expectations*. New York: WW Norton & Company.

Le Bon, Gustave. 1897. *The Crowd: A Study of the Popular Mind*. London: Fisher.

Lessig, Lawrence. 2011. *Republic, Lost: How Money Corrupts Congress—And a Plan to Stop It*. London: Hachette UK.

Lotringer, S. and Christian Marazzi. 2007. *Autonomia: Post-Political Politics*. Los Angeles, CA: Semiotext(e).

Lovink, Geert. 2011. *Networks Without a Cause: A Critique of Social Media*. Cambridge, UK: Polity Press.

Lyotard, Jean-François. 1984. *The Postmodern Condition: A Report on Knowledge*. Minneapolis: University of Minnesota Press.

Lynch, Marc. 2012. *The Arab Uprising: The Unfinished Revolutions of the New Middle East*. New York: PublicAffairs.

Machado, Antonio and Robert Bly. 1983. *Times Alone: Selected Poems of Antonio Machado*. Middletown, CN: Wesleyan University Press.

Machiavelli, Niccolò. 1970. *The Discourses*. Harmondsworth, UK: Penguin.

Maeckelbergh, Marianne. 2009. *The Will of the Many: How the Alterglobalisation Movement is Changing the Face of Democracy*. Academic Library. London: Pluto Press.

BIBLIOGRAPHY

Mameli, Matteo and Lorenzo Del Savio. 2015. *Controsovranità. La democrazia oltre la democrazia rappresentativa* [Counter-sovereignty. Democracy beyond representative democracy]. Milano: Fondazione Giangiacomo Feltrinelli.

March, Luke. "From Vanguard of the Proletariat to Vox Populi: Left-populism as a 'shadow' of contemporary socialism." *SAIS Review* 27, no. 1 (2007): 63–77.

Marcos, Subcomandante and Juana Ponce de Leon. 2001. *Our Word is Our Weapon: Selected Writings*. New York: Seven Stories Press.

Marcuse, Herbert. 1964. *One-Dimensional Man: Studies in the Ideology of Advanced Industrial Society*. Boston: Beacon Press.

Marshall, Peter. *Demanding the Impossible: A History of Anarchism*. PM Press, 2009.

Marx, Karl. 1977. *The Eighteenth Brumaire of Louis Bonaparte*. Moscow: Progress Publishers.

———— 1964. *Economic and Philosophic Manuscripts of 1844*. New York: International Publishers.

Mason, Paul. 2012. *Why It's Kicking Off Everywhere: The New Global Revolutions*. London: Verso.

Masoud, Tarek. "The road to (and from) Liberation Square." *Journal of Democracy* 22, no. 3 (2011): 20–34.

Marshall, T. H. 1950. *Citizenship and Social Class, and Other Essays*. Cambridge, UK: Cambridge University Press.

Mazzarella, William. "The myth of the multitude, or, who's afraid of the crowd?" *Critical Inquiry* 36, no. 4 (2010): 697–727.

McCall, Leslie. "The Complexity of Intersectionality." *Signs* 30, no. 3 (2005): 1771–1800.

McCormick, John P. 2011. *Machiavellian Democracy*. Cambridge, UK: Cambridge University Press.

———— "Machiavelli Against Republicanism On the Cambridge School's 'Guicciardinian Moments'." *Political Theory* 31, no. 5 (2003): 615–643.

McDonald, Kevin. "From Solidarity to Fluidarity: social movements beyond 'collective identity'—The case of globalization conflicts." *Social Movement Studies* 1, no. 2 (2002): 1474–2837.

———— 2006. *Global Movements*. Oxford: Blackwell.

McLaughlin, Barry. 1969. *Studies in Social Movements: A Social Psychological Perspective*. New York, NY: Free Press.

Melucci, Alberto. 1996. *Challenging Codes: Collective Action in the Information Age*. Cambridge, UK: Cambridge University Press.

Mény, Yves, and Yves Surel. 2002. *Democracies and the Populist Challenge*. New York: Palgrave.

Michels, Robert. 1999. *Political Parties: A Sociological Study of the Oligarchical Tendencies of Modern Democracy*. New Brunswick, NJ: Transaction Publishers.

BIBLIOGRAPHY

Mills, C. Wright. 1956. *The Power Elite*. New York: Oxford University Press.

Mirowski, Philip. 2013. *Never Let a Serious Crisis Go to Waste: How Neoliberalism Survived the Financial Meltdown*. London: Verso.

Mitchell, Don. 2003. *The Right to the City: Social Justice and the Fight for Public Space*. New York: Guilford Press.

Moore, Alan and David Lloyd. 2005. *V for Vendetta*. New York: Vertigo/DC Comics.

Morgan, Edmund S. 1988. *Inventing the People: The Rise of Popular Sovereignty in England and America*. New York: Norton.

Morozov, Evgeny. "The brave new world of slacktivism." *Foreign Policy* 19, no. 5 (2009).

Mouffe, Chantal. 1992. "Democratic citizenship and the political community," in *Dimensions of Radical Democracy: Pluralism, Citizenship, Community*, 225–239.

Mudde, Cas. "The Populist Zeitgeist." *Government and Opposition* 39, no. 4, (2004): 542–563.

Negri, Antonio. 1989. *The Politics of Subversion: A Manifesto for the Twenty-First Century*. Cambridge, UK: Polity Press.

———— 1999. *Insurgencies: Constituent Power and the Modern State*. Minneapolis: University of Minnesota Press.

Ortellado, Pablo. "Reflections on The Free Fare Movement and Other "New Social Movements." *Mediações-Revista de Ciências Sociais* 18, no. 2 (2013): 110–117.

Neruda, Pablo and Ilan Stavans. 2003. *The Poetry of Pablo Neruda*. New York: Farrar, Straus and Giroux.

Norris, Pippa. 2011. *Democratic Deficit: Critical Citizens Revisited*. New York: Cambridge University Press.

Olson, Parmy. 2012. *We are Anonymous: Inside the Hacker World of Lulzsec, Anonymous, and the Global Cyber Insurgency*. New York: Little, Brown.

Panizza, Francisco. 2005. *Populism and the Mirror of Democracy*. London: Verso.

Pettit, Philip. 1999. *Republicanism: A Theory of Freedom and Government*. Oxford: Oxford University Press.

Pianta, Mario and Paolo Gerbaudo. 2015. "In Search of European Alternatives: Anti-Austerity Protests in Europe," in Kaldor, Mary and Sabine Selchow (eds). *Subterranean Politics in Europe*. Basingstoke, Hampshire: Palgrave Macmillan, 31–59.

Pickard, Victor W. "Assessing the radical democracy of Indymedi@Head A: Discursive, technical, and institutional constructions." *Critical Studies in Media Communication* 23, no. 01 (2006): 19–38.

Pickerill, Jenny and John Krinsky. "Why does Occupy Matter?." *Social Movement Studies* 11, no. 3–4 (2012): 279–287.

Piketty, Thomas. 2014. *Capital in the Twenty-First Century*. Cambridge, MA: The Belknap Press of Harvard University Press.

Pitkin, Hanna Fenichel. 1969. *Representation*. New York: Atherton Press

Pleyers, Geoffrey and Alain Touraine. 2010. *Alter-Globalization: Becoming Actors in the Global Age*. Cambridge, UK: Polity.

Polletta, Francesca. 2002. *Freedom is an Endless Meeting: Democracy in American Social Movements*. Chicago: University of Chicago Press.

Postel, Charles. 2007. *The Populist Vision*. Oxford: Oxford University Press.

Poulantzas, Nicos Ar. 1978. *State, Power, Socialism*. London: NLB.

Putnam, Robert D. 2000. *Bowling Alone: The Collapse and Revival of American Community*. New York: Simon & Schuster.

Putterman, Ethan. 2010. *Rousseau, Law and the Sovereignty of the People*. Cambridge: Cambridge University Press.

Quiggin, John. 2010. *Zombie Economics: How Dead Ideas Still Walk Among Us*. Princeton, NJ: Princeton University Press.

Rabinowitch, Alexander. 2004. *The Bolsheviks Come to Power: The Revolution of 1917 in Petrograd*. London: Pluto Press.

Rancière, Jacques. 2007. *Hatred of Democracy*. London: Verso.

Ranney, Austin. 1954. *The Doctrine of Responsible Party Government: Its Origin and Present State*. Urbana: University of Illinois Press.

Roszak, Theodore. 1969. *The Making of a Counter Culture: Reflections on the Technocratic Society and its Youthful Opposition*. Garden City, NY: Doubleday.

Rousseau, Jean-Jacques. 1968. *The Social Contract*. Harmondsworth: Penguin.

Rowbotham, Sheila. 1992. *Women in Movement: Feminism and Social Action*. New York, NY: Routledge.

Santos, Boaventura de Sousa. 2005. *Democratising Democracy: Beyond the Liberal Democratic Canon*. London: Verso.

Schumacher, E. F. 1973. *Small is Beautiful: Economics as if People Mattered*. New York: Harper & Row.

Schumpeter, Joseph A. 1950. *Capitalism, Socialism, and Democracy*. New York: Harper.

Shelley, Percy Bysshe, Geoffrey Matthews and Kelvin Everest. 2014. *The Poems of Shelley*. London: Routledge.

Shipler, David K. 2004. *The Working Poor: Invisible in America*. New York: Knopf.

Sieyès, Emmanuel Joseph. 1964. *What is the Third Estate?* New York: Praeger.

Sitrin, Marina. 2006. *Horizontalism: Voices of Popular Power in Argentina*. Edinburgh: AK Press.

——— 2012. *Everyday Revolutions: Horizontalism and Autonomy in Argentina*. London: Zed Books.

Sitrin, Marina and Dario Azzellini. 2014. *They Can't Represent Us!: Reinventing Democracy from Greece to Occupy*. London: Verso.

——— 2012. *Occupying Language*. New York: Zuccotti Park Press.

Sorkin, Michael (ed). 1992. *Variations on a Theme Park: The New American City and the End of Public Space*. New York: The Noonday Press.

BIBLIOGRAPHY

Starr, Amory and Jason Adams. "Anti-Globalization: The Global Fight for Local Autonomy." *New Political Science* 25, no. 1 (2003): 19–42.

Stiglitz, Joseph E. 2012. *The Price of Inequality: How Today's Divided Society Endangers Our Future.* New York: W.W. Norton & Co.

Streeck, Wolfgang. 2014. *Buying Time: The Delayed Crisis of Democratic Capitalism.* London: Verso.

Street, Paul Louis. 2014. *They Rule: The 1% vs. Democracy.* Boulder, CO: Paradigm Publishers.

Strauss, Anselm L. and Juliet M. Corbin. 1998. *Basics of Qualitative Research: Techniques and Procedures for Developing Grounded Theory.* Thousand Oaks, CA: Sage Publications.

Taylor, Astra. 2014. *The People's Platform: Taking Back Power and Culture in the Digital Age.* New York: Metropolitan Books.

Taylor, Blair. "From alterglobalization to Occupy Wall Street: Neoanarchism and the new spirit of the left." *City* 17, no. 6 (2013): 729–747.

Tarrow, Sidney G. "Struggle, politics, and reform: Collective action, social movements and cycles of protest." No. 21. Center for International Studies, Cornell University, (1989).

———— 1994. *Power in Movement: Social Movements, Collective Action, and Politics.* Cambridge, UK: Cambridge University Press.

Therborn, Göran. 2013. *The Killing Fields of Inequality.* Cambridge: Polity.

Tormey, Simon. 2015. *The End of Representative Politics.* Malden, MA: Polity.

Tilly, Charles. 1978. *From Mobilization to Revolution.* Reading, MA: Addison-Wesley Pub.

———— 2006. *Regimes and Repertoires.* Chicago: University of Chicago Press.

———— "Major forms of collective action in western Europe 1500–1975." *Theory and Society* 3, no. 3 (1976): 365–375.

———— 2008. *Contentious performances.* Cambridge: Cambridge University Press.

———— 2007. *Democracy.* Cambridge: Cambridge University Press.

Tocqueville, Alexis de. 2003. *Democracy in America: And Two Essays on America.* London: Penguin.

Touraine, Alain. 1971. *The Post-Industrial Society, Tomorrow's Social History: Classes, Conflicts and Culture in the Programmed Society.* New York: Random House.

———— 1977. *The Self-Production of Society.* Chicago: University of Chicago Press.

———— 1981. *The Voice and the Eye: An Analysis of Social Movements.* Cambridge: Cambridge University Press.

———— 1995. *Critique of Modernity.* Oxford, UK: Blackwell.

———— 2001. *Beyond Neoliberalism.* Cambridge, UK: Polity Press.

Touraine, Alain, Michel Wieviorka and François Dubet. 1987. *The Workers' Movement.* Cambridge: Cambridge University Press.

Vaneigem, Raul. 1983. *The Revolution of Everyday Life.* Seattle: Left Bank Books.

BIBLIOGRAPHY

Venturi, Franco. 1960. *Roots of Revolution: A History of the Populist and Socialist Movements in Nineteenth-Century Russia*. London: Weidenfeld and Nicolson.

Vials, Chris. 2009. *Realism for the Masses: Aesthetics, Popular Front Pluralism, and US Culture, 1935–1947*. Jackson: University Press of Mississippi.

Virno, Paolo and Michael Hardt. 1996. *Radical Thought in Italy: A Potential Politics*. Minneapolis, MN: University of Minnesota Press.

Virno, Paolo. 1996. "Virtuosity and revolution: The political theory of exodus," in Paolo Virno, and Michael Hardt. *Radical Thought in Italy: A Potential Politics*. 189–210.

Wainwright, Hilary. 2003. *Reclaim the State: Experiments in Popular Democracy*. London: Verso.

Wilson, Charles Morrow. 1970. *The Commoner: William Jennings Bryan*. Garden City, NY: Doubleday.

Witheford, Nick. "Autonomist Marxism and the Information Society." *Capital and Class* (1994): 85–85.

Woodcock, George. 1962. *Anarchism: A History of Libertarian Ideas and Movements*. New York: New American Library.

Wright, Steve. 2002. *Storming Heaven: Class Composition and Struggle in Italian Autonomist Marxism*. London: Pluto Press.

Writers for the 99%. 2012. *Occupying Wall Street: The Inside Story of an Action that Changed America*. Chicago, IL: Haymarket Books.

Zibechi, Raúl. 2013. "Autonomy in Brazil: Below and behind the June uprising." *Roarmag*. http://roarmag.org/essays/raul-zibechi-brazilian-uprisings, last accessed 12 Sep 2016.

Žižek, Slavoj. 2012. *The Year of Dreaming Dangerously*. London: Verso.

Žižek, Slavoj. "Occupy first. Demands come later." *The Guardian*, (26 October 2011).

Zuckerman, E. (2008). "The Cute Cat Theory Talk at ETech." (2008). http://www.ethanzuckerman.com/blog/2008/03/08/the-cute-cat-theory-talk-at-etech, last accessed 12 Sep 2016.

INDEX

15-M movement: 40, 91, 102, 112, 126–7, 154, 170, 172, 215–16, 218, 220, 222, 224, 247; ideology of, 109, 123, 129; marches of, 165; participants in, 207; social media accounts of, 146; strategies used by, 36

6 April Youth Movement: 35, 152, 194, 244; members of, 145, 158, 175; role in Egyptian Revolution (2011), 152, 217

Abramoff, Jack: memoirs of, 51
ActionAid: 67
Adbusters: 37
Adorno, Theodor: 66
Agamben, Giorgio: 25
Aganaktismenoi Polites: 7, 10, 31, 35–7, 91, 110, 120, 127, 219, 226; decline of, 38; demands for new constitution, 222; discourse of, 102; ideology of, 40; Occupation of Syntagma Square (2011), 2, 29, 31, 36, 55, 82, 84, 109–10, 120–1, 164, 166, 168, 173, 177, 198, 233; participants in, 54, 121, 129, 138, 167, 200–1; public support for, 55; use of national flags, 120–1

Ahora Madrid: 225
Aktivix: 140
Albertazzi, Daniele: 70
Algeria: Protests (2010–12), 31
Allende, Salvador: 90, 224
Alpha Bank: merger with Eurobank, 127
American International Group, Inc. (AIG): financial bailout of (2008), 41, 46
Amnesty International: 189
anarchism: 6, 12–13, 64–6, 76, 94–5, 196, 207, 211–12, 225, 237; movement of the squares as, 65; view of democracy, 63; view of protest camps, 18, 178–9
anarcho-autonomists: 21
Anderson, Benedict: 133
Anonymous: 4, 96, 136; members of, 151; OpEgypt, 136; OpTunisia, 136; use of *V for Vendetta* masks, 3
Antarsya: 215
anti-globalisation: 9, 12, 15, 20–1, 23, 26–7, 55–6, 65, 67, 69, 89–91, 94, 101, 108, 113, 115, 117–18, 130–1, 134, 137, 141, 162, 188, 195, 199–201, 209, 223, 241–2; collaboration with left-wing par-

303